Authors of the Day

GRANT OVERTON

Authors of the
Day by Grant Overton
Studies in contemporary literature

Essay Index Reprint Series

BOOKS FOR LIBRARIES PRESS
FREEPORT, NEW YORK

PR
473
.O_x 774
1971

First Published 1924
Reprinted 1971

INTERNATIONAL STANDARD BOOK NUMBER:
0-8369-2289-1

LIBRARY OF CONGRESS CATALOG CARD NUMBER:
75-156700

PRINTED IN THE UNITED STATES OF AMERICA

CONTENTS

CONTENTS

PORTRAITS

Authors of the Day

Mr. Galsworthy's
Secret Loyalties

i

IN the autumn of 1922 New York began to witness a play by John Galsworthy, called *Loyalties*. Not only the extreme smoothness of the acting by a London company but the almost unblemished perfection of the play as drama excited much praise. Because, of the two principals, one·was a Jew and the other was not, with consequent enhancement of the dramatic values in several scenes, it was said (by those who always seek an extrinsic explanation) that *Loyalties* simply could not have avoided being a success in New York. The same type of mind has long been busy with the problem of Mr. Galsworthy as a novelist. It read *The Man of Property* and found the book explained by the fact that the author was a Socialist. Confronted with *The Dark Flower*, it declared this "love life of a man" sheer sentimentalism (in 1913 there was no Freudianism to fall back on). And the powerful play called *Justice* was accounted for by a story that quiet Mr. Galsworthy had "put on old clothes, wrapped a brick in brown paper, stopped in front of a tempting-looking plate-glass window" and let 'er fly. On being "promptly arrested," he "gave an assumed name, and the magistrate, in his turn, gave Galsworthy six months. That's how he found out what the inside of English prisons was like."

A saying has it that it is always the innocent bystander who gets hurt; but the fate of the sympathetic bystander—and such a one John Galsworthy has always been—is more ironic. That peculiar sprite, George Meredith's Comic Spirit, reading all that has been written about Galsworthy would possibly find some adequate comment; but Meredith is dead and the only penetrating characterisation that occurs to me is: "Galsworthy's the kind of man who, if he were in some other station of life, would be a splendid subject for Joseph Conrad."

In the middle of *Loyalties* a character exclaims: "Prejudices—or are they loyalties—I don't know—criss-cross—we all cut each other's throats from the best of motives." Well, in a paper written in 1917 or earlier and included in their book, *Some Modern Novelists*, published in January, 1918, Helen Thomas Follett and Wilson Follett, discussing Galsworthy's early novels put down a now very remarkable sentence, as follows:

"Mr. Galsworthy does not see how two loyalties that conflict can both be right; and he is always interested in the larger loyalty."

So interesting and significant a statement, buried as seed, might easily sprout as novel or play. I have

JOHN GALSWORTHY

no atom of evidence that Mr. Galsworthy ever saw
the comment; but if he read it and forgot (buried?)
the words, then *Loyalties* was written in their
effectual disproof. For in this drama, as in all his
novels, as in all his other dramas, Mr. Galsworthy
is constantly seeing and portraying how conflicting
loyalties both are right; he is never interested in the
larger loyalty and cannot keep his eye on it through
consecutive chapters or through a single act; he is
forever presenting the two or more sides and taking
none. He once said: "I suppose the hardest lesson
we all have to learn in life is that we can't have
things both ways." He should have added:
"—and I have never learned it!"

ii

"Learned," of course, in the sense of "accepted,"
of becoming reconciled to the fact. It did not need
Mr. St. John Ervine to tell us that "Mr. Galsworthy is the most sensitive figure in the ranks of
modern letters"; for of all modern writers the
author of *Loyalties* and *The Forsyte Saga* is the
most transparent. He is transparent without being
in the smallest degree luminous; he refracts, but
he does not magnify—a prism through which we
may look at society.

Compare him for a moment with Mr. Conrad.
Mr. Conrad is by no means always transparent; his
opacity is sometimes extraordinary, as in *The Rescue;* and yet from the midst of obscure sentences,
like a gleam from those remarkably deep-set eyes,
something luminous will shine out, both light and

[15]

heat are given forth. "In a certain cool paper," explains Galsworthy, "I have tried to come at the effect of the war; but purposely pitched it in a low and sober key; and there is a much more poignant tale of change to tell of each individual human being." But even when telling the more poignant tale, as in *Saint's Progress*, the coolness is noticeable, like the air of an April night; the key is still sober, pitched low; and the trembling passion of a melody proclaimed by violins is quickly muted. Such is his habitual restraint, so strong is his inhibition, that when we hear the orchestral brasses, as we do once or twice in *Justice* and *Loyalties*, it shocks us, like a rowdy outburst in a refined assembly or a terse sentence in Henry James. But it is nothing, nothing. Mr. Galsworthy has momentarily achieved a more perfect than usual transparency; he has suddenly surrendered to the pounce of another of those multitudinous loyalties which give him no peace and the secret of which, except for its continual disclosure in his works, he would most certainly carry with him to the grave.

For he does not talk. No! "You are nearer Galsworthy in reading his books than in a meeting." Another keenly observant person summed up Galsworthy's conversational resources in the one word: "Exhausted!" St. John Ervine: "Whatever of joy and grief he has had in life has been closely retained, and the reticence characteristic of the English people . . . is most clearly to be observed in Mr. Galsworthy. . . . How often have we observed in our relationships that some garrulous person, constantly engaged in egotistical conversation, contrives

[16]

to conceal knowledge of himself from us, while some silent friend, with lips tightly closed, most amazingly gives himself away. One looks at Mr. Galsworthy's handsome, sensitive face, and is immediately aware of tightened lips! . . . But the lips are not tightened because of things done to him, but because of things done to others." Mr. Galsworthy, in a personal letter: "The fact is I cannot answer your questions. I must leave my philosophy to my work generally, or rather, to what people can make out of that work. The habit of trying to tabloid one's convictions, or lack of convictions, is a pretty fatal one; as I have found to my distaste and discredit." He conducts his own cross-examination, in new books, new plays. He acknowledges, with quiet discontent, the claims upon his sense of loyalty of a dog, a jailbird, two "star-crossed lovers," the wife of a possessive Forsyte, a De Levis unjustly used. His pen moves, with a bold stroke, across the paper; another secret is let out; his lips tighten. He is serene and indignant and completely happy.

Why not? "My experience tells me this: An artist who is by accident of independent means can, if he has talent, give the Public what he, the artist, wants, and sooner or later the public will take whatever he gives it, at his own valuation." And he speaks of such artists as able to "sit on the Public's head and pull the Public's beard, to use the old Sikh saying." Nothing else is worth while—for an artist. "The artist has got to make a stand against being exploited." But if the artist should exploit himself, or anything more human or individual than that impersonal entity, the Public, Mr. Gals-

[17]

worthy's mouth would become grim again; his loyalty would be forfeited, I think. There might be a larger cause, but his concern would be with the other fellow. And however hard you might press him for a verdict, he would bring in only a recommendation for mercy.

iii

The Galsworthys have been in Devonshire as far back as records go—"since the flood—of Saxons, at all events," as John Galsworthy once put it. His mother came of a family named Bartleet, whose county for many centuries was Worcestershire. The boy, John, was born in 1867 at Coombe, in Surrey. "From the first," continues the anonymous but authorised sketch I am quoting, "his salient characteristics were earnestness and tenacity. Not surprisingly brilliant, he was sure and steady; his understanding, not notably quick, was notably sound. At Harrow from 1881-1886 he did well in work and games. At New College, Oxford, 1886-1889, he graduated with an Honour degree in Law. After some further preparation he was called to the bar (Lincoln's Inn) in 1890. It was natural he should have taken up the law, since his father had done so. 'I read,' he says, 'in various chambers, practised almost not at all, and disliked my profession thoroughly.'

"In these circumstances he began to travel. His father, a successful and unusual man in both character and intellect, was 'not in a position to require his son to make money'; his son, therefore, travelled,

off and on, for nearly two years, going, amongst
other places, to Russia, Canada, British Columbia,
Australia, New Zealand, the Fiji Islands, and South
Africa. On a sailing-ship voyage between Adelaide
and the Cape he met and became a fast friend with
the novelist Joseph Conrad, then still a sailor. We
do not know whether this friendship influenced
Galsworthy in becoming a writer; indeed, we believe
that he has somewhere said that it did not. But
Galsworthy did take to writing, published his first
novel, *Jocelyn*, in 1899, *Villa Rubein* in 1900,
A Man of Devon and Other Stories in 1901."
Jocelyn has been dropped from the list of Galsworthy's works, *Villa Rubein* was revised in 1909,
The Island Pharisees, a satire of English weaknesses
which appeared in 1904, was revised four years
later; and it was not until the publication of *The
Man of Property* in 1906 that our author succeeded
in sitting on the Public's head and twining his fingers firmly into the Public's whiskers.

This was the first volume of the then-unplanned
Forsyte Saga and it led Conrad, who had two years
previously dedicated to Galsworthy what remains
his greatest novel (*Nostromo*), to write an article
in which he said:

"The foundation of Mr. Galsworthy's talent, it
seems to me, lies in a remarkable power of ironic
insight combined with an extremely keen and faithful eye for all the phenomena on the surface of the
life he observes. These are the purveyors of his
imagination, whose servant is a style clear, direct,
sane, illumined by a perfectly unaffected sincerity.
It is the style of a man whose sympathy with man-

[19]

kind is too genuine to allow him the smallest gratification of his vanity at the cost of his fellow-creatures . . . sufficiently pointed to carry deep his remorseless irony and grave enough to be the dignified vehicle of his profound compassion. Its sustained harmony is never interrupted by those bursts of cymbals and fifes which some deaf people acclaim for brilliance. Before all it is a style well under control, and therefore it never betrays this tender and ironic writer into an odious cynicism of laughter and tears.

"From laboriously collected information, I am led to believe that most people read novels for amusement. This is as it should be. But whatever be their motives, I entertain towards all novel-readers the feelings of warm and respectful affection. I would not try to deceive them for worlds. Never! This being understood, I go on to declare, in the peace of my heart and the serenity of my conscience, that if they want amusement they shall find it between the covers of this book. They shall find plenty of it in this episode in the history of the Forsytes, where the reconciliation of a father and son, the dramatic and poignant comedy of Soames Forsyte's marital relations, and the tragedy of Bosinney's failure are exposed to our gaze with the remorseless yet sympathetic irony of Mr. Galsworthy's art, in the light of the unquenchable fire burning on the altar of property. They shall find amusement, and perhaps also something more lasting—if they care for it. I say this with all the reserves and qualifications which strict truth requires around every statement of opinion. Mr. Galsworthy will never be found futile by anyone, and never uninteresting by the most exacting."

Twelve years after the appearance of *The Man of Property*, in the volume *Five Tales* (1918), was included a long short story, *Indian Summer of a Forsyte*. The year 1920 saw publication of the novel, *In Chancery*, and another long short story, *Awakening;* and the following year brought the novel, *To Let*. These five units, separately in the order named or together in the same chronological order in the thick volume called *The Forsyte Saga*, compose a record of three generations of an English family which has very justly been compared to the Esmonds of Thackeray. The Forsytes and their associates and connections are indeed "intensely real as individuals—real in the way that the Esmonds were real; symbolic in their traits, of a section of English society, and reflecting in their lives the changing moods of England in these years." The motif is clearly expressed by certain words of young Jolyon Forsyte in *The Man of Property:*

" 'A Forsyte is not an uncommon animal. There are hundreds among the members of this club. Hundreds out there in the streets; you meet them wherever you go! . . . We are, of course, all of us slaves of property, and I admit that it's a question of degree, but what I call a "Forsyte" is a man who is decidedly more than less a slave of property. He knows a good thing, he knows a safe thing, and his grip on property—it doesn't matter whether it be wives, houses, money, or reputation—is his hall-mark. . . . "Property and quality of a Forsyte. This little animal, disturbed by the ridicule of his own sort, is unaffected in his motions by the laughter of strange creatures (you or I). Hereditarily disposed to myopia, he recognises only the persons and habitats of his own species, amongst which he passes an existence of competitive tranquillity." . . . They are half England, and the better half, too, the safe half, the three-per-cent half, ‘the half that counts. It's their wealth and security that makes everything possible; makes your art possible, makes literature, science, even religion, possible. Without Forsytes, who believe in none of these things, but turn them all to use, where should we be?' "

One of Galsworthy's severest critics, St. John Ervine, calls *The Forsyte Saga* "his best work," and breaks the force of many strictures to declare: "The craftsmanship of *To Let* is superb—this novel is, perhaps, the most technically-correct book of our time—but its human value is even greater than its craftsmanship. In a very vivid fashion, Mr. Galsworthy shows the passing of a tradition and an age. He leaves Soames Forsyte in lonely age, but he does not leave him entirely without sympathy; for this muddleheaded man, unable to win or to keep affection on any but commercial terms, contrives in the end to win the pity and almost the love of the reader who has followed his varying fortunes through their stupid career. The frustrate love of Fleur and Jon is certainly one of the tenderest things in modern fiction."

iv

Grove Lodge, The Grove, Hampstead, London, N. W. 3, is the residence of Mr. and Mrs. Galsworthy; if you have occasion to telephone, call Hampstead 3684. The approach to the house is described by Carlton Miles in the Theatre Magazine (December, 1922):

"The Galsworthys live at the bottom of a long, rambling lane called The Grove, in that part of Hampstead that looks calmly down on the crowded chimneypots of northwestern London. To reach the house you must climb a steep hill from the underground station and pass the stone building in which Du Maurier wrote *Peter Ibbetson* and to whose memory it bears a tablet. A few minutes' walk in one direction and you are in Church Row with the historic cemetery in which Du Maurier and Beerbohm Tree rest side by side. Follow the Grove walk and you arrive on Hampstead Heath, black with thousands of workers on Bank Holiday, overlooking the little row of cottages where Leigh Hunt and his followers established their 'Vale of Health.' But, having passed the Du Maurier home, you turn fairly to your left, descend a winding pathway that takes you by the Admiral's House— designated by large signs—erected 159 years ago by an aged commander who built his home in three decks and mounted it with guns. The guns have vanished but the Admiral's House still is one of the sights of Hampstead.

"At the end of the lane a small grilled iron gate shuts off the world from a green yard and a low white house, whose rambling line suggests many passageways and sets of rooms. A sheltered, secluded spot, the place above all others where Galsworthy should live. Peace has been achieved in five minutes' walk from the noisy station. 'The Inn of Tranquillity.'

"A turn down a long hallway, up a short flight of steps—a bright, flower-decked livingroom, a tea table, a dark-eyed, low-voiced hostess, a clasping of hand by host and a bark you interpret as cautious approval from Mark, the sheepdog, lying on the hearth rug. Mark is named for one of Galsworthy's characters"—Mark Lennan in *The Dark Flower?*—
" . . . moments flee before you dare steal a look at the middle-aged gentleman sitting quietly in his chair, striving with gentle dignity to place you at the ease he feels not himself.

"Tall, grey-haired he looks astonishingly like his photographs. Reticent to a degree about his own work, he talks freely and with the utmost generosity about that of others. Opinion, formed slowly, is determined. The face, with its faint smile, looks neither disheartened nor sad, yet sometime it has met suffering. Like most Englishmen the eagerness of youth has not been crushed. . . . There is nothing chill about the novelist. He is the embodiment of easy, gracious courtesy. Conversation is far from intimidating, a long flow of material topics with now and then an upward leap of thought. And it is this swift flight that betrays his mental withdrawal. As clearly as if physically present may be seen the robed figure of his thoughts, standing behind him in his own drawingroom. You wonder what may be their burden. About him is the veil of remoteness."

His humility, adorned by his presence and made disarming by what is certainly the most beautiful

[24]

head and face among the living sons of men, does
not always save him from the charge of coldness
when manifested impersonally and at a distance.
Where nearly all men and women give essential
particulars of their lives, not to mention the human
touch of their preferred recreations, Mr. Galsworthy, in the English *Who's Who*, besides the long
list of his publications, states only the year of his
birth, his residence, and his membership in the
Athenæum Club. This would hardly support Mr.
Ervine's declaration that the Galsworthy sensitiveness "is almost totally impersonal"; and instead of
being "startled to discover how destitute of egotism
Mr. Galsworthy seems to be" the close student of
mankind might be led to speculate upon the variety
of egotism he had just encountered. "It may even
be argued," pursues Mr. Ervine, cautiously, "that
his lack of interest in himself is a sign of inadequate
artistry, that it is impossible for a man of supreme
quality to be so utterly unconcerned about himself
as Mr. Galsworthy is." With due respect to Mr.
Ervine, this is nonsense. Whatever Mr. Galsworthy
may lack, it is not interest in himself. He has
achieved countless satisfactory channels for the extrusion of that interest through other and imaginary
men, women and beasts—that is all.

v

It is as if he had long ago said to himself, as perhaps he did: "I am myself, but myself isn't a
subject I can decently be concerned about or expose
an interest in. Let me forget myself in someone—

[25]

in everyone—else!" And since then, if he has ever
repented, the spectacle of George Bernard Shaw,
and particularly the horridly fascinating spectacle
of Herbert George Wells, have been before him, to
serve as awful warnings and lasting deterrents. Mr.
Wells, in ever-new contortions, like a circus acrobat
whose nakedness was gaudily accentuated by span-
gles, began seeing it through with Ann Veronica
and is still exposing the secret places of his heart,
while dizzy recollections of marriage, God and tono-
bungay yet linger. Mr. Shaw has gone back to
. . . evolution.

"I was," Mr. Galsworthy has said in an unin-
hibited moment, "for many years devoted to the
sports of shooting and racing. I gave up shooting
because it got on my nerves. I still ride; and I
would go to a race-meeting any day if it were not
for the din, for I am still under the impression that
there is nothing alive quite so beautiful as a thoroughbred horse." His devotion to dogs and other
dumb animals is frequently spoken of as it extrudes
in *Memories*, Noel's protection of the rabbit in
Saint's Progress and "For Love of Beasts" in
A Sheaf. These shifting loyalties were—what were
they if not admirable realisations of the Self? But
let those who still believe Mr. Galsworthy selfless
but read the prefaces to the new and very handsome
Manaton Edition of his works. For these volumes
he has provided sixteen entirely new prefaces. I
quote from the announcement of the edition:

"These"—prefaces—"are peculiarly interesting,
for in them he frankly criticises his work; in
some cases, too, they reflect the response of readers

[26]

as he has sensed it. In others he tells of the thought in his mind while writing, and of the changes through which the thought has gone in the process. Again, he speculates on the art of writing in general, on the forms of fiction, on emotional expression and effect in the drama. In short, as he phrases it, 'in writing a preface, one goes into the confessional.'

"Of *The Country House* he says: 'When once Pendyce had taken the bit between his teeth, the book ran away with me, and was more swiftly finished than any of my novels, being written in seven months.'

" 'The germ of *The Patrician*,' he begins the preface to that volume, 'is traceable to a certain dinner party at the House of Commons in 1908 and the face of a young politician on the other side of the table.'

"In the preface to *Fraternity* he says: 'A novelist, however observant of type and sensitive to the shades of character, *does little but describe and dissect himself. . . .* In dissecting Hilary, for instance, in this novel, *his creator feels the knife going sharply into his own flesh, just as he could feel it when dissecting Soames Forsyte or Horace Pendyce.*' "

The italics are my own and I think they are permissible.

Probably not enough attention has hitherto been paid to Mr. Galsworthy as a writer of short tales, but that may be because no collection of his stories has shown his talent so roundly as does the new book *Captures*. This opens with the well-known story "A Feud" and offers also such variety and such virtuosity in the short story form as "The Man Who Kept His Form," "A Hedonist," "Timber," "Santa Lucia," "Blackmail," "Stroke of Lightning," "The Broken Boot," "Virtue," "Conscience," "Salta Pro Nobis," "Heat," "Philanthropy," "A Long Ago Affair," "Acmé," "Late— 299." In this book, as in similar collections, there must be put to Mr. Galsworthy's credit his frequent practice of the Continental notion of the short story —the sketch, the impression, the representation of a mood which we find in French and Russian literature and which the American short story too often sacrifices for purely mechanical effects.

Books by John Galsworthy

1900 *Villa Rubein.* Revised Edition, 1909
1904 *The Island Pharisees.* ,Revised Edition, 1908
1906 *The Man of Property*
1907 *The Country House*
1908 *A Commentary*
1909 *Fraternity*
1909 *Strife.* Drama in Three Acts
1909 *The Silver Box.* Comedy in Three Acts
1909 *Joy.* Play on the Letter "I" in Three Acts
1909 *Plays.* First Series. Containing *The Silver Box*, *Joy*, and *Strife.*
1910 *Justice.* Tragedy in Four Acts
1910 *A Motley*
1911 *The Little Dream.* Allegory in six Scenes
1911 *The Patrician*
1912 *The Inn of Tranquillity.* Studies and Essays

1912   *Moods, Songs, and Doggerels*
1912   *Memories.*   Illustrated by Maud Earl
1912   *The Eldest Son.*   Domestic Drama in Three
       Acts
1912   *The Pigeon.*   Fantasy in Three Acts
1913   *Plays.*   Second Series.   Containing *The
       Eldest Son, The Little Dream, Justice*
1913   *The Dark Flower*
1913   *The Fugitive.*   Play in Four Acts
1914   *The Mob.*   Play in Four Acts
1914   *Plays.*   Third Series.   Containing *The Fugi-
       tive, The Pigeon, The Mob*
1915   *The Little Man and Other Satires*
1915   *A Bit o' Love.*   Play in Three Acts
1915   *The Freelands*
1916   *A Sheaf*
1917   *Beyond*
1918   *Five Tales*
1919   *Another Sheaf*
1919   *Saint's Progress*
1919   *Addresses in America 1919*
1920   *Tatterdemalion*
1920   *In Chancery*
1920   *Awakening*
1920   *The Skin Game.*   A Tragi-comedy
1920   *The Foundations.*   An Extravagant Play
1920   *Plays.*   Fourth Series.   Containing *A Bit o'
       Love, The Foundations, The Skin Game*
1921   *To Let*
1921   *Six Short Plays.*   Containing *The First and
       the Last, The Little Man, Hall-marked,
       Defeat, The Sun,* and *Punch and Go*
1922   *The Forsyte Saga*

1922 *A Family Man*
1922 *Loyalties*
1923 *Windows.* Comedy in Three Acts
1923 *Plays.* Fifth Series. Containing *Loyalties,
Windows, A Family Man*
1923 *The Burning Spear* [first published anonymously in England in 1918]
1923 *Captures*

Sources on John Galsworthy

John Galsworthy: A Sketch of His Life and Works.
Booklet published by Mr. Galsworthy's publishers, CHARLES SCRIBNER'S SONS, 1922.

John Galsworthy. Booklet published by Mr. Galsworthy's English publisher, WILLIAM HEINE-
MANN, 1922. Valuable for its bibliography of
the English editions.

J. G. Pamphlet announcing the Manaton Edition
of John Galsworthy's works. Procurable from
CHARLES SCRIBNER'S SONS. This edition contains
some hitherto unpublished material and a re-
arrangement of the plays.

The Prefaces to the Manaton Edition. Practically
the only discussion of his own work by the author.

Some Modern Novelists. Helen Thomas Follett
and Wilson Follett. HENRY HOLT & CO.
Chapter X. contains a long and careful critical
consideration of Galsworthy's work up to and
including *The Freelands.*

Some Impressions of My Elders. St. John G.
Ervine. THE MACMILLAN COMPANY. For a
forceful statement from one of those who strongly

[30]

criticise Mr. Galsworthy's work, especially for its "indiscriminating pity." Analyses at length the play, *The Fugitive.*

John Galsworthy. Carlton Miles. THE THEATRE MAGAZINE, December, 1922. An interview.

A Middle-Class Family. Joseph Conrad. THE OUTLOOK (London), March 31, 1906. A review of *The Man of Property.*

The interested reader should further consult the READER'S GUIDE TO PERIODICAL LITERATURE for the years since 1906.

A complete Galsworthy bibliography, to be published in England, is now in preparation by Harold A. Marrot.

In the Kingdom of Conrad

i

"I ONCE knew such a man," declared Marlow. I don't believe any of us felt moved to reply. To have indicated, by a syllable or two, a polite interest, would have been fatal. Marlow, in the presence of anything but an aloof skepticism or a cynical reserve, becomes tiresome in his pursuit of metaphysical abstraction. He seems to think it can be caught in the butterfly-net of words. . . . Now he sat, sucking his pipe (he always cools it before re-filling) and looking attentively at each of us as the sparks of cigars momentarily threw a faint gleam on our faces. At length:

"You all know him, too," he pronounced. "Chap named Conrad, Joseph Conrad. Teodor Jozef Konrad Korzeniowski. That Polish sailor; writes novels. But he has a master's ticket. Got blackwater fever or something down at the Congo; he was out East before that. Then he settled in Kent, in a little house, where I once went to see him. Of course you've read *Lord Jim;* I don't think a lot of it. Give me *Victory* or *Youth,* or, best of all, *Nostromo*——"

"Personally, Marlow, I always look at the end first, to see how it comes out. Since you are beginning in the middle——"

[32]

JOSEPH CONRAD

"I? I'm not, but Conrad was. Did you ever read *Nostromo?* Talk about beginning a story in the middle!"

"Well, if you want to talk about *that*," sighed a voice. "My impression was, Marlow, that you were undertaking to tell us about a man who knew himself—shall we say?—singularly well."

"Exactly." Marlow uttered the word with something that might have been reluctance. He repeated it, "Exactly." It was time to re-fill his pipe and he made a long job of it. When he had it drawing nicely and began to speak again his voice was veiled, his choice of words was frequently made with a certain hesitation, and we listened without comment or any other interruption than the occasional shifting of a foot on the deck. At least, I can recall nothing; and I know we borrowed our matches by signs—when we thought to borrow them.

ii

"As you have heard something of him, I won't waste my breath on the bare biographical record," Marlow informed us. "I believe you all know he was born in the Ukraine in 1857; sixth of December happened to be the day. His father and mother were Polish patriots and Russian exiles and their death left the boy in the hands of his mother's brother, who used him affectionately and engaged a very capable tutor to fit the young Korzeniowski for the University of Cracow. It is pertinent, I think, that the father had been a man of scholarly tastes and occupation. He had succeeded in translating Shakespeare into Polish. The legendary figure of a great-uncle, whom, however, the boy had seen, made a great impression. Mr. Nicholas B., as Conrad calls him in his book, *A Personal Record*, was in the retreat from Moscow and had the strange misfortune to share in eating a Lithuanian dog. Did you ever read *Falk?* Mr. Nicholas B. transmuted into fiction, I should say. The one had eaten a dog, the other was credited with having eaten human flesh; but the effect is the same. Then there's that other story, *Heart of Darkness*—the one all the authorities acclaim as among the half-dozen greatest stories in English. I have heard Conrad narrate the actual incident as it befell him down at the Congo; I have also read, and heard him read aloud, his tale. Very interesting. Let us admit that truth is frequently stranger than fiction; what then? Why truth is so often unintelligible, void of significance, without meaning. Whereas fiction is the real truth—all we can grasp, anyway. How we abuse words! It is facts, or apparent facts, that are stranger than so-called fiction. Not truth! Let us save that word for finer purposes. The conquest of brute facts? Well, maybe.

"This Polish boy I am telling you about had an incomprehensible wish. I understand that nowadays there is no such animal as an incomprehensible wish. All wishes are fulfilled, or something of the sort. The boy's wish I am speaking of was fulfilled, safe enough, but its comprehensibility is still in doubt. At any rate, he wanted to go to sea. As almost all boys wish urgently to go to sea, this might not appear abnormal. Perhaps, after all the oddity

lay chiefly in the attitude of his uncle and tutor,
which was strongly adverse; also, to some extent,
in the fact that Poland is (or then was) purely an
interior country without ships or the enticing sight
of sailors to tempt a boy. A country of farmers.
And he left it. He has told in *A Personal Record*
of the last stand made by the tutor and his uncle.
The sight of an Englishman in the Alps had the
mysterious effect of making the lad more set in his
purpose than ever. Why, as I say, is not com-
prehensible, unless by those serious scientists who
exist in Vienna and play jokes on the rest of the
world.

"When he had got clean away, with a sorrowful
blessing, he fared to the Mediterranean. He wanted
to become not merely a sailor but a British sailor;
he knew no English. French, of course, he knew,
as befitted a Pole of a good family and some education. It was not so difficult to get berths on Mediterranean vessels. Being in his teens, he was looking for excitement and adventure. This, too,
mare nostrum provides. It does not really matter, I
take it, where one sows his wild oats, provided only
he sows thickly; and the waters of the Mediterranean received a bushel or two from Poland (a
strictly agricultural land). One harvests such a
crop from the sea uncertainly and at a long interval,
but the sea's return is often curious and beautiful.
Fragments, if you like, but of a loveliness not
yielded by the soil of the shore; mother-of-pearl'd,
glistening. And out of that uncouth time and those
bizarre experiences the man Conrad has got back
certain pages in *The Mirror of the Sea*, pages that

we all remember. *The Arrow of Gold*, also, is the return of those years when he was irregularly employed in smuggling and gun-running out of Marseilles to the loosely-guarded shores of Spain.

"There is a woman in *The Arrow of Gold*, Rita, you know . . . but it is useless to speculate about women. In a preface provided for the new uniform edition of his works, J. C. explains that the slightly demure Antonia Avellanos, in the pages of *Nostromo*, sprang from the recollection, tenderly cherished, of a young girl, a schoolmate of his back there in Poland. But I would like to know where he got Lena, in *Victory*. If I were Somerset Maugham and came unexpectedly upon Lena in another man's novel there would be no limit to my jealousy. One does not expect a sailor to understand women and I cannot for the life of me comprehend how J. C. got in the way of knowing the sex. Perhaps, for some time, he didn't. Disregarding the mysteries of feminine nature, if he observed any, the youth persisted in his weird determination to become one of the great race of sailors. He shipped on English ships. Richard Curle's book, *Joseph Conrad: A Study*, will even tell you just which English ships. For example, the story called *Youth* with its vessel, the Judæa, harks back to a passage on a hulk called the Palestine. And so on. But what are such things to you and me? I have read Curle's book and I give you my *parole d'honneur* that I found it extraordinarily confusing when not simply rhapsodical. I did! As if J. C. were not, in himself, serious enough to require close attention and profound

[36]

enough to merit it and pellucid enough to reward
our most earnest scrutiny. Along comes Curle and
roils up the surface of that clear, deep stream. I
have no forgiveness for such a man, upon my word,
I have not! May his excellent intentions pave the
road to . . . but I suppose they do force one to
re-read Conrad if only to get straightened out again.

"Anyway, he stuck to ships, this foreign blighter.
You will find all that is pertinent diffused through
the pages of *A Personal Record*. Even to the examination in which he passed for his master's ticket.
What was he reading in those years? One would
give something to have the tally; but certainly he
did not neglect the French masters. Those who
find in the earlier books, including *The Nigger of
the Narcissus*, a style 'too florid,' or 'too consciously sonorous' say it was because J. C. was long
in understanding that English prose cannot display
the crystal resonance of French. Mind you, I don't
in the least accept their premise; to me, *The Nigger
of the Narcissus* is so perfect that when I came upon
it I was seized with a most violent nostalgia. I
wanted, in a foolish, incredible way, to be back in
the fo'c's'le or on the deck of a certain squarerigger
called the Wayfarer which carried me around Cape
Stiff in—how long ago?—in 1909. It seems a
century. Youth! The splendid, the immortal time!

"The ships bore him eastward. Only the thought-
less, griped by the vain longing for empire or
inflated with a nauseating self-importance, will go
west. One goes east when one is in search of wisdom, and this man was. The greatest piece of
wisdom is the knowledge of oneself; seek that in

[37]

India or China or the ocean islands, whichever you please; the road lies eastward. You see, he had already acquired some self-knowledge; not a great deal, perhaps, but beyond the average. Or was he born with it? At a surprisingly early age he had known that he must, as the saying is, 'follow the sea.' This senseless conviction must be put down to the score of self-knowledge. When a man is not misled by that logical apparatus, his brain, it is astonishing to what clearness of perception he may attain. Do you recall that gentle, highly ironic sentence Conrad uses in *The Rescue* about d'Alcacer? 'Mr. d'Alcacer, being a Latin, was not afraid of introspection.' Exactly. J. C. isn't a Latin but neither is he afflicted like us, who shrink from a look inward in a way to arouse the recording angel's darkest suspicion. The best advice, I believe, is that which counsels a man to look into his heart and write. The best advice extant, but it can be bettered. J. C. looked into his heart a long time before he began writing.

"All that he saw there we have had steadily reflected in the succession of novels and tales of a surprisingly varied character and a deep, a very deep, inner relevance to the discovered self within him. Externals do not matter. And yet they have taken aback visitors to J. C., persons already acquainted with the true person and who should therefore have known better. They found, in a cottage in Kent, a man quitting middle age, the victim of an atrocious rheumatism (or what seemed to be rheumatism) who dosed himself with all sorts of concoctions that he had heard of, until the

[38]

house looked like a laboratory of disused patent
medicine bottles. Well, perhaps that is an exaggeration. Tall and broadly ample Jessie 'Conrad
beamed on the very infrequent visitors and would
sometimes confide to them, with a giggle: 'You
know, they say in London that Conrad lives in the
country with his cook!' But she, Jessie, Mrs. Conrad, was a great deal more than just an excellent
cook, a capable mother, all that. She was, in
J. C.'s words, 'the fortune of the house,' a pair of
eyes that guarded watchfully over this unhappy
man when, for eighteen months, hardly knowing
whether he ate or slept, and sitting all day long at
a table, he struggled desperately for 'the breath of
life' which had to be blown into the shapes of men
and women, 'Latin and Saxon, Jew and Gentile'
who people the pages of that miraculous novel,
Nostromo. That book is unique. You may get
some idea of its cost in toil and sheer creative effort
from J. C.'s own words in *A Personal Record.*
Just so; but then an American editor comes along,
some years later, and finds Conrad as nervous as a
cat. Actually! The editor particularly noticed
that Conrad would never turn his back upon him
while they were together in that room and always
sat so as to face, or partly face, the door. He appeared like a man who wanted to feel the wall at
his back; and with his deep-set eyes and the over-
hang of his forehead, the Slav contour of the cheek-
bones, the greying beard, the silences and the rest-
lessness, the jumpiness—everything—J. C. made on
the American editor a memorable and fantastic
impression. That editor came away convinced that

AMERICAN NIGHTS ENTERTAINMENT

J. C. had seen some wild goings-on and been in some devilish tight places in his seafaring days; and altogether was spending his later years like Stevenson's chap at the Admiral Benbow, waiting for some old, blind, tap-tap-tapping Pew to come along and tip him the black spot. Fact! But the editor carried no black spot, only large sums of American money which he was prepared to part with in exchange for the very best English fiction, both spot and future delivery. J. C. was then busy writing the novel called *Victory*, and gave it to the American to read. The next morning the American ripped it to pieces, on certain plot details. His, the American's, account of that interview is instructive. He says Conrad sat, fingers clawing the arms of his chair, speechless and infuriated, for nearly an hour, while our editor stressed the importance of the return of the shawl that belonged to Mrs. Schomberg in the story and other matters that the meticulous would find fault with. And finally, I suppose when he was able to speak at all, the editor tells that J. C. came around, ending up by quite handsomely admitting the editor to be right, and promising to make the necessary changes. What I cannot get over is the fact that after, as the story goes, Conrad had re-written 70,000 words and added 60,000 more, in order to run *Victory* complete in a single number, the American cut out of it everything but the conversation and the shooting. The resulting skeleton was, to some readers at least, very imperfectly articulated. That manuscript had a curious history and certainly deserves a place in a Museum. I heard lately that Gabriel Wells, the American collector, has got hold of it. J. C. had made alterations in black ink, the magazine editor had gashed it horribly in red; and when the book publisher came to restore the mangled corpus he could do so, intelligibly for the printer, only by an extravagant use of green ink. You see, there was no duplicate copy of the original. Always make duplicates. If you don't, and if you are a writer of J. C.'s size, your manuscripts may some day be priceless. Even though they are typewritten; for the fact that they are not in handwriting is offset by the touching fact that perhaps your wife got up in the middle of the night to type them off, so you could see how they would look in the neat similitude of printed words.

iii

"But there! Let us not talk about the value of manuscripts. That is adventitious, a sort of excrescence on the process of moneygetting, which, in turn, perhaps, is an excrescence on all the forms of art. Do I sound like one of those absurd persons who wail because an artist must make money? If so, I beg your pardon, I do, humbly. Perhaps you would like me to do it kneeling here on the deck. My knees are bent. I would no more absolve the artist from the urgence of making a living than I would absolve him from the necessity of drawing breath to live. After all, isn't it the same thing? So surely as you breathe, you must suffer; and what is the wage problem but a visitation, like sickness, or misfortune, or mental anguish inseparable from the

[41]

act of living? If art cannot triumph over these things, if a novelist could not continue to write novels in spite of the awful pangs of rheumatism, the element of struggle would be lost and all our values would exist in a vacuum. It is their merit, and sometimes their sole merit, that they exist in the air under atmospheric pressures averaging fifteen pounds to the square inch and of only the very slightest variation. The need to make money is the atmosphere in which we all live. By a sublime law of nature, of human nature, I should say, the more we make, the more we need. Human nature abhors a vacuum. But, as I was saying—

"What a pill it would be to a man engaged in writing his first few great novels if he had seriously to consider the fact that, some years later but yet within his lifetime, these blackened pages would be worth a modest fortune. Such a consideration might well drive him quite off his head. What actually steadies him is the indisputable fact that *this* book has simply got to earn him enough to live on for a whole year, including the younger boy's annual six pairs of shoes. Then, when the book doesn't, a way is provided. Don't snort, please. I admit that, on the face of it, such a solution is improbable. The answer to that objection is: The solution arrives. Take J. C. He came ashore with the remnants of this tropical fever infesting ·him and a definite medical mandate enjoining him from all future notion of following the sea. When a chap is nearing forty and has spent all his life from boyhood working up to a master's ticket and a ship to command, a decree of that sort is calculated to knock

[42]

him out completely. He is in splendid shape to be counted out in a prostrate condition, lying prone and never recovering consciousness. J. C. had no more idea what to do———. He dug up the manuscript of that tentative story or novel he had been working on at intervals for about five years. The one which, to the extent of about the first nine chapters, he had shown to a young Englishman on a passage between Adelaide and the Cape. This was a young Cambridge student, named Jacques, who was aboard as a passenger. You remember that Jacques handed the manuscript back and J. C. ventured to ask if the story seemed worth finishing. Jacques answered. 'Distinctly.' So the beginnings of *Almayer's Folly* escaped being thrown overboard to puzzle the fishes.

"Ashore, J. C. finished the thing and it got published. No appreciable sum of money rewarded him, of course, and he has told how he wondered whatever he should do afterward, and he submitted his dilemma to Edward Garnett one evening after the publication of *Almayer's Folly*. Finally Garnett brought forth a suggestion which, in its unoriginality, was a piece of the most authentic inspiration. 'Why don't you write another?' he asked. But, of course, that is the only safe suggestion to make to a person who has written one novel. J. C. admits that from the moment those words crossed Garnett's lips, *An Outcast of the Islands* was merely a matter of time. All the same, he had to live. Shortly, he was marrying, and at suitable intervals Boris and John were added to the family unit. Capel House was a Kentish cottage but there were rates to pay. For some years the pension provided by the Civil List was an affair of serious importance. There is a man or two now living and a man or two now dead who could throw light on this phase of J. C.'s special problem. Conrad's present American publisher dropped in one day on the late William Heinemann in London, with his usual question of what, or more accurately whom, Heinemann had got. The reply was: A comparatively new writer who would some day be as important as Kipling. However, it appeared that in order to attain this importance he would have to live. 'Suppose,' suggested Heinemann, with every aspect of intense earnestness, 'you and I back him. He has a novel he wants to do. I think if we both put in ten pounds—fifty dollars—a month——.' For a moment it seemed as if this blithe proposal might terminate the interview. And, after all, a publisher, who has to foot the cost of a book anyway on what is often the slenderest chance, might well draw back before the prospect of investing $50 a month for a year or two as a preliminary to risking as much more. But it was done. In the end, J. C. told them frankly that he could not give them the book. He had got seven-eighths of the way through and he was unable to bring the story out. Stuck for an ending would be the other way of stating the case. The two, Heinemann and Frank N. Doubleday, accepted this disappointment with a most commendable calmness. J. C. went on to write other things, *The Nigger of the Narcissus*, *Lord Jim*, since so widely hailed and at the time so little heeded and so immensely unlucrative; *Nostromo*.

[44]

IN THE KINGDOM OF CONRAD

James B. Pinker (you knew Pinker, the author's agent) handled the stuff. In the American phrase, Pinker 'grubstaked' Conrad; and among long-term investments of the very highest grade J. C. has been one of the very best in the world. Ah, yes! He has! No one who ever invested in Conrad and held on, held 'for the rise,' has ever lost a penny—or failed to make an enormous per cent. Why, take Heinemann and F. N. D. They, in effect, bought at away below par twenty-year bonds that matured and were paid off at par. For after twenty years J. C. picked up the all-but-finished novel, put it through in triumphant fashion and gave it to them under the title of *The Rescue*. By that time, he was made. He was selling in America practically seventeen times as many copies as when they put their money in—maybe more. And any publisher in America or England would, by then, have given his upper and lower teeth to possess Conrad. The Civil List was at liberty to take care of someone else and lucky if it found another half so rewarding.

"Do I give the impression that this result was brought about in the least meteorically? That would be inexcusable on my part. Let me see: There were *Almayer's Folly* and *An Outcast of the Islands* and *The Nigger* and *Lord Jim* and *Nostromo* and *The Secret Agent* and *Under Western Eyes*. Seven novels, not counting the two he wrote with Ford Madox Hueffer and four or five books of short stories. I am speaking now of the nineteen years that lay between Conrad's first book and his novel, *Chance;* and I am avoiding all exaggeration when I tell you flatly that in all those nineteen years not

[45]

one single book—not the succession of all those books—made enough money for the reasonable needs of himself and his family. Oh, I don't say that he was entirely dependent on these books and the far-sightedness of men like those investors I have mentioned. W. E. Henley serialised *The Nigger;* in America, the North American Review serialised *Under Western Eyes;* there was a bit of money, now and again from the magazine sale of one of the short-stories, no doubt. I stick to my point: The income from the books was not enough. By the way, he also wrote in those years the two autobiographical books, *The Mirror of the Sea* and *A Personal Record.* H'm. The American publishers of *A Personal Record* printed it from type. You know; print a few and throw the type away.

"*Chance* was published in 1914 and sold 20,000 copies in England and the long ordeal was over.

iv

"One ordeal, that is. Ordeals, as such, are never over. After the trial by water, the trial by fire; and you are not to suppose that because one has survived the trial of the spirit he will therefore triumph easily over the trials of the flesh. Not at all. What is the malady of rheumatism beside the torture of shyness? And Conrad has always been distinctly shy. His American publisher, for a long time, did not meet him; J. C. backed out of it, until, finally, a perfectly reasonable impatience seized upon Mr. Doubleday, who said to himself, in a mild tone: 'Confound it all. This sort of thing has got to stop.' And that sort of thing did stop. J. C. at length was induced to come to a London hotel and shake hands—about all he did do, in fact, for at once a severe attack of shyness set in. For quite a while that interview went—very badly? Goodness knows it did not even go badly; it simply did not go at all. But then, as he knew Conrad was planning a new book, Mr. Doubleday asked a few questions natural to a person who has something at stake in a prospective venture. J. C. answered with entire willingness, began explaining what he had in mind and—pouf! Where was that shyness any longer? They parted as very good friends and have remained such ever since. So it came about that at last J. C. visited America as the guest of Mr. Doubleday. As you can imagine, lecture bureaus, societies and every sort of outfit had been after J. C. for years to speak in public. He had always turned down such offers, but before coming to America he explained to Mr. Doubleday that he should like to tell a few people, not more than a dozen, over the luncheon table of his Congo experience, and then read to them from his story, *Heart of Darkness*, the same affair as it came out in fiction. 'If I am able to interest those few,' J. C. went on, 'perhaps I might try the same thing with a larger number, say fifty or even a hundred; I don't think I could ever address more than a hundred.' You see, he knew himself. He is the kind of man who is at his best in an intimate surrounding. Perhaps you have noticed the very special quality of intimacy achieved in his stories under practically all conditions. He inhabits other people's breasts.

[47]

A self-conscious tendency as great as his own or greater excites his friendly compassion. I know an American novelist, at one time editor of an American magazine and then in England meeting people and questing material. Several people were present but Conrad noticed the extreme ill-ease of the American editor. J. C. got up and came over and sat beside the stranger, who then lost some of his discomfort and eventually plucked up enough to say to J. C. that he would like to get some short stories from him. 'Ah! Short stories,' J. C. commented with that markedly foreign accent or intonation. He paused. 'I do not pick short stories out of my sleeve.' It was said with an inflection pleasantly humorous that did not conceal the seriousness of the fact. He simply wasn't that kind of a conjuror. This was not the editor who handled *Victory*. American editors, according to my impression, are a varied lot. The mixture they make is a literary cocktail which appears to go to the heads of so many American authors. I know an American editor who bought a Conrad novel as a serial when all his—confrères?—had rejected the story because of the impossible length. This man printed the 147,000 words without the sacrifice of one. This was after *Victory* and as the editor in question knew nothing of that case, his was an unconscious as well as a vicarious atonement. But let that pass. We are not concerned with American editors, and neither, except momentarily, has Conrad been. His preoccupation has been unbrokenly with the problem of a sufficient self-knowledge. Must he not know himself better than any other possibly could?

[48]

IN THE KINGDOM OF CONRAD

Of course, and for two imperative purposes: In the first place to write, in the second place, to keep his courage. It is no use being able to write unless you can keep your courage. Too, the world is full of brave souls who have bravery and . . . nothing else. No gift, I mean. Nothing in the world is so cheap as courage, so common. But look you!—if a man undertakes self-examination, his courage goes. 'The scale of values is hopelessly deranged and either the self rises to sublime heights of despair or sinks into a hopeless, sticky complacency. J. C. is not an unblemished exception to this general law, or deplorable result—whichever term you prefer. He had gone to revisit Poland and was there when the Great War unleashed itself. The story of how he got out of Europe has never been told and, in fact, I don't see how it can be. Or, well, why not? What do a few bribes matter, in a good cause? Some fairly influential persons, including an American Ambassador, were called upon to extricate Conrad from the extremely troublesome complications caused by the fact that he, a Pole by race and a Russian subject by birth, was a naturalised Englishman. The American Ambassador, appointed in the first place because of his large personal means, enabling him to support an Ambassadorship in the style to which it had been accustomed, may have used his private pocketbook; but in my judgment the matter was one to which he could quite conscientiously have devoted the public funds. Let that pass, too. They say that J. C. hates Russians and is frequently irascible. He also understands Russians, as any disbeliever may discover

[49]

by reading *Under Western Eyes*. As for his iras-
cibility, the results of self-examination justify any
reasonable amount of irritation. If it had been
one of you who had written seven-eighths of *The
Rescue* and found himself stuck for an ending I
daresay the detonations would have been terrific.
A volcano can blow its head off but an artist must
not be permitted to let a little steam escape! What
sort of a doctrine is that? J. C., of late years, has
lost a good deal of his nervousness. He has written
his *Lord Jim* long ago. He has accomplished the
most satisfactory definition we possess of the novel
—where he calls it 'a conviction of our fellowmen's
existence strong enough to take upon itself a form
of imagined life clearer than reality.' I call your
attention to the last three words. If the 'form of
imagined life' is not clearer to us than life as we
observe it, there is no novel. Now, life is never
clear unless we hold a little fragment of it in front
of the mirror of each one of us, his own heart.
Always, then, something different from what we
expected is then clear, recognisable. J. C. has never
done anything else. The story of *The Secret Sharer*,
that chap who haunted the captain's cabin and persisted in the captain's thoughts, is the symbol of all
Conrad's work. I believe he has called it his favourite story; does anyone need to ask why?
Giorgio Viola in *Nostromo*, Mrs. Gould in the same
novel, the nigger in the story of the Narcissus,
Haldin in *Under Western Eyes*, our friend, the
anarchist, in *The Secret Agent;* Captain MacWhirr
in *Typhoon* and Jim in *Lord Jim;* Axel Heyst in
Victory; Flora de Barral and others in *Chance—*

[50]

you know as well as I do that these are simply
persons we encounter and depreciate or else dismiss
as incomprehensible.   But Conrad holds them up to
the mirror of his own heart and behold! they are
reflected in new shapes, pathetic shapes, heroic
shapes, twisted and tortured shapes, but shapes that
are unfailingly intelligible.   It is not quite the same
thing as saying: 'There, but for the grace of God,
goes Joseph Conrad.'   It is equivalent, perhaps, to
saying: 'Here, by the grace of God, is the affinity
with Joseph Conrad.'   The meaning of the universe
is, as the Spaniards say, with God; but what we feel
about it is of perpetual fascination and very real
importance.   J. C. has found that out, in the course
of a fairly long and extremely surprising lifetime.
The world is a ship that will never make port, it is
fair to assume, in our lifetimes; its exact position,
then, as witnessed to by the sun and the stars, is of
little moment.   But those who are aboard—let us
have a clear understanding about them, if we can.

"To do that, one must feel the deck beneath his
feet, like that old fellow Peyrol, in Conrad's newest
novel which you will so soon be reading.   Coming
after *The Rescue*—how long it has been!   Three
years after!—*The Rover* has surprised me with an
unexpected simplicity of strain, like a clear little
thread of blue in a riot of scarlet, the bright background of Revolutionary France and Napoleon's
day.   Peyrol, I ought to tell you, was a French waif
whose sea exile led him to the coast of India and
to membership in the strange fraternity of pirates
who called themselves Brothers of the Coast.   But
this was all before; we open upon the return of

[51]

Peyrol to France and an inconspicuous repose in a little farmhouse where dwell an old woman, a bloodthirsty scarecrow, and a young girl whose eyes, having looked upon the spurting blood of the Terror, can remain fixed on nothing for consecutive instants since. And there's a young French officer sent to the farm on duty connected with the blockade. Far down below the rim of the horizon, you understand, sails the fleet commanded by Lord Nelson. The complete affair is one of those episodes in which a handful of people are wholly at the mercy of destiny if a single one of them fails to sustain his illusion, whether of love, of wrath, of mercy, of hope, or, perhaps, of a sublime despair. Despair? Why, certainly; from what other sentiment could old Peyrol have acted as he did, in the grand emergency, cutting the knot that bound up together those few lives, whose only importance was the supreme importance of the insignificant and humble? Peyrol, the ex-pirate, flashing out over the water to his final earthly adventure is the latest and most beautiful incarnation of that old sailor whom Conrad knew in the flesh and has translated so often —the 'Ulysses' we meet in *The Mirror of the Sea*, who is also Nostromo, who appears under his actual name and in his true rôle in *The Arrow of Gold*. In the closing pages of *The Rover* we get a brief glimpse of the great Nelson, but he does not dwarf Peyrol.

"A Mediterranean story, a tale of that sea which is 'the charmer and deceiver of audacious men,' like Life itself, which also keeps 'the secret of its fascination.'"

[52]

IN THE KINGDOM OF CONRAD

V

Marlow ceased to speak. It was beautifully dark. The river, in our stretch of it, was composed to the beauty of that darkness and won to the felicity of a nearly perfect silence. I can't speak for the others, of course. Personally I was absorbed in trying to remember the man Conrad's exact words—in the so long suppressed preface to *The Nigger.* You must have read them:

"The artist appeals to that part of our being that is not dependent on wisdom; to that in us which is a gift and not a mere acquisition—and, therefore, more permanently enduring. He speaks to our capacity for delight and wonder, to the sense of mystery surrounding our lives; to our sense of pity, and beauty, and pain: to the latent feeling of fellowship with all creation—and to the subtle but invincible conviction of solidarity that knits together the loneliness of innumerable hearts, to the solidarity in dreams, in joy, in sorrow, in aspirations, in illusions, in hope, in fear, which binds men to each other, which binds together all humanity—the dead to the living and the living to the unborn."

Books by Joseph Conrad

NOVELS:

1895 *Almayer's Folly*
1896 *An Outcast of the Islands*
1898 *The Nigger of the Narcissus* [first published
        in America as *The Children of the Sea*]

AMERICAN NIGHTS ENTERTAINMENT

1900 *Lord Jim*
1903 *Nostromo*
1907 *The Secret Agent*
1911 *Under Western Eyes*
1914 *Chance*
1915 *Victory*
1917 *The Shadow Line: A Confession*
1919 *The Arrow of Gold*
1920 *The Rescue*
1923 *The Rover*

NOVELS IN COLLABORATION WITH FORD MADOX HUEFFER:

1901 *The Inheritors: An Extravagant Story*
1903 *Romance*

TALES AND SHORT STORIES:

1898 *Tales of Unrest*
1902 *Youth: A Narrative; Heart of Darkness; The End of the Tether*
1903 *Typhoon and Other Stories* [in America *Typhoon* is published separately and the volume is *Falk and Other Stories*]
1908 *A Set of Six*
1912 *'Twixt Land and Sea*
1916 *Within the Tides*

AUTOBIOGRAPHICAL:

1906 *The Mirror of the Sea: Memories and Impressions*
1912 *A Personal Record* [published in England as *Some Reminiscences*]

[54]

IN THE KINGDOM OF CONRAD

1921 *Notes on Life and Letters*

Sources on Joseph Conrad

Joseph Conrad: His Romantic-Realism, by RUTH M. STAUFFER (Boston: Four Seas Company, 1922). This study of Conrad is of first importance because of its thirty pages of appendices, consisting of:

I. Conrad Bibliographies
II. Conrad's Works
    (A) Chronological List of Novels and Tales (with Original Editions)
    (B) Alphabetical List of Short Stories
    (C) Miscellaneous Writings by Conrad
III. Criticisms of Conrad
    (A) Books on Conrad. With a paragraph of characterisation of each.
    (B) Articles About Conrad. With notes as to the character of each article. There is given a "first," a "second" and a "third" list, according to the estimate of an article's value.
IV. Book Reviews. Described as a "partial list only," but recording fully 200 reviews in principal English and American magazines and newspapers.
V. Miscellaneous
    (A) Brief Articles on the Personality of Conrad

[55]

(B) Poems to Conrad
(C) A list of Portraits of Conrad

All of Conrad's short stories are credited to their respective volumes, serial publication is invariably noted, etc.

Joseph Conrad—The Man, by Elbridge L. Adams, in THE OUTLOOK for 18 April, 1923. One of the most complete accounts of a visit and report of the everyday Conrad.

The chapter on Joseph Conrad, by Leland Hall, in *English Literature During the Last Half Century*, by JOHN W. CUNLIFFE. The Macmillan Company, revised edition, 1923.

Some Modern Novelists, by HELEN THOMAS FOLLETT and WILSON FOLLETT. Henry Holt & Company, 1918.

Joseph Conrad, A Study, by RICHARD CURLE. Doubleday, Page & Company, 1914.

Private Information.

The reader may consult the references available in the New York Public Library or the Library of Congress, Washington, D. C., and should also consult the annual READER'S GUIDE TO PERIODICAL LITERATURE especially since 1914. He should also consult the map showing the locations of Conrad's stories, printed as an end-paper in some editions of his books, particularly *Victory*.

The Documents in the
Case of Arthur Train

i

THE first and most important is a volume of over
two hundred pages—very large pages, somewhat larger, in fact, than those of Cosmopolitan
magazine, a trifle smaller than those of Vanity Fair.
The volume is bound in heavy yellow paper which
says, in neat letters at the upper left, "Indictment
No. 1." Inside the cover is a long table of contents;
the printed pages that follow are made either more
enlightening or more alarming, according to your
variety of intelligence, by the presence of charts
and diagrams. One such, when unfolded, shows
green, red and black inks. The purpose is to make
it easier for the eye to trace the intricate handlings
of certain considerable sums of money. . . .

This mysterious book, possessed of no title-page
and honouring no one as its author, represents the
capacity of Arthur Train for hard work. In 1914
Henry Siegel, a New York merchant and banker,
was to be prosecuted, and Arthur Train was en-
trusted with the prosecution. Counsel for Siegel
secured a change of venue and the trial was transferred to Geneseo, New York. The case for the
prosecution, in its mathematical and extremely complicated demonstration, seemed only too likely to be

lost before a jury of farmers completely unfamiliar with Mr. Siegel's affairs. Mr. Siegel was in banking companies, merchandising corporations, realty corporations, a securities company, an express company and other enterprises. It was quite necessary to explore the labyrinth; something like $50,000 was expended by Arthur Train, the explorer, and the printed and bound book, *Indictment No. 1*, was a mere preliminary to the battle in court.

In 1914 Arthur Train was already the author of quite a number of books of fiction. In a general way, they represented pleasant recreation.

ii

Other documents are these books and stories of his, the work of leisure intervals and an active imagination. Some of them were done by dictation, dictation interrupted by telephone calls, by days in court, by this or that or the other. He acquired the faculty of dropping and picking up again in the middle of a chapter, a paragraph, a sentence. He didn't worry over the stuff; he didn't fuss about it, as some men do about their golf, when they're off their game. The business of life was transacted in the gloomy chambers of the Criminal Courts Building, New York, where the air is bad, the light poor, but the saturation with human nature, perfect. To prepare a case was rather frequently interesting, to try a case was scarcely ever without its thrill. And the cases, despite the common misconception of them, were not assorted East Side vendettas or Chinatown murders. A large percentage of them

ARTHUR TRAIN

were always on that shadowy borderline where a District Attorney must stop and ask himself if a crime has been committed, if, after all, the remedy is not to be sought in an action brought in the civil courts. And every little while there would be a case of proportions, of an almost inscrutable complexity, like that which led to the publication (in a strictly limited edition with a deluxity of coloured inks) of *Indictment No. 1*.

Arthur Train is the most agreeable of men, not tall, suave, exceedingly friendly, a good talker and with all the requisite human approaches and contacts, but if you really wish to make yourself tiresome to him you can do it by suggesting that he is a "criminal lawyer." Now there have been and are among "criminal lawyers" many men of eminence. The defence of persons accused of crime is possibly that branch of the law in which talent or genius shows most conspicuously. As a matter of fact, however, the most ingenious brains of the legal profession have preferred, for a generation past, to remain in offices and nurse the young and growing corporation or correct the adult corporation's errors in diet and underwear. Corporation law is the thing in our day and there is some very good evidence that Arthur Train is an excellent corporation lawyer.

What about the evidence that he is a novelist? Your Honours, I am coming to that directly.

iii

The document now to our purpose is his latest novel, *His Children's Children*. It represents Mr.

[59]

Train's most serious work to date. To give it its proper background of purpose, I should like to make a literary comparison. My trouble is that any sort of literary comparison seems to be extended too far. If I compare one novel with another the impression arises that I am comparing them in every respect. I compare two books, and it is assumed that I am comparing the two authors. Perhaps the two books have a single resemblance and the authors both have blue eyes. Very well, then! I was about to speak of John Galsworthy's work in *The Forsyte Saga*.

That history of a family is discussed elsewhere in this book. My present point is that it is the history of an English family whose main inheritance was the property instinct, a blending of acquisitiveness and tenaciousness, "to have and to hold." Mr. Train's *His Children's Children* is the history of an American family whose main inheritance was a most characteristically American one, the wish to "get on." Tenacity was strong in the Forsytes, it is undeveloped in the Kaynes. A Forsyte has not much to acquire, but a Kayne is always two up and three to play; the effort to acquire is his breath and he is somehow always afflicted with the feeling of short-windedness. Each in his quite distinctive way, these two novelists have concerned themselves with the situation arising from an age of materialism—the age that culminated in the Great War. I choose my words. I do not say that the Great War was a product of a materialistic age, though there is a brief for that and I think quite possibly Mr. Train would consent to argue it. But the Great War did come in our age of a materialistic civilisation, and, if not at the end of it, nearer to the end than to the beginning. When did our materialistic age begin? At the end of Mrs. Wharton's *Age of Innocence*, of course.

Mr. Train's motif is the dominant characteristic of an age we all lived in, and what that characteristic led to. He writes, of course, about old Peter B. Kayne, "The Pirate," and his children and grandchildren; these are the little group of people in the immediate foreground. They are the larger world in little, people who set the fashion and make the pace, watched and aped by thousands. Their ambitions, their discontents, their achievements in every direction, including sensation, scandal and disgrace are the best commentary on—themselves as individuals? Not at all; on certain forces and tendencies more powerful than they.

So considered, *His Children's Children* is a perfectly documented study of the third generation since the beginning of the era of "big business" in America. To the Forsytes the termination came with a sign, "To Let." With us it has more frequently come with some such scene as that closing Mr. Train's able novel; I mean old Peter B. Kayne, ill and helpless upstairs, and the auctioneer at his stand below. To the once redoubtable Pirate comes the sound of a rising murmur from down there; he manages to get up and struggle feebly to a place where he can look upon the alien affair going on in the house—in his, Peter B. Kayne's, house. The auctioneer's voice is lifted above the rest, in a louder smoothness, in an accent of barter; ambitions and ideals, so far as realised, are here knocked down to the highest bidder. What price are we offered on certain tangible results of a desire to get on? To the highest bidder. . . . Perhaps, after all, Peter B. Kayne's was the high bid.

iv

A "documented" study; I chose my word there, also. For an immense amount of work went into *His Children's Children*. You may take my word for it, as much as went into the authorship of *Indictment No. 1*. Or, no, you need not take my word. Take a fact, instead. Mr. Train is now at work upon a very remarkable novel of which it is not my privilege to speak here except to say that its first chapter exemplifies his infinitely painstaking method to-day. In common with a very few other novelists, he likes to derive clearly through several antecedent generations his principal characters. His writing undergoes many corrections but in his first draft he gives himself full rein. In the novel that is to follow *His Children's Children*, he spent much time on the first chapter. By a "cut-back" he traced his hero's family from about the year 1790 to the opening of the story, in the present. This, mind you, was with the deliberate intention that the first chapter should ultimately be of not much, if any, more than ordinary chapter length—perhaps thirty typewritten pages.

Well, he knew he had written a good deal, but the first chapter, first draft, was written and he sent it to be typed. The manuscript had been returned to him on a day when I called; it made exactly 184 typewritten pages—about half the length of an ordinary full-length novel, maybe somewhat more.

v

Arthur (Cheney) Train was born in Boston, 6 September 1875, the son of Charles Russell Train and Sarah M. (Cheney) Train. His father was Attorney-General of Massachusetts, 1873-1880. Arthur Train was graduated from Harvard (A.B.) in 1896 and received the law degree three years later. In 1897 he married Ethel Kissam, daughter of Benjamin P. Kissam, of New York. Mrs. Train, also a writer, died in the spring of 1923. Her book, *"Son" and Other Stories of Childhood and Age* is being published posthumously.

Arthur Train went almost immediately into the District Attorney's office in New York. He never entirely sacrificed his connection with it until 1916, when he became a member of the firm of Perkins & Train. As a special deputy Attorney-General of the State of New York, in 1910, he brought about the indictment of over one hundred persons, political offenders in Queens County, in the city of New York. He is a member of the Century, University and Harvard Clubs of New York, and of the Downtown Association. In his attractive home, at 113 East Seventy-third street, New York, there is a room, up one flight, occupying the whole width of the front of the house, with southerly windows, book-lined walls, an ample desk, and a roomy davenport confronting a fireplace. The fireplace is fenced about and the top of the fence is leather-cushioned,

[63]

making a comfortable seat. Nothing could be more pleasant than to sink into the davenport and face Mr. Train, who has seated himself on the fireplace fence and lighted a cigarette.

"But don't you mind the interruptions?" you ask him. "Suppose you are in the middle of a novel and a big case comes along——"

"That's very refreshing," he answers. "I come back to the novel as from a vacation."

And you recall the early writing, done, so to speak, between telephone calls.

There *has* been a change; Mr. Train freely acknowledges it. "I can't say exactly when it occurred. It was during the war. I felt differently about my writing. I felt much more intent about it. It took hold of me very strongly when I was writing about Ephraim Tutt—*Tutt and Mr. Tutt*, you know. I think those were possibly the first stories I had written which made me feel emotion."

It is easy to see why, easier, perhaps, in Mr. Train's new collection of these tales, *Tut, Tut! Mr. Tutt*, than in the first book. For the emphasis upon Ephraim Tutt's attitude is more pronounced as we see him deliberately employing the tricks of the law in the interests of justice. Himself moved by that most permanent of human emotions, the desire for the just, and by that most continual of human delights, the extraction of good from evil or even good wreaked by means of evil, and moved also by that human protest against the application of general rules to individual dilemmas, Mr. Tutt would be strange if he did not arouse in his creator the emotion inseparable from any act of art.

[64]

DOCUMENTS IN CASE OF ARTHUR TRAIN

Once felt, never without. The practise of law seems less important than once it did to Arthur Train. The number of cases that really are interesting—are they growing fewer? There is something about private practise . . . duller than the old court work, less stimulating. . . .

He has "an infinite capacity for taking pains." It has been proven. There, I think, our case rests.

Books by Arthur Train

1905 *McAllister and His Double*
1906 *The Prisoner at the Bar*
1908 *True Stories of Crime*
1909 *The Butler's Story*
1909 *Mortmain*
1909 *Confessions of Artemas Quibble*
1910 *C. Q., or In the Wireless House*
1911 *Courts, Criminals and the Camorra*
1914 *The "Goldfish."* This book, published anonymously, caused a sensation by its satirisation of American social life
1915 *The Man Who Rocked the Earth* (with ROBERT WILLIAMS WOOD)
1917 *The World and Thomas Kelly*
1918 *The Earthquake*
1920 *Tutt and Mr. Tutt*
1921 *By Advice of Counsel*
1921 *The Hermit of Turkey Hollow*
1923 *His Children's Children*
1923 *Tut, Tut! Mr. Tutt*

The Lady of a Tradition, Miss Sackville-West

THERE are two sides from which you may first profitably look at the house. One is from the park, the north side. From here the pile shows best the vastness of its size; it looks like a mediæval village. It is heaped with no attempt at symmetry; it is sombre and frowning; the grey towers rise; the battlements cut out their square regularity against the sky; the buttresses of the old twelfth-century tithe-barn give a rough impression of fortifications. There is a line of trees in one of the inner court-yards, and their green heads show above the roofs of the old breweries; but although they are actually trees of a considerable size they are dwarfed and unnoticeable against the mass of the buildings blocked behind them. The whole pile soars to a peak which is the clock-tower with its pointed roof; it might be the spire of the church on the summit of the hill crowning the mediæval village. At sunset I have seen the silhouette of the great building stand dead black on a red sky; on moonlight nights it stands black and silent, with glinting windows, like an enchanted castle. On misty autumn nights I have seen it emerging partially from the trails of

[66]

V. SACKVILLE-WEST

vapour, and heard the lonely roar of the red deer roaming under the walls."

Such is the opening page of V. Sackville-West's volume, *Knole and the Sackvilles*, a handsomely printed and illustrated account of the seat of the Earls and Dukes of Dorset. Authentic record of the family goes not beyond that Herbrand de Sackville who came to England with William the Conqueror. Knole, bought by Archbishop Bourchier in 1456, and held by Cardinal Morton, Cranmer, Henry VIII., Edward VI., Queen Mary and Elizabeth, was granted, in 1586 by Elizabeth, to Thomas Sackville, Lord Buckhurst, first Earl of Dorset. The name "West" enters with the marriage of Lady Elizabeth Sackville, sister of the fourth Duke, to John West, Earl de la Warr.

The house, of seven courts to correspond with the days of the week, fifty-two staircases matching the weeks of the year and 365 rooms answering to the days of the year * "is gentle and venerable. It has the deep inward gaiety of some very old woman who has always been beautiful, who has had many lovers and seen many generations come and go, smiled wisely over their sorrows and their joys, and learnt an imperishable secret of tolerance and humour. It is, above all, an English house." The garden side is the gay, the princely side. When, in

---

* "I cannot truthfully say," writes Miss Sackville-West in *Knole and the Sackvilles,* "that I have ever verified these counts, and it may be that their accuracy is accepted solely on the strength of the legend; but, if this is so, then it has been a very persistent legend, and I prefer to sympathise with the amusement of the ultimate architect on making the discovery that by a judicious juggling with his additions he could bring courts, stairs and rooms up to that satisfactory total."

[67]

summer, the great oak doors of the second gate-house were left open, "it has sometimes happened that I have found a stag in the banqueting hall, puzzled but still dignified, strayed in from the park since no barrier checked him."

ii

In 1825 the duchess Arabella Diana died and her estate devolved upon her two daughters, Mary and Elizabeth. Elizabeth, as has been told, became the wife of Lord de la Warr. Dying in 1870 she left Buckhurst to her elder sons and Knole to her younger sons, one of whom was Miss Sackville-West's grandfather. He was eighty and she perhaps eight, and as he shared "the family failing of unsociability" it fell to the child's lot to show the house to visitors. In this, as in more natural ways, she became highly familiar with Knole and from her earliest years must have loved the place. On receipt of a telegram that people were coming, Grandpapa would take the next train for London, "returning in the evening when the coast was clear." The Cartoon Gallery, the Leicester Gallery, the Brown Gallery; Lady Betty Germaine's bedchamber; the three principal bedrooms, the Spangled Room, the Venetian Ambassador's and the King's chamber, "the only vulgar room in the house" with furniture made entirely in silver and articles of silver, "even to a little eye-bath"—the procession of the days and years was not more certain than the procession of the curious, the inquisitive and the wonder-struck through these. You will fashion your own picture of the daughter of the Sackvilles standing before the portrait of Lady Margaret Sackville (over the fireplace in Lady Betty Germaine's sitting room) and endeavouring, quite vainly, to do her own hair in the elaborate manner of young Lady Margaret's. Or, it may be, she had been naughty that day, and had hid herself inside the pulpit of the Chapel of the Archbishops, where, in spite of private steps leading out of her bedroom straight into the Family Pew, "they never found me." Grandpapa was "a queer and silent old man," as Miss Sackville-West remembers him. "He knew nothing whatever about the works of art in the house; he spent hours gazing at the flowers, followed about the garden by two grave demoiselle cranes. . . . He and I, who so often shared the house alone between us, were companions in a shy and undemonstrative way. Although he had nothing to say to his unfortunate guests, he could understand a child. . . . When we were at Knole alone together I used to go down to his sitting-room in the evening to play draughts with him—and never knew whether I played to please him, or he played to please me— and sometimes, very rarely, he told me stories of when he was a small boy, and played with the rocking-horse, and of the journeys by coach with his father and mother from Buckhurst to Knole or from Knole to London; of their taking the silver with them under the seat; of their having outriders with pistols; and of his father and mother never addressing each other, in their children's presence, as anything but 'my Lord' and 'my Lady.' I clasped my knees and stared at him when he told me these stories

[69]

of an age which already seemed so remote, and his
pale blue eyes gazed away into the past, and suddenly his shyness would return to him and the clock
in the corner would begin to wheeze in preparation
to striking the hour, and he would say that it was
time for me to go to bed. . . ."

iii

At the age of thirteen Miss Sackville-West wrote
"an enormous novel" about the figure of Edward
Sackville, fourth Earl of Dorset, who seemed to her
the embodiment of Cavalier romance. And perhaps
he was. "He had the advantage of starting with
the Vandyck portrait in the hall, the flame-coloured
doublet, the blue Garter, the characteristic swag-
gering attitude, the sword, the love-locks, the key
of office painted dangling from his hip and the
actual key dangling on a ribbon from the frame of
the picture." The dashing career of this follower
of King Charles, who fought a duel with Lord
Bruce and whose younger son was murdered by the
Roundheads, became "a source of rich romance to a
youthful imagination nourished on *Cyrano* and *The
Three Musketeers.*" The half-grown girl re-examined
certain old nail-studded trunks in the attics, mute
witnesses to Cromwellian violence, some of them
curved to fit the roof of a barouche. "The battered
trunks were stacked near the entrance to the hiding-
place, which, without the smallest justification save
an old candlestick and a rope-ladder found therein,
I peopled with the fugitive figures of priests and
Royalists. I peeped into the trunks: they contained

[70]

only a dusty jumble of broken ironwork, some old books, some bits of hairy plaster fallen from the ceiling, some numbers of Punch for 1850. Nevertheless, there were the gaping holes where the locks had been prised off the trunks, and the lid forced back upon the hinges by an impatient hand. Down in the Poets' Parlour, where I lunched with my grandfather, taciturn unless he happened to crack one of his little stock-in-trade of jokes, Cromwell's soldiers had held their Court of Sequestration. The Guard Room was empty of arms or armour, save for a few pikes and halberds, because Cromwell's soldiers had taken all the armour away. The past mingled with the present in constant reminder; and out in the summer-house, after luncheon, with the bees blundering among the flowers of the Sunk Garden and the dragon-flies flashing over the pond, I returned to the immense ledger in which I was writing my novel, while Grandpapa retired to his little sitting-room and whittled paper-knives from the lids of cigar-boxes, and thought about—Heaven knows what *he* thought about."

iv

Miss Sackville-West is writing of Knole, of course, in her long story called *The Heir*. The manor of Blackboys with its peacocks is not Knole; I suppose no one makes the mistake of literal identification of people and places in fiction; at least, none should do so. What is truly identifiable is never anything tangible at all; it is merely an emotion. When we read *The Heir*, subtitled "A

Love Story," and acquaint ourselves in a leisurely sufficience with the fellow Chase we should be stupid indeed if we grasped at the substance and neglected the shadow. It is shadow and its correspondent sunlight for which, after all, mankind lives a life wherein the things of substance are the final unreality. . . .

But her first book, which was brought to the attention of the American publisher by Hugh Walpole, was a novel called *Heritage*, an unusual story of young lovers. The breath of distinction upon the tale more than redeemed its faults of construction, of which, perhaps, after all, the most serious was merely the device of a letter immensely longer than any epistle probable to be written. Then, in point of publication, at least, came *The Dragon in Shallow Waters*, also a novel. Some two years elapsed before the appearance of her third novel, *Challenge*, a piece of work of such a character as to demand our earnest scrutiny. *Challenge* is being followed by *Grey Wethers* and *The Heir*.

I have been speaking of American publication; in England Miss Sackville-West first came to notice as a poet. Her *Poems of West and East* was followed by another collection called *Orchard and Vineyard*. Her work in verse exhibited austerity of expression joined to an emotional and descriptive power difficult to appraise. Although it may be, as has been said, that the chief use of poetry, written when one is young, is to produce a finer prose when one is older.

Of *The Heir* it is best to say little since a few betraying words can so easily spoil its secret for

[72]

THE LADY OF A TRADITION

the reader. In the same volume appear *The Christmas Party*, *Patience*, *Her Son* and *The Parrot*, a vignette dedicated to "H. G. N." All the qualities present in *The Heir* may be found in the other tales, so varyingly shorter—delicacy, precision, dramatic power and a perception of beauty translated almost without the use of a single emotional word. In *The Christmas Party* we have the deferred revenge of a woman, a theatrical costumer, upon her strait-minded family; *Patience* is an elderly man's recollection, in perfectly domesticated surroundings, of his youthful affair; *Her Son* is the inevitable cruelty inflicted upon a mother by the passage of the years; the story of *The Parrot* points to the only escape from the . . . cage.

The "H. G. N." of its dedication is the Honourable Harold G. Nicolson. Except as an author, the lady of Knole is no longer Victoria Sackville-West but the Honourable Mrs. Harold G. Nicolson.

v

Challenge, a novel that may instructively be compared with Joseph Conrad's *Nostromo*, had the curious fortune to be published first in America and—what is more remarkable—only in America. It might seem altogether extraordinary that one of the most noteworthy novels by an Englishwoman in years should not only not be published first in England but should not be published there at all. It might seem very extraordinary; and it is. The circumstances were perhaps without a precedent and, it may be hoped, will be without a duplication.

In 1920 an English publisher had accepted *Challenge* and prepared it for issuance. That is to say, type had been set, plates had been cast, the sheets of the novel had been printed, folded and sewed. Nothing remained but to encase them in cloth—a matter of a week, usually—when the book would be ready to go on sale. It was the eleventh hour; 11.59 to be precise. Then fate intervened.

It transpired (or was allowed to transpire) that Miss Sackville-West had written her novel about an actual family, portraying that family in general and possibly in particular. The family was part of her own, or shall we say, connected with her own; and it was not without influence. This influence was immediately exerted to secure the suppression of *Challenge*. How far the influence succeeded, by virtue of its own force and considerations, and how far it was aided by the peculiarity of the English libel law, which recognises technical libel, I am unable to say; but succeed it did. *Challenge* remained unbound and the English house either put it down as a loss or, with a sanguineness born of much publishing experience, carried it in its inventory. There were all those folded and sewed sheets constituting a very fair-sized edition, as English editions go, packed away in some sufficiently dry place. At Knole and in Cornwall and it may be in other places Miss Sackville-West continued writing.

Probably the only challenge to the suppressors of the novel in England lay in the single figurative word of the title. Miss Sackville-West could be said to be writing of the actual family only in the same sense that we can say, in alluding to the manor of Blackboys in *The Heir*, that she writes of Knole. Some South American republic, indeed, any South American republic, would be equally justified in beginning suit for libel against Conrad for the picture of Costaguana in *Nostromo*—could a court be discovered in which such a suit would be justiciable? It is charitable to suppose that the suppressors beheld themselves mirrored in the pages of *Challenge* because they were victims of a narcism complex. However, the interesting disabilities of these people were of no serious importance on this side of the Atlantic; Miss Sackville-West had done no work of such importance as the unborn *Challenge;* and after all those unbound sheets had lain untouched for two years or longer the day came when an American publisher took the whole lot, together with the plates to enable him to print more, and *Challenge* saw the light in the United States early in 1923.

It is still unpublishable in England and seems destined indefinitely to remain so. Not indignation nor ridicule is likely to alter this state of affairs, since the prototypes of Miss Sackville-West's Davenants must be conceived of as resembling Galsworthy's Forsytes in one respect: They are almost certainly impervious to the wrath or derision of any except their own kind, and this will hardly be forthcoming.

Challenge, admirable in its technique, begins with an epilogue, giving us through the eyes of disinterested bystanders a glimpse of Julian Davenant many years afterward. We see him with his wife

[75]

at a great affair in London. He has power, wealth, distinction; and his wife is perfectly equipped for her rôle. Many people expect that Davenant will be the next Viceroy; he has already been in the Cabinet. A cynical man, who believes in nothing —and a philanthropist, really. His face, or his eyes, give one the impression that he has "learnt all the sorrow of the world"; they are inexpressibly weary. And the two onlookers, a man and a woman, recall that there was some "crazy adventure" in Julian Davenant's youth. "Very romantic, but we all start by being romantic until we have outgrown it."

The three parts which follow narrate in a strictly chronological order the details of that "crazy adventure." Julian Davenant was the young son of a house of English Levantines, that is to say, an English family established for several generations in the Levant and possessing, at the time of the story, besides much land, the site of valuable vineyards, prestige and influence and political power. It will be recalled that the Goulds of Costaguana in *Nostromo* constituted a similar clan. Such English exoterics (not to say exotics) are only moderately rare. It is not proper to speak of them as hybrids, since in their marriages they are careful to avoid a non-English admixture and their sons are invariably sent to England for their education. Without in any essential degree sacrificing a single one of those peculiarly tenacious English traits of character and without any alteration of the English habit of thought, they are in most other matters assimilated to the country of their holdings. They

[76]

come to understand it, its ways, its habit of thought
and policy of conduct and instinct of behaviour with
a completeness that amounts to perfection and re-
poses, as a rule and deep down, on a sincere distaste.
They are really marvellous, whether Goulds in
South America or Davenants in Greece. And their
young men . . .

In any comparison of *Nostromo* and *Challenge* it
will be found that the most obvious likenesses are
purely superficial. In *Nostromo* we have the son,
Charles Gould, determined to avenge, by a patient
commercialism and a silent political sagacity, the
fate of his Uncle Harry and the killing worry of
his father; the instrumentality to his hand is the
silver of the mine. In *Challenge* young Julian
Davenant is the victim of the romantic impulse
which causes him to respond, at any cost, to the
patriotic appeal of the Islands lying off the coast
and unwillingly a part of the tiny republic of
Herakleion. The girl, Eve, and the woman, Kato,
a native of the Islands and a famous singer, are the
personal contending forces in the struggle over
Julian Davenant. Eve is Julian's cousin. In the
developing story of her love for Julian, in its cul-
minating struggle and final disaster a precise comparison with *Nostromo*—even in respect of the
tragedy that befell Linda Viola—is a waste of our
attention.

vi

What may profitably be compared in Mr. Conrad's acknowledged masterpiece and Miss Sackville-
West's dramatic novel is the identity of method

[77]

AMERICAN NIGHTS ENTERTAINMENT

and art. I say "identity" without any hesitation,
for in both cases I think the artist has achieved a
proportionately impressive and living and beautiful
result. As to method, the reader will observe for
himself that either novel might have been written
by either author. In each case the actual knowledge
of a totally foreign country is perhaps the same; and
in neither case is it very great or very important.
Again, in each case, the imaginative creation is on
a plane so much above the level attained in other
(and very excellent) novels that the book must
definitely be set in a class apart. One accounts for
the intense imaginative insight of *The Old Wives'
Tale* and *My Antonia* (to choose two especially fine
examples) by saying that, after all, both Arnold
Bennett and Willa Cather had the immeasurable
aid of childhood's unblunted perceptiveness; and in
so partially accounting for the sheer fact, one does
quite rightly. But neither memory nor the deepest
well of sympathy serves to explain *Nostromo* and
Challenge; in these two novels the imagination had
to create something *de novo* and actively body it
forth; memories, hearsay, would be an actual
interference and the existence of an outer world a
positive interruption. They are both novels of a
perfectly valid idea recreated in terms of the subconscious personality. If that is too cloudy an explanation I will ask you to think of the subconscious
mind as a happily benevolent oyster, of the germ-
idea as an infinitesimal particle of irritant sand, and
of the accomplished story as the resulting pearl. It
is as near as I can come to conveying what I mean
. . . and know to be at least subjectively true.

[78]

THE LADY OF A TRADITION

Abandoning this difficult region and ascending to the surface on which most art and literary method lies, the comparison becomes so easy that one feels superfluous in making it. Have we not the same complexity of persons presented in an intimate relation to each other and composing a little world, complete socially, politically and in their attitudes; so that we can perfectly conceive them in any set of circumstances? Have we not also an atmosphere resulting from a multitude of impalpable small touches? Is not the effect in each case more exact than any impression to be derived from personal familiarity with either South America or Greece? Is not the same impersonal viewpoint present? the same astringent humour in evidence in its application to the incongruities of the life presented? In both cases the avoidance of any expression of emotion, the final austerity of the highest art, exercises an effect out of all predictable proportion on the emotions of the reader. He is led to feel amusement, ridicule, sympathy, indignation, dismay, horror and grief; because never is it intimated to him that it is his duty to feel any of these things.

vii

The new novel, *Grey Wethers*, taking its name from those ancient sacrificial stones of the Druids which are the symbols of the story, traces back in substance to Miss Sackville-West's *Heritage*, but is free from the faults of construction which made her first novel so unsatisfactory. The fineness of her hand upon this more familiar material is the delicate reward for her incessant painstaking. She is not a person to rest satisfied, but an artist. An artist . . .

"What was the promise of that mediocre ease beside the certainty of these exquisite privations?" So Chase questioned himself, in Miss Sackville-West's story of *The Heir*. "What was that drudgery beside this beauty, this pride, this Quixotism?" There is only one answer. If you would be an artist you do not even bother with the answer. But your heart leaps.

Books by V. Sackville-West

Poems of West and East [in England]
1921 *Orchard and Vineyard* [in England]
1918 *Heritage*
1920 *The Dragon in Shallow Waters*
1923 *Knole and the Sackvilles*
1923 *Challenge* [withdrawn in England prior to publication, 1920]
1923 *Grey Wethers*
1924 *The Heir and Other Stories*

Sources on V. Sackville-West

Knole and the Sackvilles, generally, and also pages 11, 17, 68, 82, 83, 219 and 220
Who's Who [in England]
Private Information

Harold Bell Wright

i

FROM *Who's Who in America*, 1922-1923 (Volume 12):

"WRIGHT, HAROLD BELL, author: born, Rome, Oneida County, New York, May 4, 1872; son, William A. Wright and Alma T. (Watson) Wright; student two years, preparatory department, Hiram College, Ohio; married, Frances E. Long, of Buffalo, New York, July 18, 1899; married, second, Mrs. Winifred Mary Potter Duncan, of Los Angeles, California, August 5, 1920. Painter and decorator, 1887-92; landscape painter, 1892-7; pastor, Christian (Disciples) Church, Pierce City, Missouri, 1897-8, Pittsburg, Kansas, 1898-1903, Forest Avenue Church, Kansas City, Missouri, 1903-5, Lebanon, Missouri, 1905-7, Redlands, California, 1907-8; retired from ministry, 1908. Author: *That Printer of Udell's*, 1903; *The Shepherd of the Hills*, 1907; *The Calling of Dan Matthews*, 1909; *The Uncrowned King*, 1910; *The Winning of Barbara Worth*, 1911; *Their Yesterdays*, 1912; *The Eyes of the World*, 1914; *When A Man's a Man*, 1916; *The Re-Creation of Brian Kent*, 1919; *Helen of the Old House*, 1921. Home: Tucson, Arizona."

[81]

AMERICAN NIGHTS ENTERTAINMENT

Such is the outline derived by the compilers of an invaluable work of reference whose method is to ask of the individual certain standard questions which he may answer in his discretion and which he may supplement—in the editor's discretion—by further information about himself. The latitude allowed in such a work as *Who's Who in America*, is necessarily rather small; it would, however, have permitted Mr. Wright to say that the sales of his fiction exceed those of any other living American writer—perhaps those of any other living writer anywhere. He did not say it. The impression given by the words "landscape painter" may be misleading, for Mr. Wright at that time made his living by sign painting and house painting; but also he made sketches and water colors which he sold as he went along. Let this tiny matter be as a warning that, on his own terms and in his own fashion of speech, Harold Bell Wright is to be taken literally.

Always! Is there metaphor in his writing? Was there metaphor in *Pilgrim's Progress?* Are there parables in the Bible? Do sermons contain allegories? We know that allegories embody sermons. Mr. Wright has never concealed the purpose behind his novels, stories. It is to say plainly some word that he believes will be of help, if uttered, to men and women. In his strange personal history lies the seed of a novel more absorbing, if less credible, than any he has written. The poor boy, the boy left motherless at ten, the man out of work, the man with an empty stomach and no means of filling it, the man who has been told that "the rock

HAROLD BELL WRIGHT

pile was intended for fellows like you!"—and through it all the sleazy thread of ill-health, downright sickness, and the bright scarlet stain of disease. . . . Two years at a little college, cut short by illness; two years financed by hard work and ground down in disappointment. Then the haphazard wandering, the tramping afoot outdoors, the small painting jobs, the inability to find work at times, the hardships of climate—and at last he finds himself in the Ozark Mountains looking for . . . what? For the chance to live, first of all. It was there that he preached his first sermon, and there he found a background and a setting for some of the stories he was eventually to write. They were very far off, then, those stories, below the horizon, out of sight as were so many other things that were to dawn on his life when he should be thirty.

ii

In any consideration of Harold Bell Wright as an author, the usual approaches are of no value, and not only of no value but so without meaning as to be absurd. Almost he raises the fundamental question: What is an author, anyway? Of course the word does apply to all whose writing achieves publication, especially as a book or books; and perhaps it may be used of a person who remains unpublished. But, as always, there is here a meaning within a meaning; the word generally carries with it some suggestion of literary skill or a pretension thereto—as "doctor" implies a medical training, or "lawyer" admission to practise at the bar. However, Mr. Wright neither possesses any literary skill nor ever pretended to have any, comparatively speaking. He has more than once uttered an emphatic disclaimer, but like other very popular writers his sensitiveness to adverse criticism is keen.

He is a moralist, a fabulist, a preacher of sermons, a Sayer, and an Utterer. There is in the impoverished English language no word for his rôle. The English language, so full of words for things that do not exist, has none for this type of man who has always existed among the English-speaking peoples though rather sparsely among other peoples. When forced to recognise his existence as a power for evil in politics, we borrow the word demagogue; if his activity is rather indefinitely "religious," we affix the word evangelist. There is a common factor in John Bunyan, Theodore Roosevelt, James Whitcomb Riley, Harold Bell Wright easily recognised in whatever field it operates. In the case of Mr. Wright, it has been said that he appeals "to the thousands upon thousands who crave to see their humble doings, their paper fantasies exalted and made memorable in the bright guise of a seeming romance." Unfortunately for the success of this diagnosis, it is not the great masses of mankind who are sentimental, but the minority who have accustomed themselves to the contemplation of mankind in great masses. If Mr. Roosevelt had addressed himself to the "thousands upon thousands" he would have been almost without influence; and Mr. Riley's verses are most noteworthy for their intimate personal appeal. Such a Sayer as Walt Whitman, speaking to men *en masse*, receives from men small attention. One can neither speak, write, paint, carve or build for the thousands; one must do it for the individual every time. In a short study of Roosevelt some years ago the editor of the Atlantic Monthly, Ellery Sedgwick, admirably indicated Roosevelt's real achievement, which was—not that he moulded national policies but that he made the homegoing day labourer, sitting in a trolley car, his empty lunch pail beside him, trace with a stubby forefinger in the evening newspaper the simple precept for that day, whether a command against race suicide or a "Don't flinch! Don't foul! Hit the line hard!" He who would speak to many men and women must always address each one; he must not make the mistake of appealing to a lowest common intelligence and he must perfectly understand that what is called "sentimentality" is not a weakness but a sign of health —pink thoughts like pink cheeks.

iii

"She stood before him in all the beautiful strength of her young womanhood."

"He was really a fine looking young man with the appearance of being exceptionally well-bred and well-kept. Indeed the most casual of observers would not have hesitated to pronounce him a thoroughbred and a good individual of the best type that the race has produced. . . ."

These sentences, from Wright's novel, *The Winning of Barbara Worth*, have been quoted

[85]

with the comment that Wright himself is that casual observer and that, to the more thoughtful, Abraham Lincoln, who "was anything but a thoroughbred, anything but well-kept" is the best type of individual that the race has produced. Mr. Wright could crushingly reply that Lincoln was not a type; but the failure in perception goes much deeper. The critic of the passage quoted must know very well that the respect of mankind for appearances is well-founded. Appearances can be arrived at and kept up, being thus one of the few things definitely within our powers of accomplishment and control; for what lies under the appearance may be beyond our power to make or change. It is not instinct, or even reason, but a solid regard for fact that prizes appearance. Further, in the affair in question, two subjects for a possible mating, the usual man or woman is as unromantic and unsentimental as possible in his or her satisfaction at the good looks of hero and heroine. Those good looks and good manners are something to go upon. Each has an asset with the other and there is some chance for the children, if any. Only a dangerous sentimentalist would wish the man to be a mongrel. Mr. Wright knows all this; so do we all of us; why, then, is he called a sentimentalist?

Because, I suppose, an inveterate tradition of the minority brands the majority as sentimental. Were they so, they could not live. The majority, not being victims of self-delusion, go through life, eating, sleeping, working and feeling. The capacity to feel has not in them been weakened. They may be robbed of their cheeks' pinkness, but it is more

[86]

difficult to take away the pinkness of their thoughts (the mere mental accompaniments of their feelings). Indeed, it has so far proved impossible to enslave them by any intellectual system, as they have been enslaved by this or that economic system. If it were possible to persuade these men and women that physical mongrelism should take the place of Mr. Wright's hero's thoroughbreeding, the world would have become sentimental with a vengeance likely to recoil on the heads of those who wrought the persuasion. The French Revolution would be as nothing to the new era then dawning.

In other words, the young man used to advertise linen collars (and Mr. Wright, at the young man's age, might easily have served as the model) is the people's proper hero. He represents, to a considerable extent, something within the average power to become. No more suggestive antithesis can be imagined than between a novel like *The Shepherd of the Hills* and such a work of fiction as Mr. Sinclair Lewis's *Main Street*, crammed with the things beyond the average power to alter. It is the interesting inevitability of the visitor to humble homes in out of the way American places to encounter, on the parlour table or its equivalent, a Bible, a "gift" edition of Longfellow's Poems, *The Wreck of the "Titanic"* (with complete horrors, last words of all on board, and full text of "Nearer, My God, to Thee," as played by the ship's band) and a copy of *The Shepherd of the Hills*, or, perhaps, *When a Man's a Man*. But *Main Street?* That, if it was ever in the house, has gone the way of all wood pulp very quickly. For these people have

[87]

none of that difficulty experienced by the literary critic in distinguishing books, and their applied canons are not matters of taste or sentiment or intellectual theory, but principles of living as they are compelled to practise them daily, personal and intimate, directed toward the best appearance, unsentimental, unintellectual, individual, healthful, sensibly ambitious, emotionally direct and . . . free.

iv

Suppose, instead of audibly deploring Mr. Wright, and uttering in their assaults upon him an unconscionable amount of twaddle, the literary critics were to transform themselves into students of the popular psychology. In such case they would see at once how the usual person unsentimentally proceeds through life with the assistance of attainable ideals. Of course, definitions of sentimentality may and do differ. My idea here is simply that to espouse the shadowy ideal is to come much more under the charge of being sentimental than to aspire to wear the newest style of linen collar, or acquire good manners. I think at once, too, of a writer whose best work meets the severe tests applied by the critic of literature, Mr. Arnold Bennett. What is *The Old Wives' Tale*, what is *Clayhanger*, each a work of accepted art, but a faithful transcription of the average person's utter unsentimentality and complete devotion to the attainable ideal? Mr. Bennett made the same veracious observation as Mr. Wright makes; it is only the presentation that is different—objective in the case of Bennett, im-

[88]

mersed in the case of Wright. For Bennett's purpose literary art is essential, for Wright's, literary art is a handicap. Moreover, the identification is unlike. The people Bennett writes about, with the exception of Clayhanger, would not recognise themselves in his two novels; the people of Mr. Wright, would. Why? Because Wright expresses them in their own fractions—known to themselves. Bennett carries them out to a decimal repetend— .142857142857142857 and so on, instead of 1/7, subscribed by Mr. Wright. Virtue, vice, greed, ambition, youth and the like are the simple fractions in which Mr. Wright's characters are stated. Whatever realities these names represent, it had better be realised that they are in themselves the simplest, most necessary conventions. And as such, and as such only, has Wright used them.

His method of work was, I think, the innocent source of the general misunderstanding surrounding him in the discussions of the minority. It is well-known that before writing a novel he prepares a short argument, as other writers prepare an outline or plot. "The system I use," he has explained, "may have been used for centuries, or it may be no one else has ever used it. I have wondered whether it is old or new. Whichever it may be, here it is: When I start to write a novel, the first thing I do is to figure out why I am going to write it. Not what is the story, but why? I mull this over a while, and when it is pretty straight in my mind, I write out an argument. No suggestion of plot, you see. No incidents, scenes, location, nothing done at first except the argument, but it is the heart and soul of the novel. The novel is merely this argument presented through the medium of characters, plot, incidents, and the other properties of the story. Next come the characters, each standing for some element or factor in the argument. Up to the last copying of *The Eyes of the World*, not a character had been named. They were called in the copy, Greed, Ambition, Youth, or whatever they represented to me in the writing of the story." This simple explanation has been derided by asserting that "Mr. Wright seeks to prove some abstract notion of his own concerning good and evil by means of a picked assembly of human beings." But how so? They are not picked human beings at all, but like Bunyan's characters, expressions of the One. They prove nothing and are intended to prove nothing, being merely expository, fabulous, moralistic, and the natural presentation of no easy notion but some familiar fact—far from abstract! Take *The Re-Creation of Brian Kent*, one of Wright's least satisfactory books to its author and to many readers and released by Wright with great reluctance. An abstract notion is the last thing in the world it touches upon; all is simple, vivid, commonplace, centred around the actuality that, with another chance, many a man can set his life straight.

If there is any shortcoming it arises from Wright's personal strength. The man who can do what he has done, persistently fighting tuberculosis, risking public opinion in several matters and adhering to his method in spite of a great change of personal attitude and a personal revolution in ideas—

[90]

that man is no weakling. It would be interesting to survey the personal change in Mr. Wright but as it nowhere extrudes in his work, there is no justification for an inquest. But the very circumstance has its positive value in establishing him for what he is not, namely, an artist. But there is another aspect of Mr. Wright as phenomenon (not as person) and his success cannot be understood without examining that aspect.

v

Wright's boyhood, to the age of ten when he lost her, was focussed about the personality of his mother. When she died he lost, if not perhaps his only friend, his strongest. Before he could read she had told him the Hiawatha legends, had read aloud to him the stories of the Bible (the King James version), had retold Shakespeare for him. Her death made him clutch to his heart these books, as well as the *Pilgrim's Progress* and the portions of Ruskin they read and re-read together in the home—which, by the way, was really at Wrightstown, just outside Rome, New York, though Wright's birthplace is spoken of as "Rome." A feeling that these books of his mother's were as sacred books was fixed in the boy's mind. Wright has never ceased to read them, nor to try to pour himself into those molds; and in conversation he sometimes lets slip a phrase from one of them. Without literary aptitude and with a very ragged species of formal education, he speaks in his extraordinary fashion and the millions hearken. So much so that his success from the outset may be said to have entirely reconstructed—for the purpose of merchandising his books—the retail machinery of book-selling.

The author of *That Printer of Udell's* had the means of reaching the folks in little villages and on isolated farms, people who could scarcely be reached by any of the books ordinarily being published. The very inadequate machinery of retail distribution serving the book trade was insufficient for his purpose. It is insufficient for most purposes, but its insufficiency in the case of Harold Bell Wright was painful and intolerable. With the most remarkable courage, effort and persistence the publishers constructed a new and complete retail mechanism to serve the special need. Those who have no knowledge of the problems of merchandising will be unable to appreciate what they did. A few details are in order. First, the larger book publishers in the United States seldom sell directly to retailers in cities of less than 50,000; smaller publishers seldom enter cities of less than 100,000. The needs of bookstores in little cities and towns, mixed and important only in the aggregate, are taken care of by jobbers. There are possibly 1,000 first-rate bookstores to serve a nation of well over 100,000,000 people—of whom, however, some 20,000,000 are incapable of ever reading a book of any importance in an understanding way. There are cities of 50,000 in which no first-rate bookstore exists. On the other hand a magazine like Pictorial Review, solidly established on the demand for dress patterns, or a magazine like Saturday Evening Post, promulgating fiction patterns, penetrates into places where no new book is ever seen. So, too, do certain denominational religious papers. And in vast areas of the Middle and Far West, there is a seepage from those reservoirs of modern merchandising, the mail order houses, the Roosevelt Dams of commerce, constantly seeking, more and more achieving the reclamation of the deserts of trade.

The "producers," in stage parlance, of Harold Bell Wright determined to utilise all these channels. It was a great risk of judgment and money at the outset but it succeeded. This is no place to go into the history of a unique performance in merchandising but the results have a distinct place in any record of the author exploited. For one thing, it may be asked if the success with Wright is of value in selling other authors, and while there can be no dogmatic answer to the question it is probable that in most cases it is not. And another phase of the results throws a significant light on the nature of Wright's work, confirming what we have said about the terms of his appeal to his readers. When a Wright novel is published the orders pile in from stores and places with which a publisher has ordinarily no contact; and the order from a hamlet in North Carolina is likely to exceed the order from Brentano's in New York.

This means two things. It means, naturally, that with the heavy campaigns of advertising in all sorts of periodicals from Saturday Evening Post to Zion's Herald, the publishers reach the people who buy a book a year or less often. But also it means that Wright is the moralist, the fabulist and the Sayer

we have termed him. On the technical side, perhaps the most instructive detail of this selling performance is the way in which it is initiated. Six
months before a new Wright story is to be published,
thousands of tradespeople all over the United States
know that the story is to be published, and when,
and with what enormous advertising placed in forty
specified periodicals and several dozen newspapers
it will be "pushed"; and then begins the steady
succession of personal letters and even telegrams,
circulars and placards and posters, honest-minded
persons in remote settlements discuss with enthusiasm and awe the prodigious sum of money to be ex-
pended on "just this one book, a *book*," librarians
grow anxious and advertising men eager, preachers
prepare sermons, in thousands upon thousands of
homes the Christmas gift to Mother is pre-deter-
mined,—until at last, in a wide-rolling wave of
excitement, a vast surge of the people of simple
faith and worthy ideals, the day comes when the
book is born. . . .

vi

It has been said that Wright is of magnetic
personality, with fine, clean, inspiring ideals, a man
of tireless endeavour, a person who "stirs in one
emotions of which one is not ashamed." Also that
"he radiates a Lincolnian type of rugged honesty"
. . . and much more of the same sort. All such
lingo is meaningless outside the atmosphere of
Wright's books. The language of those novels is
not one of literary conventions but of certain
inalterable thought-conventions; and so, necessarily,

[94]

is language addressed to those who read Wright. "She stood before him in all the beautiful strength of her young womanhood." . . . "It is his almost clairvoyant power of reading the human soul that has made Mr. Wright's books among the most remarkable of the present age." These two statements are demonstrably true to the many whose minds, struck by such sentences, give back the ring of silver. They are not true in themselves; but then, we know no things that are. To be "true" is simply to signify enough, at a given time, in particular circumstances, to some individual or individuals.

That truth Mr. Wright has had enormously, and still has. His newest novel, *The Mine With the Iron Door*, although in no way an elaboration of the traditional tale of that mine—it was supposed to be a wonder mine, where the old Spanish Fathers got the gold that enriched their splendid altars— weaves the old legend through its texture of incident. This gives to the novel a colour beyond the colour it has from its Arizona setting; but the point with Mr. Wright is something like this: Every life has its "mine with the iron door," its dreams that can never come true, its hopes that belong to a past that is forever dead. Nevertheless, he will have you believe, though the lost mine may never be found nor the iron door opened, some riches of happiness is still possible. Were it not for this element, this presentation of something that at a given time and in particular circumstances can signify truth to many, many people, Mr. Wright's new novel would be no more than a picturesque and exciting adventure narrative of the Arizona desert.

vii

Mr. Wright went to Tucson, Arizona, some ten years ago on a business errand. Three days after reaching the city he had bought a cottage. Now he owns eighty acres outside Tucson and has built a new home, a comfortable but by no means pretentious house with a garden transplanted from the neighbouring desert. The scale of living is modest. Wright and his wife take care of the grounds and house, to a large extent; and there is usually not more than one servant. Mr. Wright has a motor car that he has driven for six years and will continue to drive for some years yet. He is fond of horseback riding and spends as much time camping as at home. Two or three tents, the car, some tinned stuff and staples and plenty of ammunition are all Mr. and Mrs. Wright need, for both are good marksmen. They shoot for food, but Wright will not kill a deer.

The stories are frequently written, or largely written, on these expeditions into the desert. Because he is not an artist, Wright has a sadly difficult time. He will submit a story like *The Winning of Barbara Worth* to five engineers in order that they may check up his account of the irrigation of the desert. A long time was spent in worrisome "looking over the ground," visiting factory towns, interviewing employers and workmen, before *Helen of the Old House* took even preliminary shape. As a rule, the incidents Wright uses are transcribed

[96]

from life, producing the effect of extreme incredibility of which his readers sometimes complain. Being his readers, they are silenced when he tells them of the actual occurrence.

Hildegarde Hawthorne has pointed out the very great and incontestable service of Wright: He creates book readers. It requires very little examination of the facts to discover that thousands whose reading has been nothing but newspapers and magazines have been led by Wright's stories into the habit of reading a book occasionally. That is an accomplishment of an importance hard to overrate.

As for the man, there is one story I like better than any he has written. Some years ago, riding horseback on a narrow trail, Wright was struck by an automobile that came suddenly around a corner of rock. Horse and rider were pitched into a gully; the horse was killed and Wright's particularly bad lung so suffered by the fall that everyone assured him there was nothing left but to die. He said: "I won't die." Because he couldn't be moved, a tent had to be erected over him there in the gully, so that he might die in the shade. Lying there under the tent, he fulfilled his purpose by getting well. He also, under the same tent and in the same place, wrote *When a Man's a Man*. . . . And now he is again in good physical shape, riding his horses after the day's work is over through the desert or up into the foothills of the Catalina Mountains.

The preacher he began, the preacher he must probably remain. There may, perhaps, be something pitiful in the spectacle of a man struggling

[97]

with the palette of words, as there is something bizarre in the voice proceeding from the wilderness with a perfectly mundane message: That every valley had better be filled, every mountain and hill nicely graded; the crooked carefully straightened, the rough ways . . . paved with asphalt.

Books by Harold Bell Wright

1903 *That Printer of Udell's*
1907 *The Shepherd of the Hills*
1909 *The Calling of Dan Matthews*
1910 *The Uncrowned King*
1911 *The Winning of Barbara Worth*
1912 *Their Yesterdays*
1914 *The Eyes of the World*
1916 *When a Man's a Man*
1919 *The Re-Creation of Brian Kent*
1921 *Helen of the Old House*
1923 *The Mine With the Iron Door*

Sources on Harold Bell Wright

Harold Bell Wright. Booklet published by D. Appleton & Company
Harold Bell Wright, the Man Behind the Novels, by HILDEGARDE HAWTHORNE. Booklet published by D. Appleton & Company
Private Information

NOTE: Since this chapter was written Mr. Wright has put on paper his own account of his experience when death was so near. His article, practically the only autobiographical matter extant, is (as this "Note" is written) scheduled to appear in an early number of the American Magazine, and will probably have appeared therein before this book can come into the hands of readers in September, 1924. Its importance and interest hardly need to be stressed.

The Man Called
Ralph Connor

i

ONCE upon a time there was a Scotsman of Clan
Gordon, those Highlanders ye ken of Blair
Athol in the North Country, properly named with
a God-fearing name, Daniel, and a fine, stirring
preacher, too. Fire was on his lips but the flame
burning in his heart was tender and you should have
lived to hear him piping "Lochaber No More." The
pibrochs sounded something beautiful as he played;
and when he stopped piping it was to begin relating
wonderful old stories; he kenned them all. Away
back in the 1840s it was he came out to Canada
with other folk from the North of Scotland and
fetched up in a Highland settlement in Ontario,
Glengarry, in the Indian Lands. Full twenty years
this man of God spent in Glengarry, taking a wife
from among the Robertsons. Her father had come
to New England first, moving on to Sherbrooke in
the Province of Quebec. I could tell you a deal
about her family; there was a cousin, Andrew
Murray, of Clairvaux, led the Dutch Reformed
South African Church; ye'll have heard of Robertson Smith and he was another cousin; the writer
M. M. Robertson was a sister. Mary Robertson

[100]

taught philosophy as a lass of twenty in Mount Holyoke College in New England. They offered to make her principal on the death of Mary Lyons and she was duly considering for a while. She was of the Robertsons of Aberdeen, ye ken, and twenty-two years aged. But there was this young Highlander, Daniel Gordon of Glengarry in the Indian Lands, who was swaying congregations. Well, then, she turned her small, straight back on the principalship and married him, and went away from that pleasant place and company and fine position that stood waiting for her to live in the backwoods of Canada, a rare wild parish with the railway twenty-five miles off and a long journey to everywhere. She was a remarkable woman. Daniel Gordon took her to his home in the woods. In the year 1860 she bore him a son; they named the boy Charles. The laddie played about the square brick house with wide verandas that stood in a natural park of pines and maples, with a glebe of some twenty-four acres and forest all about. Two miles by a path through the woods took him to school in a clearing, and two miles back. They played games in the shadows of the pines. There was a rich green darkness and a curious coolness and a curious warmth there for them; the tops of the pines murmured like distant bagpipes and everything smelt sharp and sweet.

On a day when the boy was eleven Daniel Gordon went to sway another congregation in Western Ontario, taking his wife and the boy along, for that there were better schools for Charley to go to. What with this, and high school in a neighbouring town, the lad makes ready for Toronto and the University.

He didna do badly at the University, though he was no sober-sided student. He sang in the glee club and played quarterback at Rugby football in the champion team for Western Ontario. Some honours in classics he got and went on to the study of theology at Knox College. He was not too strong in those years and capturing scholarships and prizes in the three years' courses at Knox College did him no good bodily. So then it was settled he should take a year abroad, spent mostly in Edinburgh, where he could walk along gay Princes Street and see the grand sight of Castle Rock, or climb to Arthur's Seat and look over the Firth of Forth with its speckle of green islands and white sails and the bare country of the Kingdom of Fife, or pace slowly down the Royal Mile to Holyrood, with every step a threefold memory and an historic lesson. I'll not say this did him any harm, maybe, and what it lacked in one way he made up on his return to Canada, taking his brother and travelling deep into the forest on Lake Nipissing, they seeing no other white man for three months. To crown these journeyings and to confirm the habit of health Charles Gordon spent two more years at Banff. There, in the heart of the Rockies, he climbed mountains and rejoiced in wildness. "Yes, I ought to have been an Indian!" he used to exclaim.

ii

He was ripe to receive his call at last, and it came. It took him to a life of rough hardship as a missioner in the North-West, all among lumbermen and miners with a congregation to be gathered first, and sore deeficult to sway in assembly. He came well-shod to the work of treading out the harvest in the Lord's vineyard. He could go into the woods and come out again, or face a man mad with drink, or comfort a sick mother. A tall, slender, well set up young missioner with no very much ruddiness of complexion and a thoughtful, serious face that could yet smile, for a' that, with crinkles in the eye corners. You would know him for Scots by his look, but the rest is puir American. And he loved those men among whom his work lay. When, along in 1894 and him just well into his thirties, he was asked to a city church, he didna want to respond favourably until he saw where his duty lay. Well, then, he came to Winnipeg and to the ministry of St. Stephen's because it offered him the grand chance to help those roughened men whose needs he knew. Ye ken, perhaps, Mr. J. A. MacDonald of the Toronto Globe newspaper. MacDonald had been a classmate of Charley Gordon's and a year or two after Charley Gordon came as preacher to St. Stephen's, MacDonald was owner of a new little paper called The Westminster and concerned with Canadian Presbyterianism—a frank experiment. Into the office of The Westminster dropped Charley Gordon one fine day. He was in a great heat for money to put into the foothills and the mountain camps. They needed missions out there; I'm burning up with the wish to write an article telling about those men in the pines and along the upland lakes, Charley Gordon tells MacDonald. I've facts and figures. MacDonald was quick to say, if Charley wanted to bring home his message to people and loosen the purse-strings, he had a duty to write the thing as a tale, paint a picture with lifelike figures and a warm feeling running through it all. Gordon minded himself of what he had seen and heard in such good plenty; and he went home and sat down to write a story of Christmas Eve among the lumbermen in the Selkirk mountains. When he was fair into it, he found himself carried back and away, so much so that in reading it through after he didna see what brother clergymen might make out of the ringing speech of some of his characters. MacDonald agreed, but sent to find out what name to put on the story. Gordon invented a name, Cannor, out of the first letters of "Canada" and "North-West." MacDonald picked up the reply telegram and snorted disdain. Cannor, he commented, what sort of a name is that! I'll make it Connor. And where's a first name? Frank? Fred? Chris? No. Ralph? Aye, we'll make it that. This was the birth and christening together, ye'll ken. The tale of the lumbermen's Christmas Eve in the mountains was later to become the first chapter of the novel, *Black Rock*, the first novel by Ralph Connor, that was read everywhere.

iii

I'll not have to be telling you what it was in *Black Rock* won so many readers for Ralph Connor. Humour and pathos are bound up in the lives the young minister of St. Stephen's was writing about; ye could lay hold quickly of his sympathy for those

THE MAN CALLED RALPH CONNOR

men who were in some ways as helpless as bairns
and were half-brutalised by their work and surroundings. It's the effect they have on each other,
too. Them picking up *Black Rock* to read were
struck with something fresh and wild and clean,
withal. They sensed a tenderness about the feeling
of the story, like heather softening the bare hillside,
and more than a morsel of the everlasting hope in
which men endure hard and lonely toils. The same
held true of the books that followed *Black Rock;*
for there had to be other books. Ye mind *The Sky
Pilot* and *The Man From Glengarry* and *The Foreigner* and *Corporal Cameron* and *The Patrol of the
Sun Dance Trail*. Take *The Foreigner*. On the
edge of Winnipeg, Charles Gordon found a Settlement of Slavs—Ruthenians, Russians, Galicians
and who not. They lived in a grim little collection
of huts, a dozen in a room, all huddled up, drinking
and dirty and violent; and on them was still the
shadow of tyrannies in the Old Country. Drinking
and dirty and violent with a violence dark and beautiful, Charles Gordon found them. Aye, he found
the huts and the men, and Ralph Connor that was
in him found a story. Ralph Connor took the splendid young heart in Kalmar, the son of a nihilist,
and brought it to fight its way out of the ruck of
aliens and make for the new country beyond the
Saskatchewan, where there is prairie and where the
lakes lie on the surface of the prairie like jewels
on a woman's breasts. Then, in *Corporal Cameron*,
was Connoring the first grand tale of the North-
West Mounted Police, by a man who kenned them,
as followers in his tracks scarce can be said to. A

[105]

richt fine love story is this of the lad who was born in a Scottish glen and came to ride out in the Canadian blizzards; it's furthered in *The Patrol of the Sun Dance Trail*, which makes use of the half-breed and Indian rebellion of Louis Riel. But there's a muckle I love in the book besides the adventure—Cameron and his gold-haired, plucky wife and the hesitant wonder of the first fine feeling of the lover. It fashes me how a man says what's down in the hearts of such a many other men and women. Give me to understand how it's done! Here's the Reverend Charles Gordon dwelling this quarter century and longer in Winnipeg, building up St. Stephen's and seeing it transformed from a plain chapel of wood into a handsome church of stone, with a church house where the young men without homes can live, and where there's sewing and amateur acting and films and bowling every night of the week. In the daytime the Reverend Gordon will maybe attend court to help get some boy straightened out and become a guardian to him; or he'll be at meetings in his church where revolutionary agitators are spouting the downfall of all institutions and then voting thanks to the preacher because, as they put it, he has given us an absolutely square deal. And after supper you would find him in his home at evening prayers with the three youngsters who appeared to enjoy their devotions. There's no stiltedness in the man at all. He reads from Scripture concerning Paul taking Timothy with him to learn what were the problems of that day. And he closes the book on his finger to remark what a sensible, canny thing for

Paul to do. Some of our theological seminaries, adds the father, shut a man out from contact with life, shut him up with professors, and when he comes out of his cloister he canna recognise a social problem if it walks up to him on the street. The trouble with me, he finishes, when I had gotten out of the seminary.

But he's generous to a fault sore in a son of Scots folk. If his right hand is earning moneys with a pen, his left hand is spending lavish and free. There's his salary as minister to the kirk goes flowing out several times over in gifts and helpings to people. I mind the year quite long back when the Presbyterian General Assembly of Canada was meeting in Toronto and Doctor the Reverend Gordon put down $10,000 so every missionary minister and his wife in the breadth of Canada might attend the General Assembly, expenses paid. Some of these men and their wives hadn't been out of the woods in years. Ralph Connor knew what this meant.

iv

Then, when the Great War came thundering, our sky pilot stood up and said Canada must send a half million men. Many scoffed at him; but he was right, and we sent the half million and over sixty thousand didna come back. From St. Stephen's there was an enlistment of close on four hundred, including the minister and five members of the Session. The dominie went in the spring of 1915 after the congregation had confirmed his leave of absence—Major Charles W. Gordon, chaplain to the Forty-third Battalion Cameron Highlanders of Canada. Many St. Stephen's men were enrolled in this battalion and one of the members of the Session, Robert McDonald Thomson, was their first colonel. It was the Western Front—from the Ypres Salient, Sanctuary Wood, the bloodshed of the Somme and back again to Arras. In that time Ralph Connor saw the regiment shrunk from full strength to two officers and sixty-five men. He knelt down amid the roar of guns and the hailing of machine gun bullets to do last rites for his own men and comrades. Among them was Colonel Thomson. On the eighth day of October, 1916, the outfit stormed the Regina Trench on the Somme. Unable to advance, they wouldna retreat. So they died where they stood.

v

The Major and *The Sky Pilot in No Man's Land* are books ye'll verra well recollect; likewise the novel of twa years back, *To Him That Hath.* Since ye hanna read it, it's the new novel from the pen of Ralph Connor, I'll just speak a word of to ye. He calls it *The Gaspards of Pine Croft* and explains it is "a romance of the Windermere Valley." A story of the life and moulding of Paul Gaspard, it is. Here's a mon with two powerful strains mixed and fighting for mastery of him. From his mither, Paul inherits a rare sense of the presence of God; his father gifted him with a fine artist sense, and a bounding spirit, a passion for life to the full. The clash of the two men in the boy grows with him to manhood, so that after the death of

[108]

his mither he stands between two women, who beckon different ways. Then when a great decision is put before him the mon takes upon himself a burden and a responsibility that test him body and soul. 'Tis a life and death struggle set in the grand country Ralph Connor makes his own. There's the valley of the Windermere before you with the Gaspard ranch, Pine Croft, flanked on one side by a great bend of the Columbia River and on the other by a mountain wall of virgin forest. In this mysterious wilderness, the figures of Indians do come and go, touching the lives of the white people with disaster, with dread—with an unco beauty as well.

Books by Ralph Connor

	Beyond the Marshes
1898	*Black Rock*
1899	*The Sky Pilot*
	Ould Michael
1901	*The Man from Glengarry*
1902	*Glengarry School Days*
	Breaking the Record
1904	*The Prospector*
	The Pilot of Swan Creek
	Gwen
1906	*The Doctor of Crow's Nest*
	The Life of Dr. James Robertson
1909	*The Foreigner; A Tale of Saskatchewan*
	The Angel and the Star
	The Dawn by Galilee
	The Recall of Love

1912   *Corporal Cameron of the North-West Mounted Police: A Tale of the MacLeod Trail*
1914   *The Patrol of the Sun Dance Trail*
1917   *The Major*
1919   *The Sky Pilot in No Man's Land*
1921   *To Him That Hath*
1923   *The Gaspards of Pine Croft*

Sources on Ralph Connor

Ralph Connor, the Well-Beloved. Booklet published in 1914 by George H. Doran Company. Now out of print.

Silver Jubilee, 1895-1920, of St. Stephen's, Winnipeg. Booklet published by the congregation of St. Stephen's Presbyterian Church, Winnipeg, Manitoba.

Totalling Mr. Tarkington

i

IN the interesting procession of his work, Booth
Tarkington has pretty well paralleled the somewhat vacillating development of popular literary
taste in his country. This, there is every reason to
believe, has resulted from no conscious intention.
The fashion, in considering Mr. Tarkington, has
usually been to contrast what are called his two
natures—the romanticist who wrote *Monsieur
Beaucaire* and the realist (more or less) who wrote
The Gentleman From Indiana and *The Turmoil*.
Very sensibly has it been pointed out that the two
strains are manifest side by side in a number of his
novels, such as *The Conquest of Canaan*, where the
realism of character is sadly impaled on the rocks
of plot. But, if I may advance the idea with due
diffidence, such as Tarkington always shows in any
discussion of his work, the much more instructive
comparison lies deeper in the man and is the result
of an unrelenting pressure of environment on a personality endowed with most exceptional talent and
even unmistakable genius. One can say, I think,
although with a great deal of hesitation over its
unavoidable crudeness, that Mr. Tarkington in
some sense repeats what Mr. Van Wyck Brooks

conceives to be the tragedy of Mark Twain, only in Tarkington's case it has no air of tragedy. The common view of the author of *Alice Adams* is that he is a lucky fellow who deserves all his luck. Only in a narrow, godlike perspective would he appear tragic. And such a conclusion might easily be premature. When *Monsieur Beaucaire* appeared Mr. Frederic Taber Cooper declared it certain that we knew the extent of the author's capabilities, adding that it was unthinkable that he should ever again essay the realism of *The Gentleman From Indiana*. A couple of years ago plenty of persons qualified to have and to express an opinion asserted that Tarkington would never overcome his propensity toward a pulled-together and "happy" ending in a novel; and in the same year appeared *Alice Adams*. As Mr. Tarkington is only fifty-four, and may easily have a dozen years and a half a dozen prime novels directly in front of him, to be dogmatic is to run a perfectly unreasonable risk of stultification. I shall try to avoid that.

ii

"An unrelenting pressure of environment on a personality endowed with most exceptional talent . . ."

Newton Booth Tarkington was born in Indianapolis, 29 July 1869, the son of John Stevenson Tarkington (died 1922, aged ninety) and Elizabeth (Booth) Tarkington. The father, a Civil War soldier and a lawyer, was for some years in politics; the son was a member of the Indiana Legislature

BOOTH TARKINGTON

in 1902-3. The mother's family is not traceably connected with those Booths celebrated as actors. In his study of *Booth Tarkington* which is and will for a long time remain the chief resource and delight of those considering the novelist, Robert Cortes Holliday points out that the Indianapolis of Booth Tarkington's youth was a town, and that B. T. is neither a city nor a country boy, but a town boy. For a while in his childhood the boy was affected by nervous disorders resembling St. Vitus attacks. At about the age of eleven, he became a friend of James Whitcomb Riley, who was a neighbour. In his teens, Tarkington had the behaviour of a normal boy and a spirit of deviltry showed itself that was to last him until he was thirty. He went to Phillips Exeter, then to Purdue University, and finally to Princeton, where he "made" Ivy, than which, in the way of social success, Princeton offers nothing more beautiful. Much on the sentimental side is made to this day of Tarkington's singing of "Danny Deever" at class gatherings and reunions. After leaving Princeton, Tarkington returned to Indianapolis and pursued the busy social life possible to a young man of the town while at the same time he read a good deal and tried various styles of writing. Mr. Holliday intimates that, like Stevenson, Tarkington "played the sedulous ape" to a succession of literary masters, to find out how the thing was done. The interesting point is that the beginner kept this activity quite strictly to himself. "It was probably a consciousness of the foolish look which his unrewarded activities may have had outside that caused Mr. Tarkington at that time modestly to describe the serious schooling which he gave himself as 'fussin' with literachoor,' " Holliday tells us. The fact that the young man earned only $22.50 gross, or $62.50, or whatever it was, by his first five years of literary effort has since been as widely published as Joseph Hergesheimer's fourteen years without a single acceptance.

The junior Tarkington was under no necessity of earning his living and a notebook kept at that time by his father records the repeated return by publishers of his first novel, *The Gentleman from Indiana*. *Monsieur Beaucaire* was a long time getting accepted. The whimsical *Cherry* was bought by Henry Mills Alden for Harper's Magazine, pigeon-holed as a mistake and then unearthed and printed when *Monsieur Beaucaire* had made Tarkington "valuable." Forty thousand words of an early draft of *The Gentleman from Indiana* had had to be discarded because, having got his hero out for a walk, Tarkington could carry neither him nor the story any further. After an interruption of some length, *The Two Vanrevels* was resumed and wound up only with the greatest difficulty.

Mr. Tarkington was married in 1902 and again in 1912. He lived for a while in France and Italy (Capri). His summer home, at Kennebunkport, Maine, is usually spoken of with some reference to the study, where models of vessels of every rig, a valuable collection, are displayed. This is sometimes spoken of as "the house that *Penrod* built" and the ship models are perhaps natural to a home overlooking a New England harbour. It is also to be recollected that certain of Mr. Tarkington's ancestors hailed from Salem. Perhaps any other significance in those ships is merely fanciful.

No one who meets Booth Tarkington is insensible to the personal charm of the man. He is absolutely without affectation, and the perfect host, the staunch friend, the sympathetic listener and the contained and modest talker. Whatever the vicissitudes he has undergone, whatever the pressures put upon him, he has weathered them all with a steady helm. It seems an astonishing, unwarranted and probably an impudent thing to suggest that this man has been to a deplorable extent the victim of circumstances (largely comfortable circumstances); and that, with a less winning personality —if some outward expression for the thing must be sought—the chances are he would have been a much greater writer than, on his record, he is today.

iii

You see, of course, how handicapped he was from the start by being "a good fellow." The extent of that handicap can only be realised, I think, by knowing that to this day "nothing, apparently, so much gives Mr. Tarkington the horrors as the idea of the 'literary.' He does not want to be 'caught,' he declares, writing 'prose.'" I quote Mr. Holliday, who adds: "Some literary editor in New York told him that some of the passages in *The Turmoil*, in particular (I think) the cemetery scene, were noble English prose, worthy, I suppose, of the author of *Urn Burial*. 'He liked them,' says Mr. Tarkington with a wry face, as though, if he knew

[115]

just how, he would cut those passages out." But why should Tarkington be horrified by the thought that he may have written "literature"? What black curse lies upon "literature"? The only one I know is the contempt of "good fellows" and other philistines for an affair they know nothing of and self-defensively profess to despise. And if Mr. Tarkington thinks, as perhaps he does, that he spent painful years of reading and practise writing without the secret hope that he would some day write a piece of literature, then, I suspect, he is much mistaken. But what is it, this mental process? Why should he be "very quick to insist" that none of his family have been "offensively" literary? Who is offended by literature? "Good fellows" have been known to be very much annoyed by the presence among them of one whose possession of a taste they did not share seemed to impugn their own completeness. There is more than a suspicion that "Tark" has jekyllhyded others so long as to have concealed something very precious to him from himself. There could be no greater contrast, for example, than between Joseph Hergesheimer and Booth Tarkington (in this matter). Both are persons of some taste and genius who follow the profession of letters. I reveal nothing when I say that Hergesheimer, of whom personally I am fond, is considered by many people to be most conceited. Mr. Hergesheimer would be the first to uphold such a statement. One of the universally-praised traits of Mr. Tarkington is his utter lack of self-conceit. What is the explanation?

Nobody lacks self-conceit, least of all a person

with Tarkington's endowment. It may not be detectable, but any psychologist will tell you it exists. Hergesheimer was just as "conceited" in the days when no editor would take his stuff as he is today; only the quality wasn't visible, there being (practically speaking) no one to observe it. And the quality itself was fully engaged and enterprised in sustaining Joseph Hergesheimer, until such time as a measurable success, some rounds of applause, should sustain him. When that hour has struck in an artist's life, fortunate the artist if he can turn the "self-conceit" (which is really self-sustention) into the direct channel of his work! But to return to Booth Tarkington: The environment of the Indianapolis of the 1880s (a pleasant town), was perhaps not the most favourable for a boy of a specially nervous constitution and that excessive sensitiveness so frequently found in company with a fine imagination. It isn't to be wondered at that he was "precocious" until about the age of four, and "slow" after he began going to school. Phillips Exeter, like all such places, is devoted to finding the highest common social factor in the boy. What Purdue may have been when Tarkington went there, I have no idea; but it cannot possibly have exceeded Princeton as a place where self-disguise was imperative for self-preservation. There are plenty to remember those Princeton days, when students wore paint-stained corduroys and drank constructively, innocently mistaking eccentricities of dress and conduct for the achievement of personality. The real Tarkington underneath was forcing itself up at this time; he was writing for the college magazine such stuff as college magazines are made on. He went back to Indianapolis to continue writing; but the long era of good fellowship had done its work, a certain "self-conceit" and with it a decent open dignity had been put under battened hatches, and the young man was preparing to pay the fairly serious penalty—the penalty of an inability to take himself seriously enough, the penalty of wasted time, vitiated effort, delayed arrival, deferred achievement.

iv

Little wonder, then, that Mr. Tarkington told Mr. Holliday in 1917 that he was writing a book (*The Magnificent Ambersons*) that he didn't think anybody would read; and a year or so later he was talking in the same strain about *Alice Adams*. The last remaining vestiges of an attitude which has crippled him are perceptible in such utterances. He was ready, in 1917, to admit that he couldn't read Stevenson any longer, to confess that the stories of American politics called *In the Arena* were about all of his early work he "could stand to re-read." Popularity and unpopularity, he thought, had always been an accident with him; his idea seemed to be that "anybody can write a popular story"—of course, anybody can't—and, as for himself, he had never "played the goat to entertain anybody." And devices in his books that might have the air of being bids for popular favour were there simply because, when he wrote, he didn't know any better. As for putting them in to please an editor or reader: "Really, I'd as soon have forged a check."

TOTALLING MR. TARKINGTON

Holliday quotes him further: "I've written things only as I thought they ought to be written. I thought in my youth that life could be got into books with prettier colours and more shaping than the models actually had; and I fell in with a softer, more commonplace and more popular notion of what a *story* should be. Where that acceptance definitely stopped in *me* (though the book may not show it) was *Beauty and the Jacobin*. It was at that time that I was painting with my old ornamental picture framer. Until then, I thought they were the 'cheese,'—not for sales, but the *right* 'cheese.' "

Perfectly honest! If there is anything else, and I think there is, it is hidden from Mr. Tarkington himself, or was. We may look upon the melodrama and sentimentalism of *The Gentleman from Indiana*, or *The Conquest of Canaan* and feel less distaste for them than does Tarkington who, at their mention, looks pitifully unhappy. He is suffering the acute reaction of the years after, whereas it is possible for us to note the simple fact that what now seems conventional and cheap in those novels was much less conventional, and not nearly so cheap, in 1899 and 1905. The fact remains—doesn't it?—of Tarkington having written an essentially realistic novel, his first, when we were all wild about *Richard Carvel* and *Prisoners of Hope* and *When Knighthood Was in Flower*—that sort of thing. Although, to be sure, there was *The Honorable Peter Sterling*, there had been the earlier novels of William Dean Howells, and Theodore Dreiser was putting on paper *Sister Carrie*. Another fact that

[119]

remains is the co-existence (1905) of *In the Arena* and *The Conquest of Canaan* and the fixed, large achievement, in 1912-13, of the novel called *The Flirt*.

It is easy to agree with Mr. Holliday that the efforts at invention in the story surrounding Cora Madison are "childlike," but I am convinced that *The Flirt* is a novel for which a place must be reserved in any list of twenty distinguished American novels. The portrayals of Cora and her brother, the boy Hedrick, seem to me to settle that. Thackeray's picture of Becky Sharp is, I feel, no more biting than Tarkington's delineation of Cora; Hedrick has as much gusto as any character of Dickens; and in both cases Mr. Tarkington has accomplished the thing with less than half the effort Thackeray and Dickens brought to bear. Of Tarkington, as they would say in golf, it is all in the wrist. The same undemonstrative precision, skill and force which went into the porcelain perfection of *Monsieur Beaucaire*, which fumbled so badly in such a mixture ("the rough") as *The Two Vanrevels*, is felt on every page of *The Flirt* where Cora or Hedrick are "in play." Unfortunately, the inspired suggestion of the present Mrs. Tarkington which was responsible for the existence of Hedrick Madison is also responsible indirectly for the boy Penrod. Those Penrod stories which, Tarkington admits, cost no effort to write! Toward this variety of work several attitudes are possible. The strictest condemns it, and because of it rates down the author. Obviously, such a view is just only where the author has held his writing throughout as a sacred vocation.

[120]

TOTALLING MR. TARKINGTON

The severe, exalted standard of judgment cannot very well be applied to anyone like Arnold Bennett or Booth Tarkington, both of whom, for quite different reasons, have a lively sense of what I would call the amenities of living. A more tolerant attitude holds the author justified for one or several excuses—he may have his living to make, he may have the thing in him and need to get it out of his system, the demand for Penrodism may carry its vox-populi-vox-Dei conviction, there may be nothing else to write. . . . Between the smashing drive and the perfect strokes on the putting green, one is not allowed to intermit the bad brassy or the futile iron shot; one is required to play.

The Flirt appeared in 1913, *Penrod* in 1914, *The Turmoil* in 1915, *Penrod and Sam* in 1916, *Seventeen*, an outgrowth of *Penrod*, in 1916 also; *The Magnificent Ambersons* in 1918, and *Ramsey Milholland*, the last wring-out of Tarkington's Bad Boy in 1919. Even those who declare the creation of Penrod and William Sylvanus Baxter, Jr. (in *Seventeen*) to be "great work"—and they are numerous and their opinion is respectable—will perhaps feel, as they contemplate the prolonged attack of Penroditis, that this adolescent in literature gave his fashioner a distinct setback. They may look with admiration at a photograph of the study in The House That Penrod Built and witness all those ships, and the thought may occur to them that these beautiful toys took too long the place of ampler vessels, which, with rich cargoes, with the help of the stars and in spite of weather, might have been worked home.

AMERICAN NIGHTS ENTERTAINMENT

V

One such fine vessel, richly-freighted, made port at last, in 1921, the *Alice Adams*. To praise this novel, the first in which Mr. Tarkington made an entirely successful passage, is easy; to discriminate in regard to it is difficult, for the simple reason that Mr. Tarkington's past work has made such a performance incomparable. Here was a man who in his greatest feats had always shown corresponding blemishes. *The Flirt* had been spotted with melodrama (as if the drama of Cora and the mordancy of Hedrick did not serve to tarnish any artificial sheen). *The Turmoil*, more skilfully constructed than *The Flirt*, suffered an entire loss of the detachment which Tarkington preserved toward Cora Madison; and instead of a pitiless portrayal we had a modern morality play. *The Magnificent Ambersons* was afflicted with a pulled-around ending. But in *Alice Adams* all of these defects were met and adjusted; the movement was natural and not "plotted"; no moral underlay the exposed incidents; Mr. Tarkington was impartial without being in the least unsympathetic. Then why discriminate? Surely, *Alice Adams* has everything! Not at all. No author's one book ever has, I suppose; and in finally achieving the symmetry and truth and grace of *Alice Adams* there was the sacrifice of a nervous force which animated, in a varying extent, all three of the earlier novels. One must learn, in criticism, to value above all else what can only be called "vitality," whether in painting, or sculpture, music or literature. This mysterious but indispensable

[122]

flame burns with a different intensity in individual writers. In Mr. Galsworthy, for example, it is low in novels, somewhat higher, at times, in plays; but relatively low throughout his work. In Mr. Tarkington, I cannot help feeling, it is higher in *The Flirt* than in anything else he has written; for savage and powerful as are the stories of *In the Arena*, the material is something that the author touches with his foot, rather than shapes with his hands. Indeed, this instinctive repugnance in Mr. Tarkington, as inveterate in him as in so many American writers, is one of the strictest limitations on his art. In older cultures than ours in America, where it is well understood that admission to the human race cannot be denied by some to others, a Balzac or a Conrad or even a Dickens can write with the same manifest vitality of almost anybody, however inhumanly horrible—as, for example, the "incorruptible" Professor and mad anarchist in Conrad's tale of *The Secret Agent*. In the case of Tarkington, Mr. Holliday has cleverly observed the type of material in which our writer's vitality is most evident—the memorable procession of drunkards in his stories, the unmatched darkeys of the stable alleys, the large number of Tarkington characters vocal with song.

As to plays: the man doesn't regard them as his "real trade." All the earlier ones were written in collaboration, usually with Harry Leon Wilson; and Tarkington, with an engaging candour, admits at once that the great cost of a theatrical production must be met, if possible, by filling the house. Writing alone, he has given the stage such utter ineptitude as *Poldekin* and such delicious comedy as *Clarence*. He now writes a play, usually, because a particular producer wants one with a particular actor in mind. In his book-length fiction he is unrestricted, unless the engagement in advance of the next couple of novels for serial publication may have its oblique effect. After all, it must be very difficult, knowing that your next two books are first to be placed before a certain large constituency of women readers, not to select your material "according" and not to mould it imperceptibly somewhat nearer the—supposed, suspected, or ascertained—hearts' desire of all those ladies.

vi

Booth Tarkington's home in Indianapolis, at 1100 North Pennsylvania Street, is a plain brick house, far from new. Business creeps into the street, but there is some "lawn" still about the house, a hedge, Virginia creeper on the brick walls. Six winter months are spent here, the other six in the house at Kennebunkport, which, being newer, is furnished with more simplicity and taste. Tarkington's workshop is upstairs—a tilted drawing board beside an east window, a flexible electric lamp, plenty of large-size sheets of yellow paper, two dozen pencils kept sharp by two pencil-sharpening machines. Tarkington has never used a typewriter and dictates only letters and not all of those. His sister-in-law, Miss Louise Keifer, copies his pencilled yellow pages of manuscript on the typewriter. Spectacles of all sizes and weights lie on a table.

[124]

TOTALLING MR. TARKINGTON

The man breakfasts between nine and ten, works until 1.30, and then pauses to eat a slender lunch brought to his study on a tray. He continues working until 3.30, and sometimes writes in the evenings, although the habit of writing pretty regularly at night has been abandoned. Even so it is a longer working day than most writers can keep. Mrs. Tarkington intercepts all interruptions; no telephone call can break in, nor any thought-distracting piece of news. On evenings when there is no engagement and Tarkington is not writing, he will play double-deck solitaire for an hour, read until about one o'clock, then go to bed. In Maine the day's programme is a half-hour earlier throughout; work stops around noon; a short motor ride and a quick dip in the ocean follow; and the afternoon is most likely to be spent in a motorboat. The Maine evening frequently includes a walk of a mile to and from the movies; this is mainly for the sake of the walk, although the worse the picture is, the more restful Tarkington is likely to find it.

Notes, sometimes covering several dozen pencilled pages and undecipherable by anyone else, precede the composition of a play or novel. They are vague ideas and suggestions, the writer endeavouring not to crystallise his story too suddenly. When this occurs, it is sometimes necessary to write the next to the last chapter or scene and then go back to the general plan or the beginning. Work proceeds every day, Sundays included, and averages about 1,400 words a day of fresh output, preceded by correction of the previous day's writing. In addition to this day by day revision, Tarkington revises a story or book as a whole; it is then typed, and after that is seldom altered.

"He has never resorted to neurotic realism or the much over-exploited nastiness of high life to give zest to his fiction," says a recent utterance in praise of Mr. Tarkington. And the author is quoted as himself saying: "The problems of youth had been interesting me for some time, more than I realised"—when he turned to *Penrod*—"except the one problem that most people who call themselves realists feel that they must deal with—that is, in an untrammelled fashion—the problem of sex, which I have never felt was a subject for exploitation."

"Neurotic realism" is a phrase of wabbly connotation, but if a study of neurotic characters and tendencies be meant, there are plenty of those in Tarkington fiction. Most of the Tarkington drunkards are neurotic, Cora Madison is a victim of the narcism complex, and, as Mr. Holliday has pointed out, *"The Turmoil* is remarkable as a book of nervous diseases." One of the most unlifelike things about Penrod (still more, William Sylvanus Baxter, Jr., he of *Seventeen*) is the absolute erasure of that contact with "the facts of life" which constitutes one of the indubitable facts of boyhood. And though as many crimes have been committed in the name of realism as in the name of liberty, the painfully sincere purpose of some of our most "untrammelled" writers in their treatment of sex cannot justly be called "exploitation." One thinks of Sherwood Anderson. The analysis of Holliday, in a final quest for the secret of Tarkington's popularity as an author (not invariable, but abundant), is perhaps as good as we shall get:

"He is very much like most people. There is nothing, except its energy, peculiar about his mind; it has no strong idiosyncratic bias, no strange, abnormal quality. At first, as in *Cherry*, he may have been excessively belletristic. That was not only not odd, but quite natural in a well-educated, young writer. But, just for the joke of the thing, think for an instant of Mr. Tarkington in connection with such a writer as, let us say, George Moore. In this wearer of the literary ermine you find laid bare a soul compacted of nearly everything that is detestable to the mind of a plain citizen going about his business in the marketplace. He has confessed consuming egotism, quivering sensibility, fastidiousness, vanity, timidity coupled with calculating shamelessness, sensuality, a streak of feline cruelty, and absolute spiritual incontinence. Or try to think of Mr. Tarkington coming along with some such perverse thinking (however shrewd) as Samuel Butler's: 'the worst misfortune that can happen to any person is to lose his money; the second is to lose his health; and the loss of reputation is a bad third.' Mr. Tarkington admires all those things which every decent, ordinary, simple-hearted person admires: dash, courage, honesty, honour, feminine virtue and graciousness and beauty, and so on. He hates precisely those things hated by all honest, healthy 'American' people: sham, egoism, conceit, cruelty, affectation, and so forth. In short, though he is a red hot artist (and most Americans 'don't care a nickel for art'), he believes in all those things which make up the creed of the average sane, wholesome person in this country. He has infectious humour, and (though savage in attack upon what he feels to be vicious) abounding 'good humour.' Added to all this, he has a most winning and rich, though not at all complex, personality. He is in his own person, indeed, what most of us would like to be. In a word, doubtless his books are popular because of the same qualities that made their author popular as an undergraduate."

There are compensations of all kinds on this earth, and one of Mr. Tarkington's—the most enviable of all, I think—must be knowledge of a certain occasion in which he was of the utmost possible service to another American writer. The course he took at that time, the energy he displayed, would have been very improbable in one whose natural vanity of himself as an artist was in the least like George Moore's. If it was for too long a literary misfortune that Mr. Tarkington's "self-conceit" lay in the direction of being a good fellow, at least he made of good fellowship, in this instance, the minted gold of personal greatness. No! Now it can*not* be told; but there will be those alive to tell it.

Books by Booth Tarkington

1899   *The Gentleman from Indiana*
1900   *Monsieur Beaucaire*
1902   *The Two Vanrevels*
1903   *Cherry* earlier, in composition, than *The Gentleman from Indiana*

TOTALLING MR. TARKINGTON

1905 *In the Arena*
1905 *The Conquest of Canaan*
1905 *The Beautiful Lady*
1907 *His Own People*
1908 *The Guest of Quesnay*
1909 *Beasley's Christmas Party*
1911 *Beauty and the Jacobin*
1913 *The Flirt*
1914 *Penrod*
1915 *The Turmoil*
1916 *Penrod and Sam*
1916 *Seventeen*
1918 *The Magnificent Ambersons*
1919 *Ramsey Milholland*
1921 *Alice Adams*
1922 *Gentle Julia*
1923 *The Fascinating Stranger and Other Stories*

Plays by Booth Tarkington

1901 *Monsieur Beaucaire* with E. G. SUTHERLAND
With HARRY LEON WILSON:
    1906 *The Man from Home*
    1907 *Cameo Kirby*
    1908 *Your Humble Servant*
    1908 *Springtime*
    1909 *Getting a Polish*
    1916 *Mister Antonio*
1917 *The Country Cousin* with JULIAN STREET
With HARRY LEON WILSON:
    1919 *The Gibson Upright*
    1919 *Up from Nowhere*
1919 *Clarence*

[129]

1920   *Poldekin*
1921   *The Wren*
1921   *The Intimate Strangers*

Sources on Booth Tarkington

Booth Tarkington, by Robert Cortes Holliday. DOUBLEDAY, PAGE & COMPANY. Authoritative, honest, delightful; especially sound in its detailed criticism of the books up to and including *The Turmoil* and *Seventeen*. When Holliday's book was written, Tarkington was at work on *The Magnificent Ambersons*, for an estimate of which see Holliday's *Broome Street Straws*.

Contemporary American Novelists, 1900-1920, by Carl Van Doren. THE MACMILLAN COMPANY.

Booth Tarkington at Home, by John R. McMahon, LADIES' HOME JOURNAL, November, 1922 (page 15).

Private Information.

Articles, reviews, etc., are plentiful and the reader is advised to consult the READERS' GUIDE TO PERIOD-ICAL LITERATURE for the years since 1914.

A Parody Outline of Stewart

i

ABOUT two years ago, when Donald Ogden Stewart had just abandoned the bond business for the pursuit of a literary career, he was asked to write a brief account of his life, with the following result:

"Donald Ogden Stewart was born in Columbus, Ohio, on November 30, 1894. In his early years he gave manifold evidences of his gift for humour, and many of his bright childhood remarks are still related by his proud mother upon the slightest provocation, or in fact, upon no provocation at all. There were others, however—principally among the guests at the hotel where Donald lived—who did not think that this child prodigy was so funny. Mr. Stewart bears a long red scar on his head—such as might be made by a brick or other missile—as mute evidence of one little redheaded girl's particular lack of appreciation of his early humorous efforts.

"At the age of 14 he was sent to the Phillips Exeter Academy because it was a good preparatory school for Harvard. In the fall of 1912, Mr. Stewart entered Yale. While at New Haven, Mr.

Stewart went out for all the athletic teams possible, and was always among those of whom it was said in the college paper at the end of the season, 'And we also wish to thank those members of the third and fourth teams who have worked so faithfully without reward—and yet we cannot say without reward—for they are rewarded with the knowledge that they have worked for old Yale,' etc.

"Mr. Stewart was graduated in 1916 and selected a certain large public service corporation as the scene of his future success. It was his desire to start at the bottom and work up; the first half of this wish was readily granted him. After a brief, inspiring visit with the head of the corporation, Mr. Stewart was sent to the Birmingham, Alabama, office which was about as far away as the head of the corporation could possibly send Mr. Stewart. While in Birmingham, Mr. Stewart took a keen interest in his job and read the complete works of Anatole France, George Moore, Fyodor Dostoievski, Henrik Ibsen, Gustav Flaubert and many others. He also intended to read the Alexander Hamilton business course, but did not quite get around to it before he was sent to the Pittsburgh, Pennsylvania, office.

"In Pittsburgh, Mr. Stewart took a keen interest in his job and read the works of Leo Tolstoy, Friedrich Nietzsche, G. B. Shaw, Thomas Hardy, Joseph Conrad and others. He also started to take piano lessons and got as far as 'The Happy Farmers.' He was just on the point of reading the Alexander Hamilton business course when he was sent to Chicago. After ten months in Chicago, Mr. Stewart joined the Navy. Having never been on

[132]

DONALD OGDEN STEWART

a ship or the ocean in his life, he was at once appointed an instructor in Practical Navigation, Seamanship, Naval Ordnance, and Signals. This experience was invaluable and Mr. Stewart came out of the Great War a deepened man.

"His old position with the great corporation awaited him and Mr. Stewart went back to the work of the world in the spring of 1918. He was sent to the Minneapolis office, where he took a keen interest in his job and read the works of H. G. Wells, Havelock Ellis, and H. L. Mencken; met F. Scott Fitzgerald, and led two cotillions. He was also preparing to take up the Alexander Hamilton business course when he accepted an offer of employment in Dayton, Ohio, with a financial organisation.

"Mr. Stewart spent a delightful year in Dayton where he learned to play golf, and read the works of Max Beerbohm, Sainte-Beuve, Casanova, Swift, James Branch Cabell, James Huneker, and William Congreve. He also renewed his piano lessons, getting as far as the Bach three-part inventions and 'Easy Classics.' On December 30, 1920, he read the first volume of the Alexander Hamilton business course, after which he decided that he wanted to go in for literature. In January, 1921, Mr. Stewart came to New York City to find a job (literary if possible), but there were so many symphony concerts that month that he didn't get a chance to look around until the middle of February.

"The idea for the *Parody Outline of History* came to Mr. Stewart in March, while hearing Mr. Mengelberg conduct the National Orchestra in the Pathetique Symphony.

"Mr. Stewart is unmarried and very near-sighted. He is fond of Beethoven, Scotch, and Max Beerbohm."

ii

So much for Mr. Stewart's life up to the publication of *The Parody Outline of History*. In the following year (1922)—but let Mr. Stewart again speak:

"After the appearance of the *Parody Outline* Mr. Stewart, having heard a great deal about Europe in the course of his naval war service in Chicago, decided to go abroad. Many of his friends recommended Paris as a pleasant city in which to work, so Mr. Stewart went to Paris, which he found indeed very pleasant but not for work. So after a brief period of recuperation he journeyed to Vienna where he grew a splendid red beard and wrote *Perfect Behavior*.

"Finding, however, that the beard was exhausting too much of his creative energy, Mr. Stewart shaved and went to Budapest, where he enjoyed himself immensely at the rate of 700 Hungarian crowns to the dollar.

"But in the middle of October he began to feel strangely uneasy, and as his condition grew steadily worse he consulted an authority and learned, to his surprise and delight, that he was going to have another book.

"Bidding a hasty farewell to the gay life of Budapest, which now seemed all too empty and frivolous, Mr. Stewart journeyed with his precious secret to Capri, there, under the ever-blue Italian skies, to await the happy event. He prayed with all his heart that it might be a novel, for he had never had a novel, although he had wanted one all his life. But early in February, 1923, Mr. Stewart discovered that the 'little stranger' was to be another satire, and although it was a bit of a blow at first, after a few days he got over his disappointment at not having a novel; and when, in June, Mr. Stewart returned to America he took with him, proudly, his little third book, which he had christened *Aunt Polly's Story of Mankind*."

iii

Alexander Woollcott speaking in "Shouts and Murmurs" in the New York Herald of March 18, 1923:

"Stewart is a preposterously tall, blonde man, with an enviably large amount of his twenties still to squander. His profile is faintly reminiscent of that most delightful and fantastic of all creatures, Winsor McKay's Gertie. He knows more about the music than he does about the books of the world, and has, we suspect, gone in for reading so recently that he probably thinks all novels are like Joyce's *Ulysses*. We ran across him here and there in France last summer, starting out on one pilgrimage together from the Café Valterre, in the Place Stanislas at Nancy, that celebrated restaurant which set forth marvellous dishes even when the bombs were dropping on Nancy every evening and there was not another good meal to be found anywhere else in Lorraine. Up the street somewhere was M.

Coué, healing away for dear life, and on the out-
skirts of the town an imitation Oberammergau was
in full swing. But the two of us were minded rather
to move on to the battlefields, and for the purpose
engaged a morsel of a French car, driven by a
youngster who spoke a horrible dialect he had
picked up three years before from the Americans
stationed at Neufchateau. The memories of that
rambling excursion into a cheerless countryside,
still littered with the rusted snarls of barbed wire
and still gashed with the trenches no one has had
time or strength to obliterate, are brought flooding
back by the inscription in the copy of *Perfect
Behavior* lying open here on the desk. It is in-
scribed: 'In memory of terrible days and ghastly
nights on the battlefields of France,' and winds up
with this disconcerting proclamation: ' "It shall
never happen again."—Stewart.'

"Marc Connelly was agitated the other day by
the receipt of a cablegram from Stewart in Capri
which read thus:

" 'The Queen of Sweden is here. What shall I
do?—Stewart.'

"Connelly's cabled reply must be admired
equally for its sagacity and its thrift. It was:
'Compromise.' "

Books by Donald Ogden Stewart

1921 *A Parody Outline of History*
1922 *Perfect Behavior*
1923 *Aunt Polly's Story of Mankind*

A PARODY OUTLINE OF STEWART

Sources on Donald Ogden Stewart

The Making of a Humorist, by DONALD OGDEN STEWART, suppressed by the author, 1921.

My Naval Career, by DONALD OGDEN STEWART (Privately unpublished, 1921).

Miss Zona Gale

i

NO one any longer doubts that Zona Gale belongs in the very small company of American women novelists whose work is of the first artistic importance. Her history is interesting. Of old New England parentage, she was born in Portage, Wisconsin, where she now lives. She wrote, at thirteen, a novel "which almost simultaneously came back to me from a publisher." At sixteen, just after she ·had entered the University of Wisconsin, she submitted a 3,000-word short story to the Milwaukee Evening Wisconsin, which paid her $3. When she finished college she went to work for that newspaper. "I secured a position by attrition. I presented myself every morning at the desk of the city editor. At the end of two weeks the city editor let me write about a flower show. I have never put such emotion into anything else I have written." She was another month getting on the staff. Later, by offering a list of suggestions based on the day's news, she succeeded after many weeks in getting on the staff of the New York World.

An anonymous writer in The Bookman has pictured Miss Gale in New York: "When she was a reporter on the World, and as beautiful as any girl could be, she was put on difficult assignments that might well have terrified one as fragile and flower-like and feminine as she; but she never winced. . . . She covered murders and robberies—anything given her to do she did, at any hour of the day or night. But all the while she was writing exquisite poetry; and every day of her life she sent a letter to her mother, who was back in Wisconsin. If she was waiting for an interview with some financier of the hour, she did not dawdle her time away in the corridor of his hotel. Instead, she pulled out a pad and pencil and wrote as many pages as she could on a short story; or she dashed off a lyric; or she made copious notes for future work. I think she was about the most ambitious girl in New York at that time—too ambitious, some said; her praises were being sung—too much sung was a common rumour; her picture—how lovely she was, and is!—was published repeatedly—too repeatedly, dear enemies whispered; and everyone was waiting to see just how long it would take her to make good."

ii

It took some time. Not until the year in which she was 29 did she land anywhere "to speak of," though for ten years previous to that acceptance, by Success Magazine, she had constantly submitted stories. That was in 1903. Then, in 1911, the Delineator held a short story contest in which over 15,000 stories were received. Miss Gale took first prize with a tale called "The American Dawn." It was $2,000 and in addition her other two entries (each person was allowed to submit three stories) were deemed good enough to be purchased. But meanwhile she had written stories about Pelleas and Ettare, two old lovers, and stories about Friendship Village—some forty of the first and, ultimately, about sixty of the second—and the process of collecting her Friendship Village fiction into books had begun. Said Miss Gale, in 1919: "The first editor to whom these Friendship Village stories were submitted declined them with the word that his acquaintance with small towns was wide but that he had never seen any such people as these. . . . I am still not sure that he was not right."

She was the author of ten published books before she produced anything constituting a lien upon general attention. But then, with an effect of extreme suddenness to the world outside of Portage, there came from her pen the 402-page novel, *Birth*. Its length is a point of interest in view of the brevity of *Miss Lulu Bett* and *Faint Perfume*, both of which are so decidedly under the average novel in length. And yet *Birth* exhibits the same conciseness of phrase, the same avoidance of unnecessary words so noticeable in the two later books. It is the story of a poor little man, Marshall Pitt, who comes to an insignificant Western town as a pickle salesman and remains there as a paperhanger, a husband and a father. The book's comments on life have been aptly described as "piercing"—it is a fine needlework of satire—but there are lovely lyrical moments and the tragic action is touched with majesty. Altogether a great novel. Miss Gale considers it the finest thing she has done and for once her judgment of her own work, generally as untrustworthy as most authors' or slightly more so, is right.

Then came *Miss Lulu Bett*, read with the enthusiasm of discovery by the publisher, who telegraphed his congratulations—a thing publishers infrequently do! Except in England, where its merit was quickly noted, *Birth* had not sold at all well. Six magazine editors had rejected *Miss Lulu Bett* as a serial. Happily, all signs failed. The crisply-told little novel of the household drudge and her fortunes went into one edition after another; a play from the novel was sought and Miss Gale fashioned it herself; the annual Pulitzer prize was awarded to the play. Whether the concision of style practised so effectively in *Birth* was not carried a bit too far in *Miss Lulu Bett* must always remain a matter of opinion. The most interesting point, I think, is the change of ending which the requirements of the theatre forced upon Miss Gale. As she observed, an audience in a playhouse could not reasonably be expected to swallow the spectacle of a woman marrying two men in the space of three hours, even though the indicated lapse of time was much longer than that; she therefore, to make the play, caused Miss Bett's first marriage to turn out to be valid after all. In this matter Miss Gale was not guilty of "sweetening" her story, as has been charged. She simply was up against a limitation as definite as that which restricts the number of scenes possible in a play.

iii

And this year she has given us *Faint Perfume*, a study of a finely sensitive feminine personality stifling in the atmosphere of a quite usual sort of American family. Leda Perrin, forced to make her home with the Crumbs, is brought into a fleeting contact with Barnaby Powers, a writer with a temperament of the same response. They meet, together face the defeat of their desire, and go separately apart. At the close there is the briefest possible second meeting and a hope is held out for their eventual happiness together. This theme, of the utmost delicacy, is the occasion for a considerable display of virtuosity by Miss Gale. By means of deft and distinct individualisation of her characters —each Crumb, for instance, standing out as a complete fiery particle—she orchestrates the melodic fragment of Leda and Barnaby in a sort of free treatment (but with careful working out), as a composer might do in setting a quartette for strings. May this musical simile be helpful! The clipped style of *Miss Lulu Bett* is here carried a step further, until Miss Gale almost seems to out-Sinclair Miss May Sinclair. The style has been called precious, which is the technical word for what the ordinary person calls "affected"; and, on the other hand, one able critic has declared that it is not the style that is precious but Miss Gale's material. One thing is certain, the treatment is as far removed as possible from the literalness of such a novel as *Main Street*, and this is natural to expect when we remember that Miss Gale is, after all and perhaps fundamentally,

[142]

a poet. Some of her poems have been published in book form.

Books by Zona Gale

1906 *Romance Island*
1907 *The Loves of Pelleas and Ettarre*
1908 *Friendship Village*
1909 *Friendship Village Love Stories*
1911 *Mothers to Men*
1912 *Christmas*
1913 *When I Was a Little Girl*
1914 *Neighborhood Stories*
1915 *Heart's Kindred*
1917 *A Daughter of Tomorrow*
1918 *Birth*
1919 *Peace in Friendship Village*
1920 *Miss Lulu Bett*
1920 *Neighbors* (play)
1921 *Miss Lulu Bett* (play)
1923 *Faint Perfume*

Sources on Zona Gale

The Women Who Make Our Novels (second or third edition, 1919 or 1922). MOFFAT YARD & COMPANY.

The Literary Spotlight, XVIII: Zona Gale, in THE BOOKMAN for April, 1923. This article now forms a chapter in the book, *The Literary Spotlight*, with an introduction by John Farrar.

Zona Gale, An Artist in Fiction, by WILSON FOLLETT. Booklet published by D. Appleton & Company.

Naturalist vs. Novelist:
Gene Stratton-Porter

i

WITH Gene Stratton-Porter, the quality of enthusiasm is not strained, it droppeth as tor-
rential rains from the heaven of her state of mind.
Anyone acquainted with Mrs. Porter and regarding
her with positive affection is certain to be subject to
the recurring notion that she has, after all, confused
heaven with earth. It is not that she finds nothing
on earth to contemn, but that she finds the same
objects for perpetual glorification. The rest of us
live our wavering lives in a flux of emotions, which
we commonly mistake for accomplishments of our
intellects. We glorify this at one age, and that at
another. Mrs. Porter, from the beginning, has worshipped the same pantheon.

A pantheon it is, owing to her possibly inherited
passion for the works of nature. Her idea of art
is as clear-cut as the ordinary mortal's notion of
property. Perhaps clearer, since the ordinary
mortal often finds difficulty in distinguishing the
forms of property, whether real, personal, or mixed
(as lawyers say). To Mrs. Porter, art is any
human effort that encourages, or even possibly
forces, nature to grow. It is art when you handle

[144]

flowers with the deftness and astonishing results achieved by Mrs. Porter's mother; it is art when you write a story that tends to stimulate or fortify the natural (i.e., usual) impulses of the average man or woman to live and learn, to seek and engage in interesting work, to mate, to beget or bear children. Any art that does not tend directly toward these primary social and personal ends isn't art to her; she regards it with heavy suspicion.

Some years ago it was suggested to Mrs. Porter that she furnish autobiographical material for a booklet which should satisfy the eager requests of her readers for personal facts. Mrs. Porter assented. The result was a booklet largely in her own words, and remarkable for an accent that some would call boastful and others, refreshing. We may defer for a few moments the details that Mrs. Porter set down, but the question of her personal tone and temper is one to be considered at the very outset. Is she merely naïve? Is she self-assertive, conceited, boastful? What does she embody, and what is the secret—if it is a secret—of the enormously wide appeal of her work? To attempt an answer isn't easy. But let us see. . . .

ii

Gene Stratton-Porter is a self-made woman, with all the drawbacks that self-manufacture entails. Certain definite advantages, too! It is not meant that she owes nothing to her parentage, wifehood, motherhood—she owes much to these, and her great indebtedness to her father and mother she has herself proclaimed. And yet, in the rôle in which

[145]

the world views her, she owes nothing to anybody
except herself. For although the late Richard
Watson Gilder gave her encouragement with her
first book, and although others encouraged her with
the famous *Freckles*, she would undoubtedly have
gone on with no encouragement whatever and would
have become what she is today. Why? The explanation inheres in that phrase, "self-made."
Self-made people, whatever they may lack, are obviously people with a capacity which we don't
ordinarily bother to distinguish except by the result
they achieve with it. That is, perhaps, typical of
the mental laziness of the rest of us. But if we
ask ourselves what the capacity is, in terms other
than the easily-named result, the answer may be
extremely surprising.

Who are the persons who are so happily independent of the encouragement, the approval, the
applause without a tiny measure of which the rest
of us couldn't go on? They divide into the two
great classes of mankind, if we consider psychology
and temperament. There are the mystics—the
saints, the martyrs, and some artists. There are the
non-mystics—many artists among them, to be sure.
The mystical mind isn't the secret. The mental
make-up of those who walk (who are able to walk)
by themselves, is. They have, either from birth
or by hard-wrung conquest, a kind of self-sufficiency
more precious, for living purposes, than fine gold.
It may be the bright, unconscious self-sufficiency
of a Gene Stratton-Porter, or the admirable fortitude of a Joseph Conrad or the diffident charm of
a Booth Tarkington—the manner is nothing; it is

there. The mode of acquisition, except as it bears on work and affects personality, whether birthright or painful purchase, is nothing, either. The thing is there, like driven piles or bedrock. He who lacks that foundation must take his chance of his house, built on sands, being washed away.

With Mrs. Porter this invaluable element of personality has existed from the time of her earliest childhood. Nor is the faculty in question a superficial matter, like self-confidence. It was with a considerable lack of self-confidence that Mrs. Porter began writing; but notice that she began. How many others who had the self-confidence when they started have had to acquire the self-sufficiency, the power of self-sustention? How many have failed to do that? Self-confidence, indeed, is the most perfect of traitors. But there is a reservoir in the Self. . . .

Like every other prize, this one has its penalty. What will carry one to the top of a high rock will also, unimpeded, carry one over the rock's edge. The balance in egoism always trembles; when it comes to rest, one dies. And here is Mrs. Porter, who had in her a capacity that could have overcome mountains and that found only moderately difficult hills in its path. She must have burst into a thousand pieces if it hadn't been that she was a naturalist first and a novelist afterward, that she underwent the preoccupations of a wife and mother, that she toiled in swamps and wrote books, kept other people alive with her money as well as her courage and vitality, launched forth on self-pinions as a poet, corresponded with innumerable readers, did

[147]

this and that and the other and then hit upon something else. She was one of twelve children. "To this mother at forty-six and this father at fifty, each at intellectual topnotch," she was born, the Minerva of mature and remarkable parents, a child who kept, in her own words, "thinking things which she felt should be saved," so that she frequently tugged at her mother's skirts and begged her to "set down" what the child considered stories and poems —generally some big fact in nature that thrilled the child, usually expressed in Biblical terms. Whom have we here? An incarnation as extraordinary as the Florence Nightingale whom Lytton Strachey put on paper? I think so.

iii

Mark Stratton, the father of Gene Stratton-Porter, described his wife, at the time of their marriage, as a "ninety-pound bit of pink porcelain, pink as a wild rose, plump as a partridge, having a big rope of bright brown hair, never ill a day in her life, and bearing the loveliest name ever given a woman —Mary. God fashioned her heart to be gracious, her body to be the mother of children, and as her especial gift of Grace, He put Flower Magic into her fingers."

From tiny seeds found in rice and coffee, Mary (Shellenbarger) Stratton started little vines and climbing plants. Rooted things she soaked in water, rolled in fine sand, planted according to habit, and they almost never failed to grow. When, intent on growing a tree or shrub from a slip or

[148]

cutting that appeared hopeless, she cut the slip diagonally, inserted the lower end in a small potato and planted as if it were rooted, she was nearly always successful. Being of Dutch extraction, bulbs were her favourites—tulips, daffodils, star flowers, lilies, dahlias, little bright hyacinths that she called "blue bells." From these she distilled perfume by putting clusters, at the time of perfect bloom, in bowls lined with freshly made, unsalted butter, covering them closely, and cutting the few drops of extract thus obtained with alcohol. In Ohio a man gave her two tiny cedars of Lebanon which she brought with her to the farm in Wabash County, Indiana, planting one in her front yard and one in the small cemetery on the corner of her husband's land. It stands, thirty feet tall or over, two feet in circumference, guarding her grave.

All twelve of her children lived to be eight; an attack of scarlet fever joined with whooping cough was fatal to two of them a little over that age. The house, "Hopewell Farm," was an oblong box kept speckless. The liberal table and appetising food were known by all who travelled that way. She made the clothing for her brood. In the house that she kept so faultlessly clean, at the table she heaped with hearty dishes, Mark Stratton, conscious of his worthy British blood, praised her "tidiness" and accepted responsibility for the mental and spiritual welfare of his wife and children. It was understood that he had been named for a Mark Stratton who lived in New York and married a beauty, Anne Hutchinson. It was misunderstood that the first Mark and his wife settled on Stratton

[149]

Island, "afterward corrupted to Staten." From this point back for generations across the ocean, we are told that Mrs. Porter's father "followed his line to the family of Strattons of which the Earl of Northbrooke is the present head (1913). To his British traditions and the customs of his family, Mark Stratton clung with rigid tenacity, never swerving from his course a particle under the influence of environment or association." Perhaps, after all, he was British. "All his ideas were clear-cut; no man could influence him against his better judgment. He believed in God, in courtesy, in honour, and cleanliness, in beauty, and in education. He used to say that he would rather see a child of his the author of a book of which he could be proud than on the throne of England, which was the strongest way he knew to express himself." It is not too highly imaginative, I am sure, to believe that Mr. Stratton also planted slips and cuttings successfully; but they were slips of his own tenacious mind and they were planted most successfully in the receptive mind of his daughter, Gene.

We must note Mr. Stratton rather carefully. "His very first earnings he spent for a book; when other men rested, he read"—toiling upward in the night, in that time of Longfellowship, that has since been abandoned for fifteen minutes a day, in this era of Eliotry. The memory of Mr. Stratton enabled him to quote paragraphs at a time from Hume, Macaulay, Gibbon, Prescott and Bancroft —he was perhaps fondest of history—while as for the Bible, he could repeat it entire, his daughter

says, except for the genealogies, and give chapter
and verse. The genealogies were "a waste of grey
matter to learn." Mrs. Porter confesses: "I was
almost afraid to make these statements, although
there are many living who can corroborate them,
until John Muir published the story of his boyhood
days, and in it I found the history of such rearing
as was my father's, told of as the customary thing
among the children of Muir's time."

Sermons, lectures, talks on civic improvement and
politics, delivered without thought of personal
fatigue or selfish inconvenience at the end of journeys of many miles were Mark Stratton's contribution to the cause of Good. It seems unkind to
examine such performances dispassionately. "He
worshipped beauty: beautiful faces, souls, hearts,
beautiful landscapes, trees, animals, flowers. He
loved colour: rich, bright colour and every variation
down to the faintest shadings." Mrs. Porter keeps
a cardinal silk handkerchief that he was carrying
when stricken with apoplexy at the age of seventy-
eight. "Over inspired Biblical passages, over great
books, over sunlit landscapes, over a white violet
abloom in deep shade, over a heroic deed of man,
I have seen his brow light up, his eyes shine." He
used especially to thrill his young daughter by the
story of John Maynard, who piloted a burning boat
to safety while he slowly roasted at the wheel.
That he should tell it was natural, since the telling
gave him opportunity to reproduce, with many inflections, the captain's cry of "John Maynard!"
and the answer, "Aye, aye, sir!" echoed until it sank
to a mere gasp, a whisper. . . .

[151]

iv

Gene Stratton was only a few years old when her mother, who had once nursed three of the children through typhoid fever, contracting it herself, broke down. Mrs. Stratton lived for several years, suffering continually, frequently tortured by pain. The youngest child was therefore allowed to follow an impulse and escape the training given her sisters. She followed her father and brothers outdoors, sleeping on their coats in fence corners, awakening, sometimes, to find shy creatures peering into her face. "I trotted from one object which attracted me to another, singing a little song of made-up phrases about everything I saw while I waded, catching fish, chasing butterflies over clover fields, or following a bird with a hair in its beak; much of the time I carried the inevitable baby for a woman-child, frequently improvised from an ear of corn in the silk, wrapped in catalpa leaf blankets." She made special pets of birds. She had been taught that they were useful and had "a gift of Grace in their beauty and music, things to be rigidly protected. From this cue I evolved the idea myself that I must be extremely careful, for had not my father tied a 'kerchief over my mouth when he lifted me for a peep into the nest of the humming-bird, and did he not walk softly and whisper when he approached the spot? So I stepped lightly, made no noise, and watched until I knew what a mother bird fed her young before I began dropping bugs, worms, crumbs, and fruit into little red mouths that opened at my tap on the nest quite

[152]

as readily as at the touch of the feet of the mother bird."

All this life became a thing of memory just before the mother's death. Then they left the farm and went to town, to the city of Wabash, that Mrs. Stratton might have constant medical attention. The ninety-pound bit of pink porcelain, plump as a wild partridge, the little Dutch woman who had borne twelve children and kept a spotless farmhouse and heaped up good things on the long dinner table, lay with her head on a pillow, a cinnamon pink or a trillium placed where its fragrance would reach her with every breath she drew. She was dying. She had helped Mark Stratton with the bush- and vine-covered fences that crept around the acres they owned in a strip of gaudy colour; she shared the achievement of that orchard, lying in a valley, with its square of apple trees in the centre, so that at the time of blossoming it appeared as if a great pink-bordered white blanket had been let down on the earth. To her equally with her husband was due the presence on shale, which they might have drained, of sheets of blue flag, marigold and butter-cups. All this was going out of her children's life and she was going out with it. The youngest child, in particular, had been leading a harum-scarum existence; if she reported promptly three times a day when the bell rang at meal times, with enough clothing to constitute a decent covering, nothing more was asked of her until the Sabbath. Mary Stratton was perhaps about to be released, to receive the benefit of a freedom in which, if her hands were not busy, it was not likely she would be happy or

[153]

know what to do. Gene Stratton, whose father permitted his youngest to idolise him, was to be taken from outdoor freedom, her feet shod, her body restricted by the burden of Sunday clothing, her active legs stilled to a shuffle beneath the desk of a close schoolroom, and her mind set to droning over books. Unfortunately she came to the ordeal with no purely feminine resources of inattention, preoccupation or indifference. Her father had seen to that. It was he who was responsible for the child that revelled in *Paul and Virginia*, *Undine*, *Picciola*, *The Vicar of Wakefield*, *Pilgrim's Progress* —"exquisitely expressed and conceived stories" that "may have done much in forming high conceptions of what really constitutes literature, and in furthering the lofty ideals instilled by my parents." Mrs. Porter adds: "One of these stories formed the basis of my first publicly recognised literary effort." She was assigned to write a class composition on "Mathematical Law." She postponed, rebelled, wrote a paper retelling the story of *Picciola* and in fear and defiance read it aloud in class. After one page the teacher halted her while she summoned in the superintendent of city schools to hear the sixteen foolscap pages from the beginning. "One instant the room was in laughter, the next the boys bowed their heads, and the girls who had forgotten their handkerchiefs cried in their aprons. Never again was a subject forced upon me." She was her father's daughter, and her father was Mark Stratton.

"My mother went out too soon to know, and my father never saw one of my books; but he knew I

[154]

was boiling and bubbling like a yeast jar in July over some literary work, and if I timidly slipped to him with a composition, or a faulty poem, he saw good in it, and made suggestions for its betterment. When I wanted to express something in colour, he went to an artist, sketched a design for an easel, personally superintended the carpenter who built it, and provided tuition. On that same easel I painted the water colours for *Moths of the Limber-lost*, and one of the most poignant regrets of my life is that he was not there to see them, and to know that the easel which he built through his faith in me was finally used in illustrating a book.

"If I thought it was music through which I could express myself, he paid for lessons and detected hidden ability which should be developed. Through the days of struggle he stood fast; firm in his belief in me. He was half the battle. It was he who demanded a physical standard that developed strength to endure the rigours of scientific field and darkroom work, and the building of ten books in ten years, five of which were on nature subjects, having my own illustrations, and five novels, literally teeming with natural history, true to nature. It was he who demanded of me from birth the finishing of any task I attempted and who taught me to cultivate patience to watch and wait, even years, if necessary, to find and secure the material I wanted. It was he who daily lived before me the life of exactly such a man as I portrayed in *The Harvester*, and who constantly used every atom of brain and body power to help and to encourage all men to do the same."

[155]

No further illumination should be needed on the most extraordinary personal influence in Mrs. Porter's life.

V

Gene Stratton was married in 1886, at the age of eighteen, to Charles Darwin Porter, of Wabash, Indiana. Marriage, a home of her own, and a daughter were successively brought to bear upon a nature already powerful; none of them succeeded in eradicating the impress of Mark Stratton. The new home was a cabin of fourteen rooms (at first), standing on some fifteen acres near the Limberlost Swamp. The familiar address runs: "Limberlost Cabin, Rome City, Indiana." Red, white, pink, blue, lavender and yellow flower-beds of an acre apiece were laid off in the deep woods running down the shore of a lake; the cabin stands in the middle of the yellow bed, a dwelling of large rooms and four fireplaces, two of which Mrs. Porter built, to a large extent, herself. One is of pudden stone, red and blue pebbles; another, in the living room, is constructed of field boulders split to expose their quartz crystals that sparkle under artificial light. The windows were built with broad, deep casements especially to furnish feeding-tables for birds. On the open, cement-floored porch may stand in winter wheat, apples, cabbage and celery bunches. Chickadees, titmice, nuthatches, sapsuckers, flickers, song sparrows, jays, cardinals and squirrels come to the sills to eat the chopped wheat, ground corn and suet put out for them.

But this is to mix past and the comparative present. It was not long before Mrs. Porter's daughter was old enough to go to school. "I knew how to manage life to make it meet my needs, thanks to even the small amount I had seen of my mother. I kept a cabin of fourteen rooms and kept it im-maculate. I made most of my daughter's clothes, I kept a conservatory in which there bloomed from three to six hundred bulbs every winter, tended a house of canaries and linnets, and cooked and washed dishes, besides, three times a day. In my spare time (mark the word, there was time to spare else the books never would have been written and the pictures made) I mastered photography . . ." but we need not go with her into the details of this one among many of her personal triumphs. She was for two years editor of the camera department of Recreation, for two years on the natural history staff of Outing, for four years specialist in natural history photography on the Photographic Times Annual Almanac. She had a dread of failure and, at first, carried on her special work as secretly as possible. "My husband owned a drug and book store that carried magazines, but only a few people in our locality read these, none were interested in nature photography or natural science; so what I was trying to do was not realised even by my own family. I did not want to fail before my man person and my daughter and our respective fam-ilies." She was further afraid of ridicule in a com-munity "where I was already severely criticised on account of my ideas of housekeeping, dress and social customs." When she first attempted "nature studies sugar-coated with fiction" she proceeded

[157]

with the same furtiveness. "I who waded morass, fought quicksands, crept, worked from ladders high in air, and crossed water on improvised rafts without a tremor, slipped with many misgivings into the postoffice and rented a box for myself, so that if I met with failure my husband and the men in the bank"—Mr. Porter was president of the Bank of Geneva—"need not know." Through loss of her address at the New York end, she waited unanswered until one day, months later, when she went into "our store" on an errand and the storekeeper said: "I read your story in the Metropolitan last night. It was great! Did you ever write any fiction before?" Mrs. Porter relates: "My head whirled, but I had learned to keep my own counsels, so I said as lightly as I could, while my heart beat until I feared he could hear it, 'No. Just a simple little thing! Have you any spare copies? My sister might want one.'"

The appearance of her first story led to an order for a second, to be illustrated with her own photographs. She had a day, or less, to fill the request for photographs, and kept a number of persons up all night to pose for her. The genesis of *Freckles*, her second book, was the discovery by lumbermen of a nest of the black vulture in the Limberlost Swamp. Her husband, whose business had compelled him to allow her to work alone but who was also a natural history enthusiast, insisted that he must go with her. "A Limberlost trip at that time was not to be joked about. The swamp had not been shorn, branded, and tamed. There were most excellent reasons why I should not go there. Much of it was impenetrable. Only a few trees had been taken out; oilmen were just invading it. In its physical aspect it was a treacherous swamp and quagmire filled with every plant, animal, and human danger known in the worst of such locations in the Central States.

"A rod inside the swamp on a road leading to an oil well we mired to the carriage hubs. I shielded my camera in my arms and before we reached the well I thought the conveyance would be torn to pieces and the horse stalled. At the well we started on foot, Mr. Porter in kneeboots, I in waist-high waders. The time was late June; we forced our way between steaming, fetid pools, through swarms of gnats, flies, mosquitoes, poisonous insects, keeping a sharp watch for rattlesnakes. We sank ankle deep at every step, and logs we thought solid broke under us. Our progress was a steady succession of prying and pulling each other to the surface. Our clothing was wringing wet, and the exposed parts of our bodies lumpy with bites and stings. My husband found the tree, cleared the opening to the great prostrate log, traversed its unspeakable odours for nearly forty feet to its farthest recess, and brought the baby and egg to the light in his leaf-lined hat.

"We could endure the location only by dipping napkins in deodorant and binding them over our mouths and nostrils. Every third day for almost three months we made this trip, until Little Chicken was able to take wing."

The idea of *Freckles* came one day when they were leaving the swamp. A big feather with a shaft over twenty inches long came spinning and swirling earthward, and fell in Mrs. Porter's path. It was an eagle's feather, but although she instantly looked aloft, Mrs. Porter's well-trained eyes could not catch sight of the bird. She has always regretted that to her story the title *Freckles* was given; her wish was for "The Falling Feather"—that tangible thing drifting down out of Nowhere, just as the boy came in the story of her fashioning.

The insertion of marginal drawings of nature subjects in *Freckles* made a distinct impression get abroad that it was simply a nature book, with the result that three long years were required for the novel to attain its enormous popularity. Published in 1904, the book had sold, ten years later, 670,733 copies in the regular edition.

vi

Mrs. Porter as an author is now fairly before us and may be considered profitably before we take a look at her newest novel, *The White Flag*. So familiar a phenomenon calls for incisive comment. She writes her stories "exactly as they take shape in my mind" and the excisions are sometimes—as in the case of *Her Father's Daughter*, which yet remained overlong—quite heavy. The edited and published fiction is of itself remarkable for an unrestraint, a vigorous emphasis, a masculine zeal, with which there is generally combined freshness of feeling and a transparent sincerity. It is this sincerity, proceeding as it so often does from a total unconsciousness of what lies behind it, that the popular instinct detects at once in the pages of a work of fiction. It has, of course, nothing whatever to do with literary art, it is never shamed or enriched by the processes of introspection, and in this it conforms to the wilful egoism fundamental with the Northern races in a new country and exploitable environment. The student of psychology may be interested, for more reasons than the inheritance of Holland ancestry, to compare the late Theodore Roosevelt and Gene Stratton-Porter in personalities and characters. Each has swayed the millions; each, beyond all possible question, has influenced human lives. Neither was oppressed by the enormous responsibility attached to such a rôle. I would not say that the one had more education than has the other, but, their educations were different.

"To spend time writing a book based wholly upon human passion and its outworking I would not," exclaims Mrs. Porter, to whom art is an expression of flower-beds and children a-plenty, censored books and human lives lived on sober and industrious models. And she compromised on a book "into which I put all the nature work that came naturally within its scope, and seasoned it with little bits of imagination and straight copy from the lives of men and women I had known intimately, folk who lived in a simple, common way with which I was familiar." In simple justice it should be pointed out that she insisted upon alternating nature books and novels, although far more money could be earned by writing only fiction.

Just as the child was taken from the fields, shoed and harnessed in "Sunday clothes" and put into

[161]

school, so the naturalist was torn, though somewhat more gently and gradually, from her proper enjoyments and placed in the trammels of book-length fiction. What wonder that she revolted?—but the rebellion of *Picciola*, though ending in personal triumph, was not the end of school; and the rebellion of the novelist, though rewarded with a tremendous personal triumph, did not end her ordeal of novel-writing. What people like Mrs. Porter never achieve is a successful rebellion from, within, themselves. Something more powerful than they quells their self-insurrections; they go on; money seems worth while for what can be done with it to give happiness and widen opportunity for others; the task is good—why? It is a task; something that must be done very thoroughly. The father, Mark Stratton, to whom his daughter was so observably devoted, gave her a set of ideals that were to lift her up, like strong links of iron, and then to turn into rigid chains. She who owes so much to him owes to him more than she has ever suspected, a compulsion put upon her from within herself, the final reward or fate of every worshipper.

She has tried to escape. She has written poetry. There was *The Fire Bird;* and lately there has been *Euphorbia*, a long narrative published serially to the astonishment of readers of Good Housekeeping. The subject of *Euphorbia* is interesting—a woman to whom marriage brings non-fulfilment, whose husband tramples and uproots the red-and-white wild flower she loves. When at length the man dies, the mother has one fearful moment in which her child reaches toward a bit of euphorbia

[162]

with she knows not which intention. But he loves it. Escape! It is not necessary to make as much of this as the psychoanalyst would make of it, nor, perhaps, to miss the mark so widely. "My life has been fortunate," Mrs. Porter admits, "in one glad way: I have lived mostly in the country and worked in the woods. For every bad man and woman I have known I have met, lived with, and am intimately acquainted with an overwhelming number of thoroughly clean and decent people who still believe in God and cherish high ideals, and it is *upon the lives of these that I base what I write.*" There is a puzzling fierceness in the attacks she launches on those who write otherwise; she is vulnerable somewhere in this connection or she would show less heat and animosity. And, to some extent, her active resentment is justified, for she has had a heavy experience of misleading praise and some experience of hypocrisy. I remember an occasion upon which she wrote to me, with scornful inflections, to lay before me the evidence in the case of a certain well-known writer who had enthusiastically praised her work, though "not for publication." It was a course which, like herself, I should join in condemning; but was it so much of a matter? Did, could, the voice of a single one, count for much where she had heard already the open voices of praise from so many thousands? And if it was so, then why?

Who answers that will make possibly the largest single contribution to the psychology of literature, for this identical question finally arises in the case of writers great and small.

[163]

Never, perhaps, has Mrs. Porter been more herself than in her latest book, *The White Flag;* although *Her Father's Daughter*, as originally written, was overgrown. Both these books are autobiography— *Her Father's Daughter* of the heart, *The White Flag* of mind and memory. If Mrs. Porter has but one story to tell, no one has succeeded in telling it so often with such freshness of feeling or such repeated success in the matter of readers. *The White Flag* is the story of Mahala Spellman, daughter and only child of Mahlon and Elizabeth Spellman. The opening scenes are laid in the Indiana of the 1880s. The village is called Ashwater. For what seems an excessive time our attention is concentrated upon Elizabeth as a little girl and Junior Moreland as a little boy. Nothing could be more typical of Mrs. Porter than the attention she bestows upon her heroine in childhood—the exact detail of Mahala's dress, the recorded precision of her unfailingly correct behaviour. If there is something unnatural about the child, there is everything natural to a child in Mrs. Porter's fiction. In picturing the richest man in the village Mrs. Porter blackens his villainy to a pitch where Mr. Moreland is neither more nor less credible than some of the characters in, let us say, *Way Down East.*

Mahala, in ensuing chapters, refuses Junior Moreland in the face of the fact that his father could save her father from ruin. Her father fails, and, broken, dies. Her mother becomes an invalid. When finally Mahala can truthfully say that all is

10st except self-respect and courage, a deadly blow is levelled at her self-respect. Some money is stolen. Circumstantial evidence accuses Mahala, and Ashwater shuns her.

It will not be supposed that Mrs. Porter fails to raise up a champion in her heroine's hour of need. All along we have been in touch, in close touch, with Jason. We knew him as a boy, apparently the washerwoman's son. We know him as a young man, springing to Mahala's relief. There is no real reason why, in such a situation and with two such principal characters, Mrs. Porter should not work miracles. She does. . . . Of course her point is that the virtue, goodness and courage of Mahala and Jason earn their own ample rewards; and the thousands who are reading *The White Flag* will accept this as so.

Books by Gene Stratton-Porter

1903 *The Song of the Cardinal*
1904 *Freckles*
1907 *What I Have Done With Birds* (republished, 1917, as *Friends in Feathers*)
1908 *At the Foot of the Rainbow*
1909 *A Girl of the Limberlost*
1909 *Birds of the Bible*
1910 *Music of the Wild*
1911 *The Harvester*
1912 *Moths of the Limberlost*
1913 *Laddie*
1915 *Michael O'Halloran*
1916 *Morning Face*

1918   *A Daughter of the Land*
1920   *Homing With the Birds*
1921   *Her Father's Daughter*
1922   *The Fire Bird*
1923   *White Flag*
          Euphorbia appeared as a serial in Good
            Housekeeping: January, February, March
            numbers, 1923.

Sources on Gene Stratton-Porter

*Gene Stratton-Porter, A Little Story of Her Life
and Work.* This is the booklet, now out of
print, published some ten years ago by DOUBLE-
DAY, PAGE & COMPANY, based upon the long self-
account written by Mrs. Porter and prepared by
Eugene F. Saxton.
"An American Bird-Woman." Anonymous article
in CHAMBERS'S JOURNAL (London and Edinburgh.
New York: International News Company), Part
46, October 1, 1914: page 636.
Private Information.

Joseph C. Lincoln
Discovers Cape Cod

i

ON 13 February, 1870, in the town of Brewster, Massachusetts, which is on Cape Cod, there was born to Joseph Lincoln and Emily (Crosby) Lincoln a son whom they named Joseph Crosby Lincoln. The child's father was a seaman, so had been his father's father and his father's father's father; and so were all his uncles. His mother's people followed the sea. For a mile in each direction from the plain little house of the Lincolns every house contained a Cap'n. When the boy was a year old, his father died of a fever in Charleston, South Carolina. Emily Crosby Lincoln had made voyages with her husband, whose death made it necessary to move up toward Boston. In summers, however, the boy got back to the Cape with its sand dunes and cranberry bogs, its chance to fish and swim. "He rode the old stage coach from Harwick to Chatham; he knew the lightkeepers, the fishermen, the life savers, and the cracker-box oracles in the village stores. The perfume of the green salt meadows, the pungent pines and bayberries . . . the fishing boats, the dripping nets, 'the mighty surge and thunder of the surf along the shores' were part of his very existence." The description is reminiscent of Walt Whitman's account of his young manhood. "I suppose if I had been born a few years earlier, I would have had my own ship," Joseph C. Lincoln says. But the day of steam had begun. He went to school at Brewster and Chelsea. As he grew up, college was seen to be out of the question. The youth and his mother went to Brooklyn and he entered a broker's office. This work he hated. "I have always felt that they were fully as glad to get rid of me as I was to leave them." Wishing to draw, he fell under the guidance of Henry Sandham ("Hy") and went to Boston where, with another fellow, an office was opened for commercial work. To make a picture sell better, Lincoln sometimes wrote a verse or joke to go with it. Sometimes the verse or joke sold when the drawing did not. It was the day of universal bicycling. The League of American Wheelmen Bulletin had a circulation of over 125,000 and Sterling Elliott, its editor, offered Lincoln a job as associate editor. His verses were thus brought to the attention of a considerable public. He married in 1897 Florence E. Sargent, of Chelsea, Massachusetts, and he was writing verse, mostly in the vernacular of Cape Cod, for a number of publications. In 1899 the passion for bicycling began to wane and Lincoln definitely moved from Boston to New York to try to make a living as a writer on his own. He had written a first short story, a Cape Cod narrative, and sold it to Saturday Evening Post. That magazine, Harper's Weekly, The Youth's Companion and Puck were taking his verse, which was sometimes in a swinging

[168]

JOSEPH C. LINCOLN

metre and sometimes humour tinctured with philosophy. In 1902 Albert Brandt, of Trenton, New Jersey, published Lincoln's *Cape Cod Ballads*, in a yellow-backed volume with illustrations by E. W. Kemble. It was Lincoln's first book. Now he was writing short stories in earnest and with some success and he began a novel which could only be written by labouring at it on a corner of the dining room table from midnight on Saturdays through Sunday mornings until the manuscript was completed. It was the story of three old sea captains who, despairing of their joint efforts at housekeeping, advertised for a wife. Published in 1904 as *Cap'n Eri*, this affair settled two large doubts in Lincoln's mind; first, that he could sustain the interest of readers through a long story; second, that he could make a living by writing, and by writing books.

ii

Many have been the editions of *Cap'n Eri* since its appearance, nineteen years ago. The outline of those nineteen years in Joseph C. Lincoln's life is only pleasantly eventful. A friendship with Sewell Ford led him to become a resident of Hackensack, New Jersey. There he has built a house of "Colonial" lines, the sight of which is not good for less successful writers. A very handsome summer home stands on a terrace at Chatham, Cape Cod. In 1912 the Lincolns lived for a while in England and travelled to some extent on the Continent, visiting Switzerland. Frequently Mr. Lincoln has gone to one or another part of the United States, even unto California, to deliver, before crowded houses, his lecture on "Cape Cod Folks" or to give readings from his own books. And every year since 1904 has seen the publication of one, sometimes two, Lincoln novels.

In Hackensack Mr. Lincoln attends the Unitarian Church—he is a member of its Board of Trustees—and he was at one time a member of the Hackensack Board of Education. He used to belong to the Salmagundi Club in New York but resigned because he used the club and its privileges so little. He still belongs to The Players in New York; but in any ordinary sense of the word he is not a clubman. The family usually goes to Cape Cod in a motor car and while there Mr. Lincoln fishes and swims and sails all he can. In Hackensack golf is his principal diversion and he tries to play daily, "although there are times, particularly in my brand of golf, when there seems to be more hard work and moral strain than amusement, by a good deal." The man is a red-cheeked, rotund and comfortable man, with a bright eye and a catching smile and a great fund of stories such as the following:

"An old salt of my acquaintance spent a recent winter in Florida and found in the fishing of the region a fascinating but pretty strenuous pastime. As a skipper of the old school he scorned modern devices for fishing, such as reels. In fact he went out to fish tarpons in good Cape Cod fashion with merely a fishing line and his own bare hands. He hooked a tarpon and for a couple of hours there was waged a terrific battle between the fish and the stubborn old Cape Codder, whose hands were torn

[170]

and blistered. Proudly he exhibited his 79-pound catch to the natives. 'Not much of a haul,' was their comment. 'Why, a little woman, no size at all, just brought in a tarpon that tipped the scales at 100 pounds.' Would he like to see a real fish? 'Thunder, no!' roared the Cap'n. 'Show me the woman!' "

iii

Hamlin Garland, the author of some accounts of American life which have not omitted the sombre, the discouraging, the bitter scenes and places, has written:

"Joseph Lincoln is not only a novelist of wide reputation, he is a public benefactor. His success has in it something heartening and corrective. In the midst of work which appeals to the base and cynical in human life (American city life) his clean, wholesome, humorous stories of Cape Cod sea captains and their neighbours give evidence of the fact that there is a huge public for decent and homely fiction, just as the success of his play, '*Shavings*,' is evidence that there is a paying audience for a decent and homely drama. His books can be read aloud in the family circle with joy to all the members of it—I know, for I have myself read eight or ten of them to my wife and daughters. They make no pretense of being profound, or new, or 'smart.' They are filled with the characters and the humour which are native to the Cape. Lincoln knows these Cape towns and their inhabitants as Irving Bacheller knows his men of the North Woods, for he was raised among them and lives in

[171]

their neighbourhood several months of each year. He looks like one of them, like an old skipper, hearty, unassuming and kindly. The task which he has set himself is one which calls for a keen sense of character, democracy of sentiment and a fancy which never—or very seldom—loses its hold on the solid ground of experience. His plots are sometimes negligible, but his characters, even when they seem a bit repetitious, are a joy. His prosperity is well earned."

This undoubtedly expresses a general sentiment, although it does not express it so vividly as a sentence that appeared in the Los Angeles Express:

"One enjoys a Joe Lincoln novel as one does a long, cool, thirst-quenching drink on a hot day."

However, before examining the novels them- selves, it is proper to put down here some things that Mr. Lincoln has said, at one time or another, showing his attitude toward them. Of course his attitude toward other kinds of fiction is a part of his general attitude, and so:

"I read all sorts of books and at all times. I don't know that I can name any particular author who may be called my favourite. I am very fond of Stevenson, for instance—but then, so I am of Kipling, except his more recent stories, which have a bit too much British Empire in them to please me,—of Mark Twain, of W. J. Locke, and many others. I think I like a story for the story's sake. I like to like my characters or dislike them in the old-fashioned way. It is for this reason perhaps that the work of such writers as Arnold Bennett, William De Morgan, Joseph Conrad, and others, of the realistic school, so-called, does not appeal to me as much as—well, as Mr. Locke's work, for instance. I realise,—no one can help realising—the fine literary craftsmanship in a book like *Lord Jim*. It is a wonderful piece of character mosaic, and yet in reading it I am always conscious of the literary work. I say to myself, 'This is marvellous; see how the writer is picking his hero to pieces, thought by thought, motive by motive.' And being so conscious of the writer, I do not lose myself in the story. This is not offered as a criticism; certainly I should not presume to criticise Mr. Bennett or Mr. Conrad. It is more of a confession of something lacking on my part. I enjoy reading *Lord Jim*, or *The Old Wives' Tale*, but I do not return to them again and again as I do to *The Beloved Vagabond* or *The Morals of Marcus Ordeyne*. Perhaps this is, as some of my realistically inclined friends tell me, a childish love for romance on my part. Well, perhaps it is. If it is, I can't help it; as I said, this statement is not offered as an excuse, but a confession.

"This sort of thing shows in my own stories. It would be very hard for me to write a long story which should end dismally. It is only too true that stories in real life frequently end that way, but I don't like my yarns to do so. So it is fair to presume that in whatever books I may hereafter write, the hero and the heroine will be united, virtue rewarded and vice punished, as has happened in those for which I am already responsible. Perhaps this same weakness for a story, a cheerful story, makes me care little for the so-called problem novel. It

[173]

doesn't mean that I am not fond of novels dealing with certain kinds of problems. Winston Churchill's *The Inside of the Cup* I liked immensely; but the sex problem, the divorce question, and all that sort of thing does not appeal to me. A morbid lot of disagreeable people, married or otherwise, moping and quarrelling through a long story seem to me scarcely worth while. To a specialist in nervous diseases such a study might be interesting, but I really doubt if the average healthy man or woman finds it so. Certainly we should not care to associate with such people were they living near us. We should get away from them if we could.

"Perhaps I *could* write a story with gloomy situations and an unhappy ending, but I wouldn't like to try it. I would much rather try to make people cheerful and keep myself cheerful at the same time. There's enough sorrow in this world without finding it in books."

So he spoke ten years ago; so, with possibly the change of an illustration or two, would he speak today. From nine in the morning until noon or one o'clock he disappears into his workshop, frequently a place known only to himself, and either writes (with a soft, stubby pencil, on large sheets of yellow paper) or thinks about characters and the very attenuated skeleton which, for Mr. Lincoln, constitutes the "plot."

"I know there are people who can turn out a short story in two or three hours and it will be good enough to sell, but I cannot help feeling that it would have been much better if the writer had devoted more time to it. In my case, doing work

[174]

that is satisfactory to me in any degree means that I must fairly sweat it out, if I may use the expression." There usually comes a time when he gets "a letter about once a week asking how the thing is coming along. That has been a frequent experience, especially when there are a lot of characters in my story, and I'm having more or less trouble with them. The story keeps stretching itself out. I think I may have to adopt Mark Twain's method, and begin throwing my people down the well." There is a genial artifice about nearly all his tales. Some years ago an interviewer for the Boston Globe touched on the subject of "specialty" writing, which was a natural topic, as all of Mr. Lincoln's fiction is a highly specialised affair, not only in its general localisation on Cape Cod but in its characterisation and homely wit and humour. The author said:

"A man writes what he knows. If he tries anything else it must fall—show hollow. And I find that it is necessary to write to your audience—that one must consider that a large number of his readers are to be women, and he must write things that will appeal to the women of today."

"You don't mean that you would consider the women to the point of writing stuff that would be saleable, and refrain from writing stuff which appealed to you, but might not be saleable?"

"Well," said Mr. Lincoln, slowly, "I haven't any 'message' that I know of. I'm not much of a highbrow. I have standards, though. And if I am to do the thing I want to do, I must get my book printed. But I've never been satisfied—although I did like *The Postmaster* pretty well."

[175]

This was ten years ago, and Mr. Lincoln has gone on, unchanging. He has the most enviable record of any living American writer. No book of his has been a failure. Some have done better than others, but with no serious qualification of the statement it can be said that each book has added to his audience, so that he has for some years been an unfailing best seller. Perhaps there has been a noticeable increase in his popularity with and since *The Portygee* (1919), which was published serially and then surprised the publishers by beating Lincoln records as a book. Or the gain may be traceable to the preceding book, *"Shavings,"* and its successful dramatisation. But in his sustained, unbroken and increasing popularity as a fictionist Mr. Lincoln has no competitor. There are others whose individual books have sold more heavily, whose total sales may be larger, but they have had lapses, and their popularity has either been impaired or lost. Even as I write the process known in the trade as "slipping" is observable, here and there, in the case of one of the most popular American authors, a person with a long record of immediate successes, one of whose work the American soldier, in 1917-18, could not apparently get enough. Time does this thing, but apparently it cannot touch, except to enhance, the passion for the work of this native of Cape Cod, who clips his words a little and sometimes says "hev" and "hed" for "have" and "had"—about whom there is even a suspicion of the Down East nasal twanging as he talks. A wholly lovable personality. He once wrote:

"Bless the children. They are the most con-

[176]

venient excuses in creation. Probably, if it were not for them, you wouldn't get to the zoological gardens or the aquarium or the fairy play oftener than once a year or so. And as for the circus—but that's an old story."

iv

We have not finished, though, with the man's own account of his relation to his work.

"You can't use actual people. People aren't as dramatic in actual life as you want them to be. Of course, you may hear a phrase, or a story—you may talk with a person and get an impression and build up your character from those things. But using an actual person wouldn't work. Besides, it would be rather mean.

"In writing of a Cape Cod town or village, although I purposely refrain from describing it as any one town in particular, I have tried conscientiously to give the characteristics of Cape Cod towns I am acquainted with. The promontories and inlets and hills and marshes in 'my' Cape Cod may not be found where I have located them, but I have tried very hard to make them like those which are on the real Cape. And so with the Cape Codders in my stories. I have never knowingly drawn the exact, recognisable portrait of an individual. I have of course, received hundreds of letters from readers who inform me, in strict confidence, that they know the original of 'Cap'n ——' and recognised him at once. Nevertheless they are wrong. I have endeavoured always to be true to type, and

[177]

in writing of the old deep-sea captain, the coasting skipper, the longshoreman or the people of the Cape villages, I have done my best to portray each as I have seen and known specimens of his or her kind. And in attempting to transcribe the habit of language I have made it a rule never to use an expression or idiom I have not heard used by a native of the old colony."

The differentiation of the various types of sea-man has been carefully made by Mr. Lincoln, and is perhaps valuable to a full appreciation of his fiction.

"The type of sea captain who figures in my stories has not necessarily an accurately corresponding type in my acquaintance. Going back to the Cape after having lived in New York and Boston, I was able to get varying angles on the lives of the men and women I had known in my childhood. The old sea captains that I remembered best as a child were of more than one character, classified according to their work. One was the dignified old man who had travelled to some far-away corner of the earth and returned prosperous, to spend the rest of his days as an autocrat among his own people. He had met strange peoples, he had been trusted with a ship, and, as in the days I write of there were no instantaneous means of talking across the oceans, he was shrewd at bargaining and, being one of the owners of the ship, he lost no chance to bring home a cargo that would bring rich returns. In other words, he was a shrewd trader as well as a sailing master. The same dignified bearing that he used in his trade followed him on land, and, though jovial in manner, he was developed in dignity and character.

"The other type of captain was more popular with the youngsters. He may have been as shrewd, and possibly made as much money, but he was filled with a greater sense of humour, and took life as a pastime. Men of this description would gather round the stove and tell wonderful stories, though all sea captains talk shop when they get together.

"Then too there were what are termed the 'long-shore captains.' These were mostly engaged in fishing, or in trading with coast towns and cities. They were necessarily more limited in their views, for they spent more time ashore, often working a good-sized garden, fishing when the spirit moved, and running a schooner to New York or Boston if the chance came.

"Of all the sea-captains, however, those that I knew best were those who were actually sailing in the 1870's and 1880's, and who were largely engaged in carrying oranges and lemons from Mediterranean ports. These men were really the last of our sailing captains. I have one friend in particular who was in the fruit trade, and his stories of how they crowded sail and took every risk to bring in their cargoes are many and thrilling. Fruit, of course, is highly perishable, and while it might be a valuable cargo one day, a week later it would be worthless; therefore the sea races and adventures."

In an article, "Some Samples of Yankee Shrewdness," appearing in the American Magazine, Mr. Lincoln has told stories of Cape Cod captains he has known. Acuity of observation, caution joined to a quality of going in head-first if one goes in at all, and a singularly dry humour are a large part of the "shrewdness," as Lincoln makes it out. In the course of the article he offers this admittedly serious statement:

"In all my forty-odd years of experience with Yankees I do not remember ever having met one who habitually whittled. I have, of course, known some who whittled occasionally, when they were making a 'bow 'n' arrer' or a boat for one of the children. But I never knew one who whittled when he was making a trade." *Sic transit* the "Yankee" of one species of "fiction" and drama. But it is time to look at Mr. Lincoln's own fiction; then, perhaps, we may revert for a closing glance at the puzzle of Yankee shrewdness.

v

The newest Lincoln novel (1923) is *Doctor Nye of North Ostable*—Mr. Lincoln has something of a gift in titles for his special kind of book. There is a comfortable assurance in knowing that one is going to read about Dr. Nye, or a place called Fair Harbour, or an individual named Keziah Coffin, or the sure-to-be-amusing process of *Extricating Obadiah*. That last has a music of the syllables; it is solitary in this respect among Lincoln titles which are also easily affected by climatic changes, so that *Galusha the Magnificent* had to be altered in England to *The Magnificent Mr. Bangs*. But to return to our fishing—

Ephraim Nye, M.D., a "sympathetic" hero,

self-sacrificing, a man with a deal of humour, has a black cloud over his past, as all North Ostable knows. The story opens with his return to that Cape Cod village. All that day Marietta Lamb ("Mary's Lamb") had been scrubbing away at a great rate in the old Dillingham house, so long untenanted, and Henry Ward Beecher Payson, in full working regalia of overalls and wooden leg (for "best" and Sundays he had a cork leg) was busy in the yard. Miss Althea Bemis, who lived across the road and missed nothing that went on among her neighbours, asked innumerable questions, learning nothing. Judge Copeland, Cyrenus Stone and Cap'n Mark Bearse, "natives," and "the three most influential men in North Ostable" appeared on the scene. The Judge and Stone were bitter political enemies, always flying at each other's throats. Stone, who owned the empty house, admitted to Cap'n Mark Bearse that the place was being made ready for someone whose coming would be a great surprise.

Then, at nightfall, Doctor Eph arrived in a ramshackle gig.

People sat up late that night in North Ostable. In the home of Shubal Bash discussion ran high as Shubal and his wife, Angelina, tried to tell deaf old Aunt Lidy the story of Ephraim Nye. After studying medicine, the young Ephraim had married Judge Copeland's sister, Fanny, and had returned to his native town to practise. Fanny was fond of clothes and jewels and the Doctor worked hard to give them to her. Respected and liked, everyone turned against him when it was discovered that $7,200 of the $10,000 in the fund for the new meeting-house, of which he was treasurer, had been stolen. The bank had exhibited a check for $7,200 signed "Ephraim Nye, Treasurer," and the Doctor admitted the check to be his. His wife was very ill at the time. After her death, which occurred shortly, Ephraim Nye was tried and sentenced to five years in State's prison. Later the money began to come back in instalments until it was all paid up. Always the sums were sent through Doctor Nye's lawyer.

The two enemies, Cyrenus Stone and Judge Copeland, have, respectively, a son and a daughter; and Tom Stone and Faith Copeland are young lovers.

The stage is now set for Mr. Lincoln's story. And immediately, in a backward glance, one gets the rapid impression that the plot consists entirely of typhoid fever. Such an impression, however, is quite unjust. *Doctor Nye* is one of the more carefully articulated (or more carefully complicated) Lincoln novels. In addition to the revelation forming the climax of the story and putting Ephraim Nye in a heroic light, there is a fully-constituted early love affair for the Doctor, brought back and actively developed; there is the pair of young lovers, Tom and Faith; there is the prolonged duel between Judge Copeland and the Doctor; there is a considerable variety of minor incidents essential to the movement of the tale and to its final outworking. All this, mind you, aside from the real end sought by most readers of Mr. Lincoln's work—the exposition of "characters" and the continuous oscillation into humour.

[182]

JOSEPH C. LINCOLN DISCOVERS CAPE COD

It is the humour, then, that most deserves our scrutiny; for many of the Lincoln novels, practically plotless beside such a tale as *Doctor Nye*, have only the assets of their "characters" and humour to sustain a popular interest which they have not failed to feed. If there is any question about this, a glance at the technical "descriptions" of half a dozen of the books ought to settle the matter. Here, in a sentence, is what some of them simmer down to:

Partners of the Tide. Cap'n Ezra Titcomb and young Bradley Nickerson go into the wrecking business and meet with a series of surprising adventures and difficulties.

Cy Whittaker's Place. Old Cy Whittaker, bachelor, adopted a little girl. He and an old crony form a "Board of Strategy" for her upbringing.

Keziah Coffin. Keziah Coffin, typical Cape Cod old maid, proves the good angel of the minister in his courtship. Incidentally, she turns out not to be incurably an old maid.

The Postmaster. Cap'n Zeb Snow is discontented with inactivity after retiring from the sea. As postmaster he finds all the activity he wants.

Thankful's Inheritance. Thankful Barnes and her helper Emily lose their boarders when the house proves to be "ha'nted," but they gain a Cape Cod sea captain and also a handsome young lawyer—for life.

"Shavings." The quaint, unbusinesslike windmill-maker has no success in posing as a bank robber, but his loyalty and shrewdness bring happiness to all his friends.

The Portygee. The temperament and "calf love"

of the son of a Spanish opera singer make difficulties with his Yankee grandfather.

vi

No plots, only complications; but there must be admitted to be, within somewhat narrow bounds, a considerable display of "characters." Although even here certain stock figures are (probably necessarily) much employed—the gossiping old maid, Mis' Somebody-or-Other; the village comedian, like Henry Ward Beecher Payson, who periodically lapses from good behaviour and goes on sprees. One of the most interesting of Lincoln's portrayals is Albert in *The Portygee*, a young fellow half Spanish, half New Englander, with poetic and artistic impulses. "Set there in the small hamlet, chafing at the restraints and humdrumness of the place, Albert makes a delicious contrast to the native population," says Hildegarde Hawthorne. "We understand the passionate, temperamental boy as well as his old Grandfather, with his fury against all that sort of 'foolishness,' because their author understands them." I cannot go so far as Hildegarde Hawthorne in praise of the variety or depth of Mr. Lincoln's characters, while cheerfully granting, as I do, their frequent colour and whimsical charm. Often and inevitably, I suppose, in the work of one who has written two dozen books the "characters" are not *character*, but a selected idiosyncrasy or two. Often and inevitably in the case of one who is not the inexhaustible and fecund creator, like Dickens.

[184]

JOSEPH C. LINCOLN DISCOVERS CAPE COD

But there is the humour. . . .

Now we have come to it. In the first place, Mr. Lincoln shows the quick faculty evidenced from the outset by Mary Roberts Rinehart of getting the humour on every page. Mrs. Rinehart has not always practised with that intention, but Mr. Lincoln has never neglected the rapid shift of the reader's mood. To insure it, he does not hesitate to sacrifice something of his more important scenes, making them if necessary less dramatic. The commonsensicality running through his stories is a solvent to drama and a feeder to the spirit of fun; if it makes it impossible for his story ever to leave the ground, it also kills to a large extent the language, or lingo, of sentimentality so-called, that terrible jargon in which so much popular fiction is sugared and preserved. Mr. Lincoln pickles his stories in this salty common-sensibleness, rather—a breath of Cape Cod air and a dip in the ocean brine. All his "atmosphere" is as matter of fact as a dip in the ocean, and the temperature is much more unvarying and satisfactory . . . unless you may find it tepid. He is a funmaker, resorting without hesitation to such crude and cheerful devices as the spree in which Henry Ward Beecher Payson breaks his "Sunday best," or cork, leg. And yet fun warms the heart. We laugh inanely, and afterward we have the feeling of having laughed inanely, a sense of a slight immoderacy or excess, of a mild dissipation which perhaps has not really done us any good (though the harm be passing and inconsiderable); but when the moment comes we are ready to laugh again.

[185]

A final note on that debateable Yankee shrewd-ness, then. . . .

Can we not find its fruitful exercise in Mr. Lincoln's own case? I think we can. Here was a man of around thirty whose observation was keen, whose caution was used to direct him in a proper self-committal, whose own personal sense of humour was of a sufficient dryness to keep him from the easy trails of self-deception. Just as his friend, Captain Lorenzo Baker, of Wellfleet, Massachusetts, was able to discern in the casual remarks of a West Indian the commercial possibilities of the yellow banana, so Joseph C. Lincoln could perceive from a token or two the personal possibilities of Cape Cod as he could put it on paper. And acuteness, or, as the Yankee says, 'cuteness, having done its work, that other trait of Yankee shrewdness, the caution which restrains and then goes in headlong, was brought into play. Mr. Lincoln committed himself wholeheartedly to his fictional enterprise. He put all his money, or rather, the energy which was his equivalent for money, on the bob-tailed nag—in a little sloop which was his own boat rather than in somebody else's two-masted schooner. The rest was plain sailing and persistence that could have been fatally spoiled if that inner dryness of wit and clearness of perception had ever failed him. But he never forgot that it was his own little sloop, the sailing of which must be kept within the manœuvres she could execute. He has never, for example, tried to write the great American novel which, consciously or unconsciously, has brought up into the wind, all sails shaking and way lost, the craft of more than one of his fellow sailors. A Yankee and shrewd, earning many rewards, including that of a very widespread affection.

Books by Joseph C. Lincoln

1902   *Cape Cod Ballads*
1904   *Cap'n Eri*
1905   *Partners of the Tide*
1906   *Mr. Pratt*
1907   *The "Old Home House"*
1908   *Cy Whittaker's Place*
1909   *Our Village*
1909   *Keziah Coffin*
1910   *The Depot Master*
1911   *Cap'n Warren's Wards*
1911   *The Woman-Haters*
1912   *The Postmaster*
1912   *The Rise of Roscoe Paine*
1913   *Mr. Pratt's Patients*
1914   *Cap'n Dan's Daughter*
1914   *Kent Knowles: Quahaug*
1915   *Thankful's Inheritance*
1916   *Mary-'Gusta*
1917   *Extricating Obadiah*
1918   *"Shavings"*
1919   *The Portygee*
1921   *Galusha the Magnificent*
1922   *Fair Harbor*
1923   *Doctor Nye of North Ostable*

All fiction, except *Cape Cod Ballads* (verse) and *Our Village* (sketches of life and people on the Cape).

Sources on Joseph C. Lincoln

Joseph Crosby Lincoln. Booklet published by D. APPLETON & COMPANY, 1921.

Joseph C. Lincoln's America, by Hildegarde Hawthorne. Booklet. D. APPLETON & COMPANY, 1921.

Some Samples of Yankee Shrewdness, by Joseph C. Lincoln. Article in AMERICAN MAGAZINE, July, 1919.

My Types: An Interview with Joseph C. Lincoln, by Charles Francis Reed, THE FORUM MAGAZINE, February, 1919.

Cape Cod's Genial Chronicler: An Appreciation by Hamlin Garland. PUBLISHER'S WEEKLY, 17 April, 1920.

The Men Who Make Our Novels, by George Gordon. MOFFAT, YARD & COMPANY, 1919.

Joseph Crosby Lincoln, by Adam C. Haeselbarth. BOOK NEWS MONTHLY, 1913.

Edith Wharton and the Time Spirit

i

AT just past sixty Edith Wharton's is still a name for the literary conjuror in search of an impressive effect. She has lived a long time—in the literary sense—and comparisons are not easy; she has outlived, as a writer, most comparisons, including the one which would probably have been fatal to anyone else, the comparison with Henry James. She has outlived, in the physical sense, Henry James himself; there are no more of his frequent letters to "Dear Edith." It is among the subtler tributes to Mrs. Wharton, the person, that the intellectual relation between her and the man who was once called her "Master" is now seen in a light which considerably enhances the dignity of the woman who was once called "Pupil." For who, after reading the correspondence of Henry James, published since his death, believes any longer that Mrs. Wharton ever owed anything to that man's patronage so nicely tinctured with snobbery? Victor Hugo permitted himself to be surrounded by those who worshipped him as a god, but Hugo posed, god-like; whereas Henry James——

Mrs. Atherton is several years older than Edith Wharton, both as person and author; Mary Johnston, born eight years later, is of almost exactly the same literary age; but the first is a superb journalist and a born storyteller and the second is a mystic and a historian. Mrs. Wharton's journalism in fiction is pretty well confined to *The House of Mirth* and *The Fruit of the Tree;* she invites comparison with Mary Johnston only in that ambitious novel of mediæval Italy, *The Valley of Decision.* In the two books on which Mrs. Wharton's fame definitely rests at the present, *Ethan Frome* and *The Age of Innocence*, she achieves a success and an individuality only the more interesting because it finds so strikingly different expressions.

In fact, on the evidence of the two stories, it would be superficially impossible to assert that the "sterile" tragedy of New England hillsides was from the same hand that wrote the minutely detailed story of New York society in the 1870s. Considered for their meaning and origin, *Ethan Frome* and *The Age of Innocence* are both seen to be tales of frustration, both tales of the America that Mrs. Wharton quitted some fifteen years ago but can't get out of her system, and both stories in which the background is responsible for the actors themselves as well as the play.

ii

Edith Newbold Jones was born in New York, 24 January, 1862, the daughter of Frederic Jones who had married Lucretia Stevens Rhinelander. One grandparent was a Stevens, another a Schermerhorn. A great deal of her childhood was spent in

[190]

EDITH WHARTON

EDITH WHARTON AND THE TIME SPIRIT

Europe—there was one stretch of five years in which the family didn't return to America—and education proceeded wholly with the aid of tutors and governesses. The child learned French, German and Italian. Such summers as the family devoted to America were lived in a house at Newport, on the bay, halfway out towards Fort Adams. When Miss Jones was twenty-three she became the wife of Edward Wharton, of Boston. They lived in New York and Newport and later at Lenox in the summer, frequent visits to Europe continuing. Miss Jones and Mrs. Wharton were equally interested in writing and read extensively Goethe, Balzac, Thackeray, Dickens, Flaubert, George Eliot, Meredith and—Henry James? That last one had begun as author while Miss Jones was still in her teens. Twenty years were to pass before she started to overtake him. Mrs. Wharton was thirty-seven in the year when her first book was published, *The Greater Inclination*, containing, according to Katharine Fullerton Gerould, "two of the best stories she ever wrote" ("The Pelican" and "Souls Belated").

Six years later came *The House of Mirth*, "the tragedy of the woman who is a little too weak to do without money and what it buys, or to earn it for herself, and a little too good to sell herself." The story of Lily Bart had to a high degree that provocative quality which can generally be relied upon to make a novel a best-seller; and a best-seller it became. Soon afterward, with a feeling in which satisfaction, distaste, caution and physical preferences were obscurely blended, Mrs. Wharton settled in France—winter home in Provence, summer home near Paris. In 1914 she opened a workroom for skilled woman workers thrown out of employment by the miscalculations of Napoleon III. a generation earlier. She also opened restaurants where French and Belgian refugees were fed at less than cost, and lodgings where they might sleep. Mrs. Wharton took full charge of over 600 Belgian children who had been withdrawn from orphanages near Furnes and Poperinghe and established them, with the nuns who had the children's care, in four colonies, where the girls were taught fine sewing and lace-making, in anticipation of a day when fine sewing and lace-making would again be demanded. For these services the French Government, in 1915, conferred on the American novelist the cross of the Legion of Honour. During the war Mrs. Wharton wrote little. *Fighting France* records her visits to the French fronts; she contributed to *The Book of the Homeless;* in 1918 was published her long short story of an American boy in the war, under the title, *The Marne;* in 1920, *In Morocco* gave an account of a visit to that country which she made with General Lyautey, by invitation of the French Government. *French Ways and Their Meaning* appeared in 1919. The total roll of Mrs. Wharton's non-fiction is considerable and includes *Italian Villas and Their Gardens* (1904), *Italian Backgrounds* (1905), *A Motor-Flight Through France* (1908), *Artemis to Actæon and Other Verse* (1909), *The Decoration of Houses*, as well as the books just mentioned. No article on Mrs. Wharton would be complete unless mention was made of her passion for gardening and her art in developing

[192]

beautiful gardens, both at her home in Hyères and at St. Brice, near Paris.

iii

We have had it all carefully explained for us by Mrs. Gerould how much more desirable it is that Mrs. Wharton should give us—as she has generally given us—studies of sophisticated people. Speaking of *Ethan Frome*, and, in fact, merely mentioning that masterpiece, for which, it would appear, she is without admiration, Mrs. Gerould says of Mrs. Wharton:

"She did not abandon her civilised and sophisticated folk, for any length of time, to deal with rustics. Let us hope that she never will abandon them. There is vital truth in the Shakesperean dictum that 'the hand of little employment hath the daintier sense.' To put it roughly"—as a rustic, no doubt, might put it—"the people who have leisure to experience their own emotions, and the education to show them how the emotions fit into the traditions of the race, are more interesting in themselves than the people whose emotions are bound to be on a more nearly animal plane. It is less interesting, morally, to the average man to know how the sub-average man conducts himself than to know how the super-average man conducts himself. It does not in the least matter to the average intelligent citizen —except as it may touch his social conscience—how the characters in certain modern novels behave, because those characters are not the real fruit of civilisation. They are, at best, its sorry by-products.

[193]

They do not help him out in his own problems; they do not stand to him for vicarious experience. Whereas it is of interest to a civilised man to know how other civilised beings, in situations his own or other, behave; even if they behave badly. Theirs are dramas that he can feel, theirs is conduct that he is competent to judge; they respond, or fail to respond, to an admitted code of moral taste. No creature was beyond the range of Shakespeare's sympathetic understanding; but when he wished to probe the human heart most deeply, he usually chose the heart of a king. The insensitive and the sub-normal served him chiefly for comedy.

"So that a positive purpose is served by the competent novelist's choosing to deal with the more fortunate classes. Inhibitions have more chance; and inhibitions are as necessary to real drama as are passions. There is also—naturally—more opportunity for satire; and satiric comment is inveterate in Mrs. Wharton's work. If the person who has had every chance is not fine, then he is relatively uglier than the person who has had no chance at all. She does not spare her aristocrats who had an opportunity for moral fineness and neglected it. The baser emotions are more shocking in a world where there is less excuse for them. And since it is real life with which Mrs. Wharton is dealing, the baser emotions frequently appear."

These words were written after, not before, the publication of Mrs. Wharton's novel, *The Glimpses of the Moon* (1922).

At sixty, one either prepares to die or one faces life anew. In the latter event one knows, if one chances

to be a writer, the heavenly and earthly certitudes
. . . and the escape from platitudes is final. Thus,
for example, it is given to understand that a reputation will at least last for the remainder of a lifetime
but that markets change. And, after all, as Mrs.
Wharton once remarked, cleanliness and comfort
are the two most expensive things on earth—comfort implying whatever degree of luxury is essential
to a state of mind in which one can do work to purchase continued comfort. At sixty, though one may
now and again bounce it high in the air, the real
and right concern is to keep the ball a-rolling. . . .
Let people think what they like and say what they
like (and the follies of attack and fence are always
equal), the unerring perception is directed toward
the next thing that is to be written. One may
exercise a choice from the very limited amount of
material one has or can acquire; at sixty, it is too
late to acquire much additional. Of course, a finely
cultivated imagination in early years might come
to the rescue with a second blooming; but suppose
one's imagination has always moved in the best
society? No, it doesn't do, it most decidedly
doesn't do to speculate any longer about anything;
let others pretend what they like, there is a positive
relief in the knowledge that one writes what one
can when one has to—and be it good, bad, indif-
ferent or astonishing the aim was an honest aim and
the result achieved was, at least, intelligent.

And what could place Mrs. Wharton in a clearer, finer light than just this situation of fact? What could be more in keeping with the two traditions that have bound her life?—the tradition of an older New York and the literary tradition of France, both strict and both congenial, both so severe as by their very classicism to give the greatest possible scope to personality. The New York of the Age of Innocence into which she was born, the literary Europe of the nineteenth century to which she so early attached herself—these were the ideal forcing-beds of a personality such as hers. You come upon her expressing in vigorous words her delighted enthusiasm for the first novel of William Gerhardi: "You not only make your people live, but move and grow —and that's the very devil to achieve. Do, for all our sakes, keep it up!" There is no flabbiness about her. She is past the pitfall of fanaticism and safe beyond the quagmire of adulation. She does not need to practise the conventional literary dishonesties which close like traps upon novelists whose fame is on the make and who still have much to lose. She can say frankly: "There are moments —to me at least—in the greatest of Russian novels, and just as I feel the directing pressure of the novelist most strongly on my shoulder, when somehow I stumble, the path fades to a trail, the trail to a sand-heap, and hopelessly I perceive that the clue is gone, and that I no longer know which way the master is seeking to propel me, because his people are behaving as I never knew people to behave."

EDITH WHARTON AND THE TIME SPIRIT

What heresy! Here we all are kneeling on the ground, touching foreheads and breathing the overpowering incense burnt before the shrine of Dostoievsky, and a voice is distinctly heard to remark that the literary deity is perhaps not as luminous as he should be! How many would dare such a remark, or, if they ventured it, would command from any of us the bravery of timid, relieved assents? Not many; scarcely a one.

She has not always been so free; who, indeed, is born to freedom? Saint Paul said he was, but a price had been paid formerly; it always is. Henry James, tormented to the end of his days by the fact that his books really didn't sell, wasn't able to pay the price. Thomas Hardy paid it at the cost of silence as a novelist after the reception accorded to *Jude the Obscure*. O. Henry, confronted with the heavy total, shivered and shuddered. Every man has his price, indeed, in quite another sense from what that saying was coined to convey; it is a price he must manage if he is to have the truth for himself or tell it about others.

Mrs. Wharton's greatest good fortune has probably consisted, after all, in her realisation of this. Did she learn it in France, that country where truth lies at the bottom of a well . . . and is not drawn up but used as a mirror? You can see the perception through nearly all of Mrs. Wharton's work. In her long novel of eighteenth century Italy, *The Valley of Decision*, she is painting away with grand strokes on a magnificent canvas; she wants to find out if she really is suited to the execution of fictions like the *Romola* of that George Eliot she once read so attentively. Well, no; the result satisfies her that she isn't. So then she goes on with those short stories in the writing of which she is so proficient, and, a few years later, produces *The House of Mirth.* The result is instructive; one might almost say it was destructive. Mrs. Wharton definitely learned that here was a kind of thing she could successfully do, in terms of money and popularity. But in other terms?

This was a question less easily answered. Two years after *The House of Mirth* came *The Fruit of the Tree*, with its highly interesting "problem" as to whether it can ever be right for a physician or nurse to accelerate and ease the death of a doomed patient. This has been called, by the Folletts, Mrs. Wharton's "one lapse into artistic disintegration." But Mrs. Wharton was not thinking of art, but of life. It had sharply come over her that the pursuit of art in one or another form of preciosity would land her where she didn't wish to be landed. She might be, as was charged, the woman who of all women wrote most like a man; but she didn't desire to write like some men. If she could have been Gustave Flaubert, perhaps . . . but she saw no use in being George Moore or—Henry James? The whole contemporary French school left her unaffected; she read them, but experienced no wish to write like them; and in the midst of a freshly-running sea of Continental literature she became more than ever aware of her absolute and inescapable Americanism. In a way, it was a tragedy. To think that one could grow up in Europe, be, as it were, a part of Europe, definitely adopt Europe, and yet

[198]

not to Europe belong! After steadily eyeing this situation for a while she reacted without either tears or temperament; and her reaction took the form of a short novel which is among the most perfect pieces of workmanship in English, the story of *Ethan Frome.* The "hard shapeliness" of that tale was the hard shapeliness of a full self-recognition, the so-called "sterility" was the result of an individual adjustment to the deepest personal need of her remarkable nature. What she would once have so wanted to give, she now knew she never could give to the world, and her awakened consciousness strove for the fit expression of this discovery in terms of an art of which she knew something. *Ethan Frome,* whatever else it may be (and it is many things, some strange and all beautiful) is the Magnificat of a woman in the hour of profoundest personal disappointment. Such works of fiction are especially rare, but, given the genuinely capable writer, given the one hour of a lifetime, the masterpiece is quite possible, yes, almost certain.

Ah! She had written it at last . . . and she could afford to let it stand there to her credit while, with calmness and admirable fortitude she returned to the region of *The House of Mirth* and *The Fruit of the Tree* to add a study of divorce and parasitic marriage called *The Custom of the Country.* The resumption of the general warfare which has been the custom of Europe during odd generations for several centuries didn't interfere with *Summer* (1917), wherein Mrs. Wharton tried to combine her established "material" with some of the qualities of *Ethan Frome*—an experiment only mod-

[199]

erately a success. When she came later to write
The Age of Innocence she was, to all appearances,
in the happy position of desiring only to do a definite and modest thing, a first-rate story of very
marketable quality, and then achieving something
distinctly beyond that.

v

Mrs. Wharton's new novel, *A Son at the Front*,
is primarily a study of character and a portrayal of
the relation between a father and his son. The
father is Campton, a lame painter of some distinction living in Paris. His son, George, has just
finished his education and the father is counting
on a trip to Italy for the chance, at last, to get
acquainted with the boy. Campton's wife, Julia,
after divorcing him, married a rich American named
Brandt. The two also live in Paris and George has
for some years been supported by the Brandts,
spending part of his time with them. With this
position when the novel opens, end of July, 1914,
war intervenes, taking George from them because
of his French birth. Campton and Brandt, drawn
together by a common interest, pull what wires they
can to secure a clerical appointment for George.
The intensity of the war and initial reverses bring
Campton to regret that George should have been
willing to remain behind the lines. But word comes
that the son is lying wounded in hospital; he has
all the time been at the front but has concealed the
fact in writing home. Brought back to Paris, an
effort is made to keep him there, a shallow little

[200]

married woman of George's acquaintance lending what help she can; the huge compulsion of the war is too great, however, and on his return to the front George is again wounded, this time fatally. He lives to hear that America is at last in the conflict and to know that Campton and the rest have an undivided aim while the war lasts. When George dies, the others, feeling they have lost everything except the hope of victory, bend themselves to help toward that with such courage as they have left.

The record of wartime Paris, the shift of ideals and the gradual sacrifice of all lesser purposes, the resolution of smaller loyalties in a larger, the intimacy of personal emotions—these, of course, are the true substance of Mrs. Wharton's story.

vi

You may comprehend her, in discourse with that familiar of hers, the Time Spirit, in a dialogue running somewhat as follows:

TIME SPIRIT: So, then, you've settled it with yourself? You haven't too many regrets, I hope?

MRS. WHARTON: Oh, no, thank you. You can't know what a sense of freedom, of satisfaction both outer and inner, it gives! You see, I always had, for ever so long, a few illusions—about myself and my own work, I mean.

TIME SPIRIT (*dryly*): Most writers do. But now that you are rid of them all, you aren't finding it impossible to go on?

MRS. WHARTON: I find it far more possible to go on. I go on with ease and a lightness of heart.

AMERICAN NIGHTS ENTERTAINMENT

There isn't anything I wouldn't write now, that I
mightn't wake up and find myself to have written,
except the kind of thing I once was determined to
write. That sounds cloudy, no doubt; but what
I mean is very simple: I discovered that, contrary
to the old saying, it is life that is long and art that's
fleeting.

TIME SPIRIT: Yes?

MRS. WHARTON: Exactly. We live a long time,
and we write for a time not so long but pretty long,
too. If in those years of writing we achieve art
once or twice, we are among the rare, fortunate ones.

TIME SPIRIT: And the rest of the time?

MRS. WHARTON: The rest of the time we must
be industrious, but it is so much better if we are
clear in our own minds about it.

TIME SPIRIT: But, you know, you are really an
artist!

MRS. WHARTON: *Retro me, Sathanas!* I beg
your pardon, though; you couldn't tempt me. I
know what I know. There are things I have had,
and have, to do without; but I don't live with them;
I live with what I have. Of course, all kinds of
aims, and quite possibly some forms of achievement
will be conferred upon me by those who practise
the craft of fiction under the guise of criticism.
But I am clearly not responsible for what they say,
and it may not be used against me. I am only
responsible for what I myself say—and that is:
Nothing.

TIME SPIRIT: So you refuse to answer? On the
usual ground, of course; it might tend to incriminate
or degrade you?

[202]

EDITH WHARTON AND THE TIME SPIRIT

MRS. WHARTON: I refuse to answer on the ground that it might incriminate and degrade others who write about me like this: *"The House of Mirth, Ethan Frome*—these are orchestral in their richly subtle clashing of overtones, a sort of infra-discordance which is among the rare improbable finenesses accessible to the artist, on condition of his readiness to take infinite pains for infinitesimal effects."

TIME SPIRIT: Madame, permit me to deal lightly with you.

MRS. WHARTON: *Merci, monsieur.* But I think we have concluded our bargain, haven't we? *Au 'voir.*

Books by Edith Wharton

1899   *The Greater Inclination*
1900   *The Touchstone*
1901   *Crucial Instances*
1902   *The Valley of Decision*
1903   *Sanctuary*
1904   *The Descent of Man, and Other Stories*
1904   *Italian Villas and Their Gardens*
1905   *Italian Backgrounds*
1905   *The House of Mirth*
1907   *Madame de Treymes*
1907   *The Fruit of the Tree*
1908   *The Hermit and the Wild Woman*
1908   *A Motor-Flight Through France*
1909   *Artemis to Actæon and Other Verse*
1910   *Tales of Men and Ghosts*
1911   *Ethan Frome*

1912 *The Reef*
1913 *The Custom of the Country*
1915 *The Book of the Homeless*
1915 *Fighting France*
       The Decoration of Houses
       The Joy of Living
1917 *Xingu and Other Stories*
1917 *Summer*
1918 *The Marne*
1919 *French Ways and Their Meaning*
1919 *In Morocco*
1920 *The Age of Innocence*
1922 *The Glimpses of the Moon*
1923 *A Son at the Front*

Sources on Edith Wharton

Contemporary American Novelists, 1900–1920, by Carl Van Doren. THE MACMILLAN COMPANY, 1922.

Some Modern Novelists, by Helen Thomas Follett and Wilson Follett. HENRY HOLT & COMPANY, 1918. The chapter deals with Mrs. Wharton's work up to and including *Summer.* Her novel, *The Valley of Decision,* is singled out for especial emphasis.

Edith Wharton, A Critical Study, by Katharine Fullerton Gerould. Booklet published by D. APPLETON & COMPANY, 1922. A spirited exposition of what are conceived to be Mrs. Wharton's special qualities by a woman whose interest lies particularly in Mrs. Wharton's material.

[204]

The Unclassified Case of Christopher Morley

i

TO know Christopher Morley is to be interested, amused, enthusiastic, sceptical or even secretly puzzled; but to have him for a friend is to learn the meaning of friendliness in a degree that is very exceptional. And few escape being his friends, though this is less true than formerly. There was, indeed, once a time when the friendship of Morley was among the two or three serious responsibilities of an individual's life—like marriage, or filial duty or a conscience in regard to one's chosen craft. Practically every day, sometimes twice in a day, the evidence of Morley's friendliness would appear in a brief letter or hastily-penned note about this or that or the other thing under the sun.

An image arose of an ever-active, a sleepless mind; of an emotional nature more unresting than the Atlantic and quantitatively as great. This awful abstraction slowly faded out into a visual image of a "burly" man with a smiling face and a lighted pipe, and that, in turn, gave place to the fear lest so much confidence in the human race should prove fatally misplaced. . . . Somewhat, it has; but what we didn't foresee was that the change,

[205]

coming about gradually, would operate as a gradual salvation of (1) his friends from Morley, (2) Morley from his friends, (3) Morley's work from Friend Morley.

Yet this beneficial and important transformation has been accomplished in the most salutary manner, with a result that may accrue with permanence and advantage to American literature.

ii

As lately as 1920 one estimating American talents could observe of Morley: "His gift is purely journalistic, isn't it?" and receive the answer from Morley's friend: "Purely"—an answer conceived in entire truthfulness. Both the asker and the answerer were pretty certain to regard the assumed fact as a great pity. But as to the fact!—why, what further evidence was needed to establish it? Morley had been writing for several years, had averaged several books a year of prose and verse, and nowhere gave the least sign of doing work of a different character. What, then, was the character of his work in those years? He began at Oxford with a book of verse; from a more actual standpoint his beginnings had been made with *Parnassus on Wheels*, published in 1917. This really capital conceit had engendered a sequel, *The Haunted Bookshop*, published two years later. There were certain books of essays—*Shandygaff*, *Mince Pie*, *Pipefuls*—pleasant, partly serious, sometimes sentimental and showing a deplorable fondness for the pun. There were books of verse—*Songs for a*

CHRISTOPHER MORLEY

THE CASE OF CHRISTOPHER MORLEY

*Little House, The Rocking Horse, Hide and Seek.
Travels in Philadelphia*, the short story, *Kathleen*,
and an unfortunate collaboration called *In the
Sweet Dry and Dry* completed the roll. It is no
reflection upon these volumes to say that they gave
the impression of a talent strictly journalistic; the
best journalism is more than ephemeral and most of
the titles enumerated are still actively in demand.
The quality we call "journalism" is not an affair of
perishability but something very difficult to define,
something in the approach, something in the treatment rather than in the choice of subjects. In the
last analysis it is probable that the effort to define
it would end with hands flung out hopelessly before
the mystery of a personal temperament.

The facts were these: Morley had been educated
at Haverford College and Oxford; he had then
come to Garden City to work for the publishing
house which, principally, has published his prose,
and his first enterprises as an author were pre-
cociously instructed by an "inside" acquaintance
with what James Branch Cabell would call the
auctorial career. The influence upon his own work
of this very special knowledge is not easy to estimate. He saw, as only one in a publishing house
sees, the facts of authorship after the author's child
is born. For example: the immense effect upon the
fortunes of a writer's book, or books, of the attitude
toward them of the bookseller. And that attitude
is quite rightly fixed by what the bookseller (1)
knows he can sell, or, less frequently (2), by what
he thinks he can sell.

Morley saw that books are sold through bookstores. Looking a little further, he discerned that books which are not in bookstores are, with certain class exceptions, very rarely sold. He learned, as everyone in a publishing house learns, that three-quarters of the books that are sold to retail purchasers are bought because retail purchasers have had these books thrust directly under their noses. He suffered, no doubt, the customary amazement on discovering the vast number of people who (1) either enter the bookstore with no particular book in mind, or (2), on being unable to obtain the book in mind, readily take something else. It was brought to his keen attention that, as Frank Swinnerton reiterates in his admirable brochure on "Authors and Advertising," direct advertising, as in newspapers and magazines (the commonest mediums) does not sell books. Being a young man of alert perceptions, it cannot have been lost upon him that book reviews do not, with any reliability, sell books, either. What does sell books is talk—in some instances—but the hard rock foundation of book sales is a favourable attitude on the part of "the trade."

To know the people in the bookstore, to have and to cultivate and to deserve their good will (for, in the long run, you must deserve it), and thus to insure the sale of your book to the bookseller and to enlist his energy and enterprise in re-selling it to his customers—this is the "favourable attitude" just mentioned. Few authors succeed in establishing it; fewer succeed in maintaining it. Mr. Morley has done both, with the result that in five years from the time of his *Parnassus on Wheels* he

has been able to publish a highly imaginative, refined and polished satire and see it become, in its
field, a pronounced best seller.

iii

One would about as soon expect to see a fantasy
by Lord Dunsany a best seller as witness the sale,
in tens of thousands, of Morley's *Where the Blue
Begins*—if one were making one's estimate solely
on the work itself. *Where the Blue Begins* is the
story of the dog Gissing's search for God—a search
conducted in various places and circumstances
parallel to human life of the present day by an
animal discreetly analogued to the human animal.
Such a piece of writing has ordinarily no hope except from unusual and very favourable (or acutely
controversial) critical attention; and the hope from
that quarter is relatively small. By "hope," of
course, is meant a hope of a considerable sale.
Where the Blue Begins belongs to that class of
literature which is written because it has lain in the
author's heart to write it, regardless of its fate after
it lies on paper. In the case of Mr. Morley, the
work has received merited praise; but it would be
naïve to suppose that this notice and commendation
sold the book; and the book trade might even
justifiably be indignant at such a supposition. Did
not they, the booksellers, buy *Where the Blue
Begins* because it was Morley's new book? And
did not they and their clerks "push" the book for
the same reason? The Ayes have it, to both questions, and unanimously.

[209]

On the other hand, the sceptical soul who argues that Chris Morley wrote *Parnassus on Wheels*, in the first place, because it was a story about a bookseller calculated to "get him in right" with the trade—that man does not know Morley and shows that he does not know him. It is possible to detect in the character of Morley's work, in the circumstance of its publication and in the accessories provided for that publication evidences of a singularly intelligent literary campaign; it is possible to detect them and believe them to be such; but it is not possible to over-estimate the part played by Morley's own naïveté, affectionate nature and formerly unchecked and indiscriminate enthusiasm.

Such an attitude is always open to misconstruction. But it takes real intelligence to go beneath the surface; and among Morley's friends were many who could do that. These perceived his genuineness without being in the least able to predict the outcome of his generosity. Ours is a world thus and thus and so and so. The ultimate effect upon Morley himself of a disposition which he would unquestionably see suffer and change was the problem. It would be very easy for him to come a tremendous cropper of any one of several sorts; and then should we have a soured, an embittered young man? Prophecy was worthless.

Meanwhile, with the auspicious beginning of *Parnassus on Wheels*, the young man went gaily on. His first book of verse (barring the Oxford experiment) was published in the same year under the valuable title, *Songs for a Little House;* and at once the small beginnings of a Morley vogue were faintly perceptible. The suspicion that such a title harboured a spirit committed to the sentimental attitude toward life was confirmed within a year by the publication of a book of essays, *Shandygaff*, named after a reputed or actual beverage and got up with a deliberately quaint title page. One was left in no doubt that Morley liked Stevenson, was affectionately fond of Robert Cortes Holliday, and worshipped the genius of Don Marquis. The seeds of literary jealousy were sown, to be harvested several years later in accusations of log-rolling * that were levelled at others a-plenty besides Morley. Here, however, it should be explained that Morley had come from Oxford to go to work, at the age of twenty-three, at Garden City; that while learning the publishing business he had married Miss Helen Booth Fairchild, a New York girl whom he

---

* The term is borrowed from the Congress of the United States, where it has long been employed, quite unofficially, to describe an exchange of favors among Congressmen, some voting for another's bill in exchange for his favorable vote upon their pet measures. As here used, it refers to the alleged praise of one writer by another in tacit exchange for similar praise back; the public being expected to take both encomiums at face value and without any discounting for personal friendship, etc. Whether the public has ever quite done so is possibly to be doubted; but, at any rate, in the winter of 1921-22, New York and some other literary circles were so openly under suspicion of log-rolling that the suspects were not able to ignore the charges openly made. The boldest method of counter-attack adopted was that of Heywood Broun, who ridiculed the accusation, not quite successfully from every standpoint. There was, however, an immediate and noticeable diminution of enthusiasm among some of the younger writers for each other's work, publicly expressed. Morley himself, discussing the matter of log-rolling, explained that the accusers had the cart before the horse; that commonly one liked another man's work and praised it, and in consequence thereof came into a personal acquaintance. This is without doubt frequently the true situation.

had met in England. If, therefore, he modestly undertook to become the American poet of domesticity with his songs for households "of two or more," the guilt should by no means be made personal to him, but may justly be laid at the door of the race.

The year following *Shandygaff* witnessed the appearance of another book of verse, *The Rocking Horse;* the sequel to *Parnassus on Wheels*, entitled *The Haunted Bookshop;* and a book done in collaboration with Bart Haley. Called *In the Sweet Dry and Dry*, this is quite exceptional among Morley books, and not too common among any books, for its badness. An extravaganza on the subject of prohibition, the plot may be said to have resided mainly in incessant and outrageous puns, at that time a pronounced Morley weakness. But again it is necessary to point out a detail which, taken in one light, and, as I think, the proper light, reflects great personal credit on Mr. Morley; he has never disowned the bad book. He could not do so openly, of course—copies probably exist—but he has not done so tacitly, as he might have without question or comment. I have in mind a little booklet on Christopher Morley published in 1922 and concluding with a bibliography. There it stands: "*In the Sweet Dry and Dry*, Boni and Liveright, 1919. (In collaboration with Bart Haley, out of print.)" The book, no doubt. George Moore and Henry James, not to mention other men of literary genius, have had occasion to be ashamed of their work and to drop it quietly from the roll. I like Mr. Morley for not doing so.

THE CASE OF CHRISTOPHER MORLEY

iv

Christopher Darlington Morley was born at Haverford, Pennsylvania, 5 May, 1890, of parents both English by birth but long Americans by residence. Dr. Frank Morley, an English Quaker of Woodbridge, Suffolk—the home of Edward Fitzgerald—was graduated at Cambridge and came to Haverford in 1887 as professor of mathematics. His wife was Lilian Janet Bird, of Hayward's Heath, in Sussex, a woman of some musical and poetical gifts, the daughter of a man at one time with the London publishing house of Chapman and Hall. CDM frequently praises her cooking, which blended as an influence on his boyhood with the Haverford campus, where cricket is played. In 1900 Professor Morley went to Baltimore and Johns Hopkins. His son entered Haverford in 1906, was graduated in 1910 and, in the same year, was chosen as Rhodes Scholar representing Maryland. The three years at Oxford were spent at New College. In the title-poem of a new book of verse, *Parson's Pleasure*—the name of the old bathing pool on the Cherwell at Oxford—occur the lines:

> Two breeding-places I have known
> Where germinal my heart was sown;
> Two places from which I inherit
> The present business of my spirit:
> Haverford, Oxford, quietly
> May make a poet out of me.

The confused exigencies of his native land, however, were, more immediately, to make something else out of him. Repairing to Garden City, he interviewed Mr. F. N. Doubleday, otherwise FND ("Effendi") on the matter of a job. Mr. Doubleday has preserved the record of that interview in an amusing account which fully displays the youth, eagerness, enthusiasm and amiable audacity of the twenty-three-year-old. The noted Effendi, whose philosophy of life is not without its Oriental suggestions and whose sense of humour is at such times gently active, was feeling "a little weighted down that morning with the difficulties of the job which the President of Doubleday, Page & Company takes as a daily routine," and therefore finally told Morley "to go to work at all his manifold plans and literary philanderings, reserving the right to restrain his commitments if necessary."

It was Morley who discovered William McFee. English sheets of that long and very fine novel, *Casuals of the Sea*, had been submitted to the firm for consideration and possible purchase. Ultimately it became necessary to set up type for the novel in America. "We were accustomed," Mr. Doubleday explains, "to hold what we called a 'book-meeting,' when each member of the staff gave his suggestion about authors and books. For months when it came Christopher's turn to speak he always began, 'Now, about McFee—we don't appreciate what a comer he is' and so on for five minutes without taking a breath until finally it became the joke of the meeting that nothing could be done until Morley's McFee speech had been made. Our jibes influenced him not at all. His only reply to our efforts in humour was to bring on a look of great seriousness and the eternal phrase, 'Now, about McFee.' "

In leaving Garden City after a stay of nearly four years to become, in his own phrase, one of the "little group of wilful men who edit the Ladies' Home Journal," CDM departed from the well-established tradition under which so many men in the book publishing business have fallen. It is some kind of a tribute to Doubleday, Page & Company that the house has been the training-place of a considerable number of the heads in other publishing houses. In Philadelphia a term on the Ladies' Home Journal was followed by work as a columnist on the Evening Public Ledger, the direct preliminary to Morley's column on the editorial page of the New York Evening Post, with which he has been since 1920. The book, *Travels in Philadelphia;* the personal acquaintance of A. Edward Newton, author of *The Amenities of Book Collecting and Kindred Affections;* and a deepened interest in Walt Whitman, are some of the concomitants of the Philadelphia period. Also, I think, Morley's gradual disillusionment began then. The collection of essays called *Mince Pie* was published late in 1919 and there were still to appear, in 1920, certain overflowings of the Morley of the first period—the story of an Oxford undergraduate prank, called *Kathleen;* a book of verse, *Hide and Seek;* and more essays in *Pipefuls.* But that was to be about all. Something very definite had happened to the young man who was so friendly with everybody, who was forever talking about William McFee, who wrote forty-leven letters and notes a day, who had made a cult of quaintness and who liked to be called Kit and to have the resemblance of his name to that of Christopher Marlowe's stretched into a fanciful resemblance of personalities and writing. Some lone reviewer, speaking harshly; or some slight wound received in the house of one of his friends; or the shifts and vicissitudes of commercial enterprise—dissatisfaction with what he had already done, a thirtieth birthday, a wish to do something he had yet to do—together or singly may have been the agents of the change. Only the change itself matters. And what was that? It was not that Chris became less friendly, or autographed fewer dozens of copies of a new book of his, or loved the Elizabethans less or the work of Theodore Dreiser more. But a retractation took place, an alteration of ideas went on . . . aided, it may be, by the uniformity with which American magazine editors rejected a short story called "Referred to the Author," one of the contents of Morley's book *Tales from a Rolltop Desk*—a story which Morley himself thinks marks the definite line between his old work and new.

v

Those who care for the poet of "households of two or more" will find him most readily now in the volume called *Chimneysmoke* (1921), which is a representative selection from the earlier books of verse, *Songs for a Little House*, *The Rocking Horse*, and *Hide and Seek*. Vincent O'Sullivan has said that the Morley here represented belongs with "the

[216]

THE CASE OF CHRISTOPHER MORLEY

English intimists, Herrick, George Herbert, Cowper, Crabbe." Writing an introduction for the English edition of *Chimneysmoke*, E. V. Lucas remarked: "Domesticity has had many celebrants, but I cannot remember any one work in which such a number of the expressions of Everyman, in his capacity as householder, husband and father, have been touched upon, and touched upon so happily and with such deep and simple sincerity. The poet of 'The Angel in the House' was, I suppose, a predecessor; but Coventry Patmore was a mystic and a rhapsodist, whereas Mr. Morley keeps on a more normal plane and puts in verse, thoughts and feelings and excitements that most of us have known but have lacked the skill or will to epigrammatise. If we are to look in literature for a kindred spirit to Mr. Morley's we find it rather in the author of 'The Cotter's Saturday Night.' "

Morley's new book of essays, *The Powder of Sympathy*, shows the man changed and changing. It would be impossible to detect any loss of humour or cheerfulness in such papers as those on Sir Kenelm Digby or the Morley automobile, Dame Quickly (to be succeeded some day by the more impressive Dean Swift). But the satire in "The Story of Ginger Cubes" is not less complete or sharp for being throughout good-natured; and in his piece on "The Unknown Citizen" Morley seems to me to strike a single magnificent chord in which satire and humour are simply notes underlain by the deep bass of pathos and truth. The new book of poems, *Parson's Pleasure*, shows that where there was so much *Chimneysmoke* a fire burns also. This book

[217]

AMERICAN NIGHTS ENTERTAINMENT

has an inspiring and inspiriting essay for preface—
one far too quotable; I must resist it. Instead, let
me give the first sonnet in the "Memoranda for a
Sonnet Sequence":

> The herb Lunaria, old books aver,
> If gathered thus and so, in moony patches,
> Has property of mystic opener
> When laid upon the fastest locks and latches.
> In this respect, the moonplant duly matches
> The magic of the poets, who bestir
> Their art to loosen spirit's careful catches
> And split our secret bolts like gossamer.
>
> To sprinkle moonseed on the tight-locked soul
> Bidding it open, or stand soft ajar—
> To sprinkle moonseed, gathered thus and so,
> This is the poet's honourable rôle.
> Like some old Tudor captain bound afar
> I hear him crying *Inward! Inward Ho!*

Books by Christopher Morley

1912 *The Eighth Sin.* Oxford: B. H. BLACKWELL.
Out of print
1917 *Parnassus on Wheels*
1917 *Songs for a Little House*
1918 *Shandygaff*
1919 *The Rocking Horse*
1919 *The Haunted Bookshop*
1919 *In the Sweet Dry and Dry.* Written in
collaboration with Bart Haley. Out of
print
1919 *Mince Pie*
1920 *Travels in Philadelphia.* DAVID MCKAY
COMPANY

[218]

1920   *Kathleen*
1920   *Hide and Seek*
1920   *Pipefuls*
1921   *Tales from a Rolltop Desk*
1921   *Plum Pudding*
1921   *Chimneysmoke*
1921   *Modern Essays* (an anthology, selected and with an introduction and biographical notes by Christopher Morley).   HARCOURT, BRACE & COMPANY
1922   *Thursday Evening* (a one-act play).   STEWART & KIDD COMPANY
1922   *Translations from the Chinese*
1922   *Where the Blue Begins*
1922   *Rehearsal* (a one-act play, included in *A Treasury of Plays for Women*, edited by Frank Shay.   LITTLE, BROWN & COMPANY
1923   *The Powder of Sympathy*
1923   *Pandora Lifts the Lid* (with DON MARQUIS)
1923   *Parson's Pleasure*

Sources on Christopher Morley

Christopher Morley: A Biographical Sketch.   Booklet published by DOUBLEDAY, PAGE & CO., 1922. Private Information.

The Prophecies of
Lothrop Stoddard

i

PROPHECY is a very old business. It has become our habit to think of ourselves as a people without prophets; and yet there was never a time when mankind had more seers or more interesting ones. What is H. G. Wells but a prophesier, and from whom do we receive counsel if not from Mr. Chesterton? Mr. Shaw is our Job's comforter, and George Horace Lorimer, on the editorial page of Saturday Evening Post, calls us to repentance. A few years ago I had the adventure of reading Madison Grant's *The Passing of the Great Race*, an impassioned proclamation of the merits of the blond Nordic race, and a lamentation over its decay. At that time such a book was in the nature of a revelation whether you gave faith to its assertions and proofs or scoffed at them. The thing that struck me was the impossibility (as it seemed to me) of any reader remaining unmoved; I thought him bound to be carried to a high pitch of enthusiastic affirmation or else roused to fierce resentment and furious denial. And so, in the event, I believe it mainly turned out. At that time, although he was the author of several books, I had not heard of Lothrop Stoddard, unless as a special writer and correspondent for magazines. It was not until April, 1920, that *The Rising Tide of Color Against White World-Supremacy* was published. Even so, attention is not readily attracted to a book of this type. Many who have since read it with excitement knew nothing of the volume until, in a speech at Birmingham, Alabama, on 26 October, 1921, President Harding said: "Whoever will take the time to read and ponder Mr. Lothrop Stoddard's book on *The Rising Tide of Color* . . . must realise that our race problem here in the United States is only a phase of a race issue that the whole world confronts." The late Lord Northcliffe, returning from a trip around the world, declared: "Two far-seeing books, *The New World of Islam* and *The Rising Tide of Color*, should be in the library of every one who wants to know something about the world of 1950." Several months before he died, Northcliffe spoke again to a newspaper correspondent: "Have you read *The Rising Tide of Color*? Then I want you to read it. I want every white man to read it."

ii

The New World of Islam followed *The Rising Tide of Color* from Mr. Stoddard's pen, or more probably, as authors work nowadays, from his typewriter. It brings out with detail and vividness a situation which Hilaire Belloc made vivid also in his American lectures in the spring of 1923, when he remarked that, after all, we must remember it

[221]

was only two hundred years since the armies of Mohammed stood outside the walls of Vienna. But Mr. Belloc in a lecture had no time for details; he stressed the remarkable spiritual unity (something beyond merely religious unity) of Islam, tending to match the condition of Europe in those centuries when it was possible to lead Crusade after Crusade. Mr. Stoddard, however, is a master of detail. His book on the Mohammedan world is compact of facts and figures, and concludes with one of the most significant maps the world allows to be drawn today. For it is not a day of satisfactory map-making; too much is changing; but the great patches of green on the chart at the close of *The New World of Islam* do not change. The day is never past when some dark-skinned Mahdi, like that false one in Lytton Strachey's portrait of "Chinese" Gordon, may sit his horse "letting the scene grow under his eyes," watching the assembly of turbulent but vast and unanimous armies, looking down upon the thousands of upturned, fanatical faces, in a scene "dark and violent and beautiful" . . . and of enormous import to the peoples of the earth.

His study of the coloured races and their gradual predominance and his account of Islam seem to me to be but preparatory, however, to Mr. Stoddard's book on *The Revolt Against Civilization*. This has already passed through many editions, like the two preceding volumes. "The reason why *The Revolt Against Civilization* has attracted such an extraordinary amount of attention is not far to seek," comments the Saturday Evening Post. "It is, so far as we know, the first successful attempt to present a scientific explanation of the worldwide epidemic of unrest that broke out during the Great War and still rages in both hemispheres." The book is a considered and noteworthily documented argument against the Underman—to be conceived of as the opposite of Nietzsche's Superman. It was Macaulay who remarked that if civilization is again overthrown it will not be by the barbarian from without but by the barbarian within—and Mr. Stoddard's case is, quite simply, that we have in our civilisation an immense mass of inferior men, of Undermen, who will drag us down and whom we cannot lift up. Nor is he among those who advocate terrorism. He would grant and secure to those whom he regards as the foes of civilisation a wider freedom of thought and speech than would many who share his view of the actual situation. And as a prophet is not allowed any longer to prophesy unless he is prepared with a programme—must not cry, "Woe! Woe!" unless he does so constructively—Mr. Stoddard closes his book with two chapters in which he disregards with something like a surgeon's magnificence and coolness the rooted prejudices and inherited opinions of ordinary men and women. This, he says very clearly and with precision, is the path out; and he suggests that we go to no further compromise than may be absolutely inevitable in our mixed circumstances. Nothing is more admirable in this American prophet than his daring unless it is the level admixture of his common sense.

Who is Lothrop Stoddard? In the first place, his name is Theodore Lothrop Stoddard. He is the son of John Lawson Stoddard, and both father and son were born in Brookline, Massachusetts, where at 1768 Beacon Street, the son now has his residence. The senior Stoddard travelled widely and was known as the promoter of the Stoddard lectures in the larger American cities for over twenty years. His travel lectures fill fifteen volumes. Mr. Stoddard retired from the platform in 1897 and lives in the Italian Tyrol. The son, born in 1883, was graduated from Harvard in 1905. He is unmarried. The interests that lie back of his volumes are reflected in his membership in the American Historical Association, the American Political Science Association, the American Sociological Society, the Academy of Political Science, the National Institute of Social Sciences, the American Genetic Association and the Galton Society. But let Mr. Stoddard speak for himself:

"I have aways been interested in world affairs. I spent a good deal of my early life in Europe and as an undergraduate at Harvard most of my work was along those lines, that is, history, politics, sociology, and so forth. The four men who stimulated me most were Professors A. C. Coolidge, T. N. Carver, Toy, and R. M. Johnston. At that time, however, I was intending to make the law my profession and I took the law course and was admitted to the Massachusetts bar at the beginning of 1908. The immediate occasion for my undertaking my present profession was a trip to Europe which I took at that time. This trip was an extensive journey through western and central Europe, occupying most of the year 1908; it was in the nature of a 'grand tour' before settling down to the practice of law. But when I was in Europe during that year (the year of the second great political crisis preceding the European War) I became convinced of what I had already suspected, that a cataclysm was inevitable in Europe within a relatively short time. I further realised that in any such cataclysmic struggle the United States would either be directly involved or would at least be drawn out of its isolation into the stream of world affairs. The idea shaped itself strongly in my mind to fit myself to become an expert on world affairs. I believe that such experts were at that time very few in number in America. However, I realised that if America should be situated as I felt she would be after a European disaster, such experts would be greatly needed. To me such a career implied extensive preparation and special training. In my opinion the expert on world affairs must have a high degree of technical knowledge such as cannot result from the knowledge gained by travel, ordinary reading or experience, however accurate that knowledge may be. Especially is a thorough historical background a prime necessity.

"Accordingly I proceeded to acquire the technical knowledge and training which I judged necessary by entering the Harvard Graduate School where I spent four and a half years, from the autumn of 1909 to January, 1914, gaining incidentally my

[225]

A.M. and Ph.D. degrees. I was ready then actively to practise my new profession. Nevertheless for the first two or three years I did much more research work on contemporary world affairs and future tendencies than actual writing. I planned out a long schedule of writing; and *The Rising Tide of Color* is the first large item in that schedule."

Books by Lothrop Stoddard

1914 *The French Revolution in San Domingo*
1917 *Present-Day Europe—Its National States of Mind*
1918 *The Stakes of the War*
1919 Harper's Pictorial Library of the World War (Volume 6, *The World at War*)
1920 *The Rising Tide of Color Against White World Supremacy*
1921 *The New World of Islam*
1923 *The Revolt Against Civilization*

Sources on Lothrop Stoddard

Who's Who in America, Volume 12, 1922-23. Private Information.

THE COURAGE OF HUGH WALPOLE

i

SAYS his American contemporary, Joseph Hergesheimer, in an appreciation of Hugh Walpole: "Mr. Walpole's courage in the face of the widest scepticism is nowhere more daring than in *The Golden Scarecrow.*" Mr. Walpole's courage, I shall always hold, is nowhere more apparent than in the choice of his birthplace. He was born in the Antipodes. Yes! In that magical, unpronounceable realm one reads about and intends to look up in the dictionary. . . . The precise Antipodean spot was Auckland, New Zealand, and the year was 1884.

In this somewhat remote and unlikely spot he was to pass the unremembering years. Before he was forty he was to be one of the few novelists of distinction possessing an international reputation—as familiarly known and as widely popular in America as in Britain.

The Right Reverend George Henry Somerset Walpole, D.D., Bishop of Edinburgh since 1910, had been sent in 1882 to Auckland as Incumbent of St. Mary's Pro-Cathedral, and the same ecclesi-

[227]

astical fates which took charge of Hugh Seymour Walpole's birthplace provided that, at the age of five, the immature novelist should be transferred to New York. Dr. Walpole spent the next seven years in imparting to students of the General Theological Seminary, New York, their knowledge of Dogmatic Theology. Hugh Seymour Walpole spent the seven years in attaining the age of twelve.

Then, in 1896, the family returned to England. Perhaps a tendency to travel had by this time become implanted in Hugh, for now, in his late thirties, he is one of the most peripatetic of writers. He is here, he is there. You write to him in London and receive a reply from Cornwall or the Continent. And, regularly, he comes over to America. Of all the English novelists who have visited this country he is easily the most popular personally on this side. His visit this autumn (1922) will undoubtedly multiply earlier welcomes.

Interest in Walpole the man and Walpole the novelist shows an increasing tendency to become identical. It is all very well to say that the man is one thing, his books are quite another; but suppose the man cannot be separated from his books? The Walpole that loved Cornwall as a lad can't be dissevered from the "Hugh Seymour" of *The Golden Scarecrow;* without his Red Cross service in Russia during the Great War, Walpole could not have written *The Dark Forest;* and I

[228]

HUGH WALPOLE

think the new novel he offers us this autumn must owe a good deal to direct reminiscence of such a cathedral town as Durham, to which the family returned when Hugh was twelve.

The Cathedral, as the new book is called, rests the whole of its effect upon just such an edifice as young Hugh was familiar with. The Cathedral of the story stands in Polchester, in the west of England, in the county of Glebeshire—that mythical yet actual county of Walpole's other novels. Like such tales as *The Green Mirror* and *The Duchess of Wrexe*, the aim is threefold—to give a history of a certain group of people and, at the same time, (2) to be a comment on English life, and, beyond that, (3) to offer a philosophy of life itself.

The innermost of the three circles of interest created in this powerful novel—like concentric rings formed by dropping stones in water—concerns the life of Archdeacon Brandon. When the story opens he is ruling Polchester, all its life, religious and civic and social, with an iron rod. A good man, kindly and virtuous and simple, power has been too much for him. In the first chapter a parallel is made between Brandon and a great mediæval ecclesiastic of the Cathedral, the Black Bishop, who came to think of himself as God and who was killed by his enemies. All through the book this parallel is followed.

A certain Canon Ronder arrives to take up a post in the Cathedral. The main thread of the

[229]

novel now emerges as the history of the rivalry of these two men, one simple and elemental, the other calculating, selfish and sure. Ronder sees at once that Brandon is in his way and at once begins his work to overthrow the Archdeacon, not because he dislikes him at all (he *likes* him), but because he wants his place; too, because Brandon represents the Victorian church, while Ronder is on the side of the modernists.

Brandon is threatened through his son Stephen and through his wife. His source of strength,—a source of which he is unaware—lies in his daughter, Joan, a charming girl just growing up. The first part of the novel ends with everything that is to follow implicit in what has been told; the story centres in Brandon but more sharply in the Cathedral, which is depicted as a living organism with all its great history behind it working quickly, ceaselessly, for its own purposes. Every part of the Cathedral life is brought in to effect this, the Bishop, the Dean, the Canons—down to the Verger's smallest child. All the town life also is brought in, from the Cathedral on the hill to the mysterious little riverside inn. Behind the town is seen the Glebeshire country, behind that, England; behind England, the world, all moving toward set purposes.

The four parts of the novel markedly resemble, in structure, acts of a play; in particular, the striking third part, entirely concerned with the events of a week and full of flashing pictures, such as the scene of the Town Ball. But the culmination of this part, indeed, the climax of the whole book, comes in the scene of the Fair, with its atmosphere of carnival, its delirium of outdoor mood, and its tremendous encounter between Brandon and his wife. The novel closes upon a moment both fugitive and eternal—Brandon watching across the fields the Cathedral, lovely and powerful, in the evening distance. The Cathedral, lovely and powerful, forever victorious, served by the generations of men. . . .

ii

Courage, for Hugh, must have made its demand to be exercised early. We have the "Hugh Seymour" of *The Golden Scarecrow* who "was sent from Ceylon, where his parents lived, to be educated in England. His relations having for the most part settled in foreign countries, he spent his holidays as a minute and pale-faced 'paying guest' in various houses where other children were of more importance than he, or where children as a race were of no importance at all." It would be a mistake to confer on such a fictional passage a strict autobiographical importance; but I think it significant that the novel with which Walpole first won an American following, *Fortitude*, should derive from a theme as simple and as strong as that of a classic symphony—from those

[231]

words with which it opens: " 'T isn't life that matters! 'T is the courage you bring to it." From that moment on, the novel follows the struggle of Peter Westcott, in boyhood and young manhood, with antagonists, inner and outer. At the end we have him partly defeated, wholly triumphant, still fighting, still pledged to fight.

Not to confuse fiction with fact: Hugh Walpole was educated at Kings School, Canterbury, and at Emmanuel College, Cambridge. When he left the university he drifted into newspaper work in London. He also had a brief experience as master in a boys' school (the experiential-imaginative source of *The Gods and Mr. Perrin*, that superb novel of underpaid teachers in a secondrate boarding school). The war brought Red Cross work in Russia and also a mission to Petrograd to promote pro-Ally sentiment. For these services Walpole was decorated with the Georgian Medal.

What is Hugh Walpole like personally? Arnold Bennett, in an article which appeared in the Book News Monthly and which was reprinted in a booklet, says: "About the time of the publication of *The Gods and Mr. Perrin*, I made the acquaintance of Mr. Walpole and found a man of youthful appearance, rather dark, with a spacious forehead, a very highly sensitised nervous organisation, and that reassuring matter-of-factness of demeanour which one usually does find in an expert. He was then busy at his task of seeing life in London. He seems to give about one-third of the year to the tasting of all the heterogeneous sensations which London can provide for the connoisseur and two-thirds to the exercise of his vocation in some withdrawn spot in Cornwall that nobody save a postman or so, and Mr. Walpole, has ever beheld. During one month it is impossible to 'go out' in London without meeting Mr. Walpole—and then for a long period he is a mere legend of dinner tables. He returns to the dinner tables with a novel complete."

In the same magazine, in an article reprinted in the same booklet, Mrs. Belloc Lowndes, that excellent weaver of mystery stories and sister of Hilaire Belloc, said: "Before all things Hugh Walpole is an optimist, with a great love for and a great belief in human nature. His outlook is essentially sane, essentially normal. He has had his reverses and difficulties, living in lodgings in remote Chelsea, depending entirely upon his own efforts. Tall and strongly built, clean-shaven, with a wide, high forehead and kindly sympathetic expression, the author of *Fortitude* has a refreshing boyishness and zest for enjoyment which are pleasant to his close friends. London, the home of his adoption, Cornwall, the home of his youth, have each an equal spell for him and he divides his year roughly into two parts: the tiny fishing town of Polperro, Cornwall, and the pleasure of friendships in London. 'What a wonderful day!' he was heard to say, his voice sounding

[233]

muffled through the thickest variety of a pea-soup fog. 'It wouldn't really be London without an occasional day like this! I'm off to tramp the city.' It is one of Hugh Walpole's superstitions that he should always begin his novels on Christmas Eve. He has always done so, and he believes it brings him luck. Often it means the exercise of no small measure of self-control, for the story has matured in his mind and he is aching to commence it. But he vigorously adheres to his custom, and by the time he begins to write his book lies before him like a map. 'I could tell it you now, practically in the very words in which I shall write it,' he has said. Nevertheless, he takes infinite trouble with the work as it progresses. A great reader, Hugh Walpole reads with method. Tracts of history, periods of fiction and poetry, are studied seriously; and he has a really exhaustive heritage of modern poetry and fiction."

Perhaps since Mrs. Lowndes wrote those words, Mr. Walpole has departed from his Christmas Eve custom. At any rate, I notice on the last page in his very long novel *The Captives* (the work by which, I think, he sets most store of all his books so far published) the dates:

POLPERRO, JAN. 1916,
POLPERRO, MAY 1920.

[234]

iii

The demand for the exercise of that courage of which we have spoken can be seen from these further details, supplied by Arnold Bennett:

"At the age of twenty, as an undergraduate of Cambridge, Walpole wrote two novels. One of these, a very long book, the author had the imprudence to destroy. The other was *The Wooden Horse*, his first printed novel. It is not to be presumed that *The Wooden Horse* was published at once. For years it waited in manuscript until Walpole had become a master in a certain provincial school in England. There he showed the novel to a fellow-master, who, having kept the novel for a period, spoke thus: 'I have tried to read your novel, Walpole, but I can't. Whatever else you may be fitted for, you aren't fitted to be a novelist.' Mr. Walpole was grieved. Perhaps he was unaware, then, that a similar experience had happened to Joseph Conrad. I am unable to judge the schoolmaster's fitness to be a critic, because I have not read *The Wooden Horse*. Walpole once promised to send me a copy so that I might come to some conclusion as to the schoolmaster, but he did not send it. Soon after this deplorable incident, Walpole met Charles Marriott, a novelist of a remarkable distinction. Mr. Marriott did not agree with the schoolmaster as to *The Wooden Horse*. The result of the conflict of opinion between Mr. Mar-

[235]

riott and the schoolmaster was that Mr. Walpole left the school abruptly—perhaps without the approval of his family, but certainly with a sum of £30 which he had saved. His destination was London.

"In Chelsea he took a room at four shillings a week. He was twenty-three and (in theory) a professional author at last. Through the favouring influence of Mr. Marriott he obtained a temporary job on the London Standard as a critic of fiction. It lasted three weeks. Then he got a regular situation on the same paper, a situation which I think he kept for several years. *The Wooden Horse* was published by a historic firm. Statistics are interesting and valuable—*The Wooden Horse* sold seven hundred copies. The author's profits therefrom were less than the cost of typewriting the novel. History is constantly repeating itself.

"Mr. Walpole was quite incurable, and he kept on writing novels. *Maradick at Forty* was the next one. It sold eleven hundred copies, but with no greater net monetary profit to the author than the first one. He made, however, a more shining profit of glory. *Maradick at Forty*—as the phrase runs—'attracted attention.' I myself, though in a foreign country, heard of it, and registered the name of Hugh Walpole as one whose progress must be watched."

iv

Not so long ago there was published in England, in a series of pocket-sized books called the *Kings Treasuries of Literature* (under the general editorship of Sir A. T. Quiller-Couch), a small volume called *A Hugh Walpole Anthology*. This consisted of selections from Mr. Walpole's novels up to and including *The Captives*. The selection was made by Mr. Walpole himself.

I think that the six divisions into which the selections fell are interesting as giving, in a few words, a prospectus of Walpole's work. The titles of the sections were "Some Children," "Men and Women," "Some Incidents," "London," "Country Places," and "Russia." The excerpts under the heading "Some Children" are all from *Jeremy* and *The Golden Scarecrow*. The "Men and Women" are Mr. Perrin and Mrs. Comber, from *The Gods and Mr. Perrin;* Mr. Trenchard and Aunt Aggie, from *The Green Mirror;* and Mr. Crashaw, from *The Captives*. The "Incidents" are chosen with an equal felicity—we have the theft of an umbrella from *The Gods and Mr. Perrin* and, out of the same book, the whole passage in which Mr. Perrin sees double. There is also a scene from *Fortitude*, "After Defeat." After two episodes from *The Green Mirror*, this portion of the anthology is closed with the tragic passage from *The Captives* in which Maggie finds her uncle.

WHEN WINTER COMES TO MAIN STREET

Among the London places pictured by Mr. Walpole in his novels and in this pleasant anthology are Fleet Street, Chelsea, Portland Place, The Strand, and Marble Arch. The selections under the heading "Country Places" are bits about a cove, the sea, dusk, a fire and homecoming. The passages that relate to Russia are taken, of course, from *The Dark Forest* and *The Secret City*.

Not the least interesting thing in this small volume is a short introductory note by Joseph Conrad, who speaks of the anthology as "intelligently compiled," and as offering, within its limits, a sample of literary shade for every reader's sympathy. "Sophistication," adds Mr. Conrad, "is the only shade that does not exist in Mr. Walpole's prose." He goes on:

"Of the general soundness of Mr. Walpole's work I am perfectly convinced. Let no modern and malicious mind take this declaration for a left-handed compliment. Mr. Walpole's soundness is not of conventions but of convictions; and even as to these, let no one suppose that Mr. Walpole's convictions are old-fashioned. He is distinctly a man of his time; and it is just because of that modernity, informed by a sane judgment of urgent problems and wide and deep sympathy with all mankind, that we look forward hopefully to the growth and increased importance of his work. In his style, so level, so consistent, Mr. Hugh Walpole does not seek so much for novel as for individual expression; and this search, this

ambition so natural to an artist, is often rewarded
by success. Old and young interest him alike and
he treats both with a sure touch and in the kindest
manner. In each of these passages we see Mr.
Walpole grappling with the truth of things spiritual and material with his characteristic earnestness, and in the whole we can discern the characteristics of this acute and sympathetic explorer
of human nature: His love of adventure and the
serious audacity he brings to the task of recording
the changes of human fate and the moments of
human emotion, in the quiet backwaters or in the
tumultuous open streams of existence."

v

There is not space here to reprint all of Joseph
Hergesheimer's Appreciation of Hugh Walpole,
published in a booklet in 1919—a booklet still
obtainable—but I would like to quote a few
sentences from the close of Mr. Hergesheimer's
essay, where he says:

"As a whole, Hugh Walpole's novels maintain
an impressive unity of expression; they are the
distinguished presentation of a distinguished
mind. Singly and in a group, they hold possibilities of infinite development. This, it seems to
me, is most clearly marked in their superiority to
the cheap materialism that has been the insistent
note of the prevailing optimistic fiction. There
is a great deal of happiness in Mr. Walpole's

pages, but it is not founded on surface vulgarity of appetite. The drama of his books is not sapped by the automatic security of invulnerable heroics. Accidents happen, tragic and humorous; the life of his novels is checked in black and white, often shrouded in grey; the sun moves and stars come out; youth grows old; charm fades; girls may or may not be pretty; his old women——

"But there he is inimitable. The old gentlewomen, or caretakers, dry and twisted, brittle and sharp, repositories of emotion—vanities and malice and self-seeking—like echoes of the past, or fat and loquacious, with alcoholic sentimentality, are wonderfully ingratiating. They gather like shadows, ghosts, about the feet of the young, and provide Mr. Walpole with one of his main resources—the restless turning away of the young from the conventions, prejudices and inhibitions of yesterday. He is singularly intent upon the injustice of locking age about the wrists of youth; and, with him, youth is very apt to escape, to defy authority set in years . . . only to become, in time, age itself."

Perhaps this is an anti-climax: The University of Edinburgh has twice awarded the Tait Black Prize for the best novel of the year to Mr. Walpole—first for *The Secret City* in 1919 and then for *The Captives* in 1920.

Books
by Hugh Walpole

Novels:

THE WOODEN HORSE
THE GODS AND MR. PERRIN
(In England, MR. PERRIN AND MR. TRAILL)
THE GREEN MIRROR
THE DARK FOREST
THE SECRET CITY
THE CAPTIVES
THE CATHEDRAL

Romances:

MARADICK AT FORTY
THE PRELUDE TO ADVENTURE
FORTITUDE
THE DUCHESS OF WREXE
THE YOUNG ENCHANTED

Short Stories:

THE GOLDEN SCARECROW
JEREMY
THE THIRTEEN TRAVELLERS

Belles-Lettres:

JOSEPH CONRAD—*A Critical Study.*

Sources
on Hugh Walpole

Hugh Walpole: An Appreciation, by Joseph Hergesheimer, GEORGE H. DORAN COMPANY.

[241]

WHEN WINTER COMES TO MAIN STREET

English Literature During the Last Half Century, by J. W. Cunliffe, THE MACMILLAN COMPANY.

A Hugh Walpole Anthology, selected by the author. LONDON: J. M. DENT & SONS. NEW YORK: E. P. DUTTON & COMPANY.

Hugh Walpole, Master Novelist. Pamphlet published by GEORGE H. DORAN COMPANY. (Out of print.)

Who's Who [In England].

STEWART EDWARD WHITE AND
ADVENTURE

i

"STEWART EDWARD WHITE," says
George Gordon in his book *The Men Who Make Our Novels*, "writes out of a vast self-made experience, draws his characters from a wide acquaintance with men, recalls situations and incidents through years of forest tramping, hunting, exploring in Africa and the less visited places of our continent, for the differing occasions of his books. In his boyhood he spent a great part of each year in lumber camps and on the river. He first found print with a series of articles on birds, 'The Birds of Mackinac Island' (he was born in Grand Rapids, March 12, 1873), brought out in pamphlet form by the Ornithologists' Union and since (perforce) referred to as his 'first book.' In the height of the gold rush he set out for the Black Hills, to return East broke and to write *The Claim Jumpers* and *The Westerners*. He followed Roosevelt into Africa, *The Land of Footprints* and of *Simba*. He has, more recently, seen serv-

[243]

ice in France as a Major in the U. S. Field Artillery. Though (certainly) no Ishmael, he has for years been a wanderer upon the face of the earth, observant and curious of the arresting and strange —and his novels and short stories mark a journey such as but few have gone upon, a trailing of rainbows, a search for gold beyond the further hills and a finding of those campfires (left behind when Mr. Kipling's *Explorer* crossed the ranges beyond the edge of cultivation) round which the resolute sit to swap lies while the tenderfoot makes a fair —and forced—pretence at belief."

ii

Spring, 1922, having advanced to that stage where one could feel confidence that summer would follow—a confidence one cannot always feel in March—a short letter came from Mr. White. He enclosed two photographs. One of them showed a trim-looking man with eyeglasses and moustache, sitting shirt-sleeved in a frail-looking craft. The letter explained that this was a collapsible canvas boat. My deduction was that the picture had been taken before the boat collapsed.

There was also a picture of another and much sturdier boat. I think the name Seattle was painted on her stern. She lay on a calm surface that stretched off to a background of towering mountains—Lake Louise Inlet. The much stur-

[244]

STEWART EDWARD WHITE

dier boat, I understood, was also the property of
S. E. White.

The letter made all these things very clear.
It said: "Fifteen tons, fifty feet, sleeps five,
thirty-seven horsepower, heavy duty engine, built
sea-going, speed nine knots. No phonograph!
No wine cellar.

"We are going north, that is all the plans we
have. We two are all there are on board, though
we are thinking of getting a cat. On second
thought, here is the crew in the canvas boat we
carry to the inland lakes to fish from. Her name
is the *Wreckless;* be careful how you spell it."

As stated, the crew in the about-to-collapse
boat was Stewart Edward White. On his way
north it was his intention to revise what will be,
in his judgment, the most important novel he has
written. But I must not say anything about that
yet. Let me say something, rather, about his new
book which you who read this have a more immediate prospect of enjoying. *On Tiptoe: A Romance of the Redwoods* is Stewart Edward White
in a somewhat unusual but entirely taking rôle.
Here we have Mr. White writing what is essentially a comedy; and yet there is an element of
fantasy in the story which, in the light of a few
opening and closing paragraphs, can be taken
seriously, too.

The story sounds, in an outline, almost baldly
implausible. Here are certain people, including
a young woman, the daughter of a captain of in-

dustry, stranded in the redwoods. Here is a young man out of nowhere, who foretells the weather in a way that is uncannily verified soon afterward. Here also is the astonishing engine which the young man has brought with him out of nowhere,—an engine likely to revolutionise the affairs of the world. . . .

I suppose that the secret of such a story as *On Tiptoe* lies entirely in the telling. I know that when I heard it outlined, the thing seemed to me to be preposterous. But then, while still under the conviction of this preposterousness, the story itself came to my hand and I began to read. Its preposterousness did not worry me any longer. It had, besides a plausibility more than sufficient, a narrative charm and a whimsical humour that would have justified any tale. The thing that links *On Tiptoe* with Stewart Edward White is the perfect picture of the redwoods—the feeling of all outdoors you get while under the spell of the story. I do not think there is any doubt that all lovers of White will enjoy this venture into the field of light romance.

iii

Stewart Edward White was the son of T. Stewart White and Mary E. (Daniell) White. He received the degree of bachelor of philosophy from the University of Michigan in 1895 and the degree of master of arts from the same institution

[246]

in 1903 (*Who's Who in America: Volume 12*).
He attended Columbia Law School in 1896-97.
He married on April 28, 1904, Elizabeth Grant
of Newport, Rhode Island. He was a major with
the 144th Field Artillery in 1917-18. He lives in
California. But these skeletal details, all right
for *Who's Who in America*, serve our purpose
poorly. I am going to try to picture the man from
two accounts of him written by friends. One
appeared as an appendix to White's novel *Gold*,
published in 1913, and was written by Eugene F.
Saxton. The other is a short newspaper article
by John Palmer Gavit (long with the New York
Evening Post) printed in the Philadelphia Ledger
for May 20, 1922.

Mr. Saxton had a talk with White a few days
before White sailed from New York for his second African exploring expedition. Saxton had
asked the novelist if he did not think it possible
to lay hold of the hearts and imaginations of a
great public through a novel which had no love
interest in it; if "man pitted against nature was
not, after all, the eternal drama."

White thought for a moment and then said:

"In the main, that is correct. Only I should
say that the one great drama is that of the individual man's struggles toward perfect adjustment
with his environment. According as he comes
into correspondence and harmony with his environment, by that much does he succeed. That
is what an environment is for. It may be finan-

cial, natural, sexual, political, and so on. The sex element is important, of course,—very important. But it is not the only element by any means; nor is it necessarily an element that exercises an instant influence on the great drama. Any one who so depicts it is violating the truth. Other elements of the great drama are as important— self-preservation, for example, is a very simple and even more important instinct than that of the propagation of the race. Properly presented, these other elements, being essentially vital, are of as much interest to the great public as the relation of the sexes."

The first eight or nine years of Mr. White's life were spent in a small mill town. Michigan was at that time the greatest of lumber states. White was still a boy when the family moved to Grand Rapids, then a city of about 30,000. Stewart Edward White did not go to school until he was sixteen, but then he entered the third year high with boys of his own age and was graduated at eighteen, president of his class. He won and, I believe, still holds the five-mile running record of the school.

The explanation is that the eight or ten years which most boys spend in grammar school were spent by Stewart Edward continually in the woods and among the rivermen, in his own town and in the lumber camps to which his father took him. Then there was a stretch of four years, from about the age of twelve on, when he was in Cali-

fornia, as he says "a very new sort of a place."
These days were spent largely in the saddle and
he saw a good deal of the old California ranch
life.

"The Birds of Mackinac Island," already referred to, was only one of thirty or forty papers
on birds which White wrote in his youth for
scientific publications. Six or seven hundred
skins that he acquired are now preserved in the
Kent Scientific Museum of Grand ·Rapids.

His summer vacations while he was in college
were spent cruising the Great Lakes in a 28-foot
cutter sloop. After graduating he spent six
months in a packing-house at $6 a week. His
adventure in the Black Hills gold rush followed.

It was during his studies at Columbia that
White wrote, as part of his class work, a story
called "A Man and His Dog" which Brander
Matthews urged him to try to sell. Short Stories
brought it for $15 and subsequent stories sold also.
One brought as much as $35!

He tried working in McClurg's bookstore in
Chicago at $9 a week. Then he set out for Hud-
son Bay. *The Claim Jumpers*, finished about
this time, was brought out as a book and was well
received. The turn of tne tide did not come until
Munsey paid $500 for the serial right in *The
Westerners*. White was paid in five dollar bills
and he says that when he stuffed the money in his
pockets he left at once for fear someone would
change his mind and want all that money back.

[249]

The Blazed Trail was written in a lumber camp in the depth of a northern winter. The only hours White could spare for writing were in the early morning, so he would begin at 4 A. M., and write until 8 A. M., then put on his snow-shoes and go out for a day's lumbering. The story finished, he gave it to Jack Boyd, the foreman, to read. Boyd began it after supper one evening and when White awoke the next morning at four o'clock he found the foreman still at it. As Boyd never even read a newspaper, White regarded this as a triumph. This is the book that an English-woman, entering a book shop where White happened to be, asked for in these words: "Have you a copy of *Blasé Tales?*"

White went out hastily in order not to overhear her cries of disappointment.

iv

Mr. Saxton asked White why he went to Africa and White said:

"My answer to that is pretty general. I went because I wanted to. About once in so often the wheels get rusty and I have to get up and do something real or else blow up. Africa seemed to me a pretty real thing. Before I went I read at least twenty books about it and yet I got no mental image of what I was going to see. That fact accounts for these books of mine. I have tried to tell in plain words what an ordinary person would see there.

"Let me add," he went on, "that I did not go for material. I never go anywhere for material; if I did I should not get it. That attitude of mind would give me merely externals, which are not worth writing about. I go places merely because, for one reason or another, they attract me. Then, if it happens that I get close enough to the life, I may later find that I have something to write about. A man rarely writes anything convincing unless he has lived the life; not with his critical faculty alert; but whole-heartedly and because, for the time being, it is his life."

v

John Palmer Gavit tells how once, when hunting, White broke his leg and had to drag himself back long miles to camp alone:

"Adventure enough, you'd say. But along the way a partridge drummed and nothing would do but he must digress a hundred yards from the shorter and sufficiently painful way, brace himself for the shot and recoil, kill the bird and have his dog retrieve it, and bring his game along with him. Just to show himself that this impossible thing could be done.

"I am not imagining when I say that in this same spirit Stewart Edward White faces the deeper problems and speculations of life. He

[251]

wants to know about things here and hereafter. With the same zest and simplicity of motive he faces the secret doors of existence; not to prove or disprove, but to see and find out. And when he comes to the Last Door he will go through without fear, with eyes open to see in the next undiscovered country what there is to be seen and to show that the heart of a brave and unshrinking man, truthful and open-handed and friendly, is at home there, as he may be anywhere under God's jurisdiction."

Books
by Stewart Edward White

THE WESTERNERS

THE CLAIM JUMPERS

THE BLAZED TRAIL

CONJUROR'S HOUSE

THE FOREST

THE MAGIC FOREST

THE SILENT PLACES

THE MOUNTAIN

BLAZED TRAIL STORIES

THE PASS

THE MYSTERY (With Samuel Hopkins Adams)

ARIZONA NIGHTS

CAMP AND TRAIL

THE RIVERMAN

THE RULES OF THE GAME

THE CABIN

[252]

STEWART EDWARD WHITE

THE ADVENTURES OF BOBBY ORDE
THE LAND OF FOOTPRINTS
AFRICAN CAMP FIRES
GOLD
THE REDISCOVERED COUNTRY
THE GREY DAWN
THE LEOPARD WOMAN
SIMBA
THE FORTY-NINERS (In The Chronicles of America
    Series)
THE ROSE DAWN
THE KILLER, AND OTHER STORIES
ON TIPTOE: A ROMANCE OF THE REDWOODS

Sources
on Stewart Edward White

The Men Who Make our Novels, by George
    Gordon. MOFFAT, YARD & COMPANY.
Who's Who in America.
Stewart Edward White: Appendix to GOLD (pub-
    lished in 1913) by Eugene F. Saxton.
    DOUBLEDAY, PAGE & COMPANY.
Stewart Edward White, by John Palmer Gavit.
    PHILADELPHIA PUBLIC LEDGER, May 20,
    1922.

REBECCA WEST: AN ARTIST

i

WHETHER Rebecca West is writing reviews of books or dramatic criticism or
novels she is an artist, above everything. I have
been reading delightedly the pages of her new
novel, *The Judge*. It is Miss West's second novel.
One is somewhat prepared for it by the excellence
of her first, *The Return of the Soldier*, published
in 1918. Somewhat, but not adequately.

Perhaps I am prejudiced. You see, I have been
in Edinburgh, and though it was the worst season
of the year—the period when, as Robert Louis
Stevenson says, that Northern city has "the vilest
climate under Heaven"—nevertheless, the charm
and dignity of that old town captured me at the
very moment when a penetrating Scotch winter
rain was coming in direct contact with my bones.
I was, I might as well confess, soaked and chilled
as no New York winter snowstorm ever wetted
and chilled me. It did not matter; here was the
long sweep of Princes Street with its gay shops on
one side and its deep valley on the other; across

[254]

REBECCA WEST

the valley the tenements of the Royal Mile lifted themselves up—the Royal Mile, which runs always uphill from the Palace that is Holyrood to the height that is the Castle. Talk about gestures! The whole city of Edinburgh is a matchless gesture.

And so, when I began the first page of *The Judge*, it was a grand delight to find myself back in the city of the East Wind:

"It was not because life was not good enough that Ellen Melville was crying as she sat by the window. The world, indeed, even so much of it as could be seen from her window, was extravagantly beautiful. The office of Mr. Mactavish James, Writer to the Signet, was in one of those decent grey streets that lie high on the Northward slope of Edinburgh New Town, and Ellen was looking up the sidestreet that opened just opposite and revealed, menacing as the rattle of spears, the black rock and bastions of the Castle against the white beamless glare of the southern sky. And it was the hour of the clear Edinburgh twilight, that strange time when the world seems to have forgotten the sun though it keeps its colour; it could still be seen that the moss between the cobblestones was a wet bright green, and that a red autumn had been busy with the wind-nipped trees, yet these things were not gay, but cold and remote as brightness might be on the bed of a deep stream, fathoms beneath the visitation of the sun. At this time all the town was ghostly, and

[255]

she loved it so. She took her mind by the arm and marched it up and down among the sights of Edinburgh, telling it that to be weeping with discontent in such a place was a scandalous turning up of the nose at good mercies. Now the Castle Esplanade, that all day had proudly supported the harsh virile sounds and colours of the drilling regiments, would show to the slums its blank surface, bleached bonewhite by the winds that raced above the city smoke. Now the Cowgate and the Canongate would be given over to the drama of the disorderly night, the slumdwellers would foregather about the rotting doors of dead men's mansions and brawl among the not less brawling ghosts of a past that here never speaks of peace, but only of blood and argument. And Holyrood, under a black bank surmounted by a low bitten cliff, would lie like the camp of an invading and terrified army. . . ."

ii

The Judge is certainly autobiographical in some of the material employed. For instance, it is a fact that Miss West went to school in Edinburgh, attending an institution not unlike John Thompson's Ladies College referred to in *The Judge* (but only referred to). It is a fact, as everyone who knows anything about Miss West knows, that Miss West was an ardent suffragette in that time before suffragettes had ceased from troubling

[256]

and Prime Ministers were at rest. An amazing legend got about some time ago that Rebecca West's real name was Regina Miriam Bloch. Then on the strength of the erring "Readers' Guide to Periodical Literature" did Miss Amy Wellington write a sprightly article for the Literary Review of the New York Evening Post. Miss Wellington referred to this mysterious Regina Miriam Bloch who had stunned everybody by her early articles written under the name of one of Ibsen's most formidable heroines; but unfortunately Miss West wrote a letter in disclaimer. She cannot help Mr. Ibsen. It may be a collision in names, but it is not a collusion. The truth about Rebecca West, who has written *The Judge*, seems to be dependably derivable from the English *Who's Who*, a standard work always worth consulting. This estimable authority says that Rebecca West was born on Christmas in 1892, and is the youngest daughter of the late Charles Fairfield of County Kerry. It further says that she was educated at George Watson's Ladies' College, Edinburgh. It states that she joined the staff of The Freewoman as a reviewer in 1911. Her club is the International Women's Franchise. Her residence is 36 Queen's Gate Terrace, London S. W. 7. Her telephone is Kensington 7285.

Now is there anything mythical left? What excuse, O everybody, is there any longer for the legend of Regina Miriam Bloch?

But I do not believe Miss West objects to leg-

[257]

ends. I imagine she loves them. The legend of
a name is perhaps unimportant; the legend of a
personality is of the highest importance. That
Miss West has a personality is evident to anyone
familiar with her work. A personality, however,
is not three-dimensionally revealed except in that
form of work which comes closest to the heart and
life of the worker. To write pungent and terri-
fyingly sane criticisms is a notable thing; but to
write novels of tender insight and intimate revelation is a far more convincing thing. *The Judge* is
such a novel.

iii

There is a prefatory sentence, as follows:
"Every mother is a Judge who sentences the
children for the sins of the father."
There is a dedication. It is:

TO THE MEMORY OF MY MOTHER

The Judge is a study of the claim of a mother
upon her son. The circumstances of Mrs. Yaverland's life were such as peculiarly to strengthen
the tie between her and Richard. On the other
hand, she had always disliked and even hated
her son Roger.

The first part of the book, however, does not
bring in Richard Yaverland's mother. It is a picture of Ellen Melville, the girl in Edinburgh, the

girl whose craving for the colour of existence has gone unsatisfied until Richard Yaverland enters her life. Yaverland, with his stories of Spain, and his imaginative appeal for that young girl, is the fulcrum of Ellen Melville's destiny.

That destiny, carried by the forces of human character to its strange termination, is handled by Miss West in a long novel the chapters of which are a series of delineative emotions. I do not mean that Miss West shrinks from externalised action, as did Henry James whom she has admired and studied. She perceives the immense value of introspection, but is not lost in its quicksands. She can devote a whole chapter to a train of thought in the mind of Ellen Melville, sitting inattentively at a public meeting; and she can follow it with another long chapter giving the sequence of thoughts in the mind of Richard Yaverland; and she can bring each chapter to a period with the words: "She (he) glanced across the hall. Their eyes met." It might be thought that this constitutes a waste of narrative space; not so. As a matter of fact, without the insight accorded by these disclosures of things thought and felt, we should be unable to understand the behaviour of these two young people.

All the first half of the book is a truly marvelous story of young lovers; all the latter end of the book is a relation scarcely paralleled in fiction of the conflict between the mother's claim and the claim of the younger woman.

[259]

Of subsidiary portraits there are plenty. Ellen's mother and Mr. Mactavish James and Mr. Philip James are like full-lengths by Velasquez. In the closing chapters of the book we have the extraordinary figure of the brother and son, Roger, accompanied by the depressing girl whom he has picked up the Lord knows where.

And, after all, this is not a first novel—that promise, which so often fails of fulfilment—but a second novel; and I have in many a day not read anything that seemed to me to get deeper into the secrets of life than this study of a man who, at the last, spoke triumphantly, "as if he had found a hidden staircase out of destiny," and a woman who, at the last, "knew that though life at its beginning was lovely as a corn of wheat it was ground down to flour that must make bitter bread between two human tendencies, the insane sexual caprice of men, the not less mad excessive steadfastness of women."

Books
by Rebecca West

THE RETURN OF THE SOLDIER
THE JUDGE

REBECCA WEST: AN ARTIST

Sources
on Rebecca West

Who's Who. [In England].
Rebecca West: Article by Amy Wellington in the LITERARY REVIEW OF THE NEW YORK EVENING POST, 1921.
Articles by Rebecca West in various English publications, frequently reprinted by THE LIVING AGE. See the READERS' GUIDE TO PERIODICAL LITERATURE.

THE VITALITY OF MARY ROBERTS RINEHART

i

THE total result . . . after twelve years is that I have learned to sit down at my desk and begin work simultaneously," wrote Mrs. Rinehart in 1917. "One thing died, however, in those years of readjustment and struggle. That was my belief in what is called 'inspiration.' I think I had it now and then in those days, moments when I felt things I had hardly words for, a breath of something much bigger than I was, a little lift in the veil.

"It does not come any more.

"Other things bothered me in those first early days. I seemed to have so many things to write about and writing was so difficult. Ideas came, but no words to clothe them. Now, when writing is easy, when the technique of my work bothers me no more than the pen I write with, I have less to say.

"I have words, but fewer ideas to clothe in them. And, coming more and more often is the

[262]

MARY ROBERTS RINEHART

feeling that, before I have commenced to do my real work, I am written out; that I have for years wasted my substance in riotous writing and that now, when my chance is here, when I have lived and adventured, when, if ever, I am to record honestly my little page of these great times in which I live, now I shall fail."

These surprising words appeared in an article in the American Magazine for 1917. Not many months later *The Amazing Interlude* was published and, quoting Mrs. Rinehart soon afterward, I said: "If her readers shared this feeling they must have murmured to themselves as they turned the absorbing pages of *The Amazing Interlude:* 'How absurd!' It is doubtful if they recalled the spoken misgiving at all."

Few novels of recent years have had so captivating a quality as had this war story. But I wish to emphasise again what I felt and tried to express at that time—the sense of Mrs. Rinehart's vitality as a writer of fiction. In what seem to me to be her best books there is a freshness of feeling I find astonishing. I felt it in *K;* I found it in *The Amazing Interlude;* and I find it in her new novel just published, *The Breaking Point.*

The Breaking Point is the story of a man's past and his inability to escape from it. If that were all, it might be a very commonplace subject indeed. It is not all, nor half.

Dr. Richard Livingstone, just past thirty, is supposedly the nephew of Dr. David Livingstone,

with whom he lives and whose practice he shares
in the town of Haverly; but at the very outset of
the novel, we have the fact that—according to a
casual visitor in Haverly—Dr. Livingstone's dead
brother had no son; was unmarried, anyway.
And then it transpires that, whatever may have
been the past, Dr. Livingstone has walled it off
from the younger man's consciousness. The elder
man has built up a powerful secondary personality—secondary in the point of time only, for
Richard Livingstone is no longer aware of any
other personality, nor scarcely of any former
existence. He does, indeed, have fugitive moments in which he recalls with a painful and unsatisfactory vagueness some manner of life that
he once had a part in. But in his young manhood, in the pleasant village where there is none
who isn't his friend, deeply centred in his work,
stayed by the affection of Dr. Livingstone, these
whispers of the past are infrequent and untroub-
ling.

The casual visitor's surprise and the undercur-
rent of talk which she starts is the beginning of a
rapid series of incidents which force the problem
of the past up to the threshold of Richard Livingstone's consciousness. There would then be
two ways of facing his difficulties, and he takes
the braver. Confronted with an increasingly
difficult situation, a situation sharpened by his
love for Elizabeth Wheeler, and her love for him,
young Dr. Dick plays the man.

[264]

The title of Mrs. Rinehart's story comes from the psychological (and physical) fact that there is in every man and woman a point at which Nature steps in and says:

"See here, you can't stand this! You've got to forget it."

This is the breaking point, the moment when amnesia intervenes. But later there may come a time when the erected wall safeguarding the secondary personality gives way. The first, submerged or walled-off personality may step across the levelled barrier. That extraordinarily dramatic moment does come in the new novel and is handled by Mrs. Rinehart with triumphant skill.

It will be seen that this new novel bears some resemblances to *K*, by many of her readers considered Mrs. Rinehart's most satisfactory story. If I may venture a personal opinion, *The Breaking Point* is a much stronger novel than *K*. To me it seems to combine the excellence of character delineation noticeable in *K* with the dramatic thrill and plot effectiveness which made *The Amazing Interlude* so irresistible as you read it.

ii

To say so much is to bear the strongest testimony to that superb vitality, which, characteristic of Mrs. Rinehart as a person, is yet more charac-

[265]

teristic of her fiction. There is, I suppose, this additional interest in regard to *The Breaking Point*, that Mrs. Rinehart is the wife of a physician and was herself, before her marriage, a trained nurse. The facts of her life are interesting, though not nearly so interesting as the way in which she tells them.

She was the daughter of Thomas Beveridge Roberts and Cornelia (Gilleland) Roberts of Pittsburgh. From the city's public and high schools she went into a training school for nurses, acquiring that familiarity with hospital scenes which served her so well when she came to write *The Amazing Adventures of Letitia Carberry*, the stories collected under the title of *Tish* and the novel *K*. She became, at nineteen, the wife of Stanley Marshall Rinehart, a Pittsburgh physician.

"Life was very good to me at the beginning," said Mrs. Rinehart in the *American Magazine* article I have referred to. "It gave me a strong body and it gave me my sons before it gave me my work. I do not know what would have happened had the work come first, but I should have had the children. I know that. I had always wanted them. Even my hospital experience, which rent the veil of life for me, and showed it often terrible, could not change that fundamental thing we call the maternal instinct. . . . I would forfeit every part of success that has come to me rather than lose any part, even the smallest, of

[266]

my family life. It is on the foundation of my home that I have builded.

"Yet, for a time, it seemed that my sons were to be all I was to have out of life. From twenty to thirty I was an invalid. . . . This last summer (1917), after forty days in the saddle through unknown mountains in Montana and Washington, I was as unwearied as they were. But I paid ten years for them."

Mrs. Rinehart had always wanted to write. She began in 1905—she was twenty-nine that year—and worked at a tiny mahogany desk or upon a card table "so low and so movable. It can sit by the fire or in a sunny window." She "learned to use a typewriter with my two forefingers with a baby on my knee!" She wrote when the children were out for a walk, asleep, playing. "It was frightfully hard. . . . I found that when I wanted to write I could not and then, when leisure came and I went to my desk, I had nothing to say."

I quote from a chapter on Mrs. Rinehart in my book *The Women Who Make Our Novels:*

"Her first work was mainly short stories and poems. Her very first work was verse for children. Her first check was for $25, the reward of a short article telling how she had systematised the work of a household with two maids and a negro 'buttons.' She sold one or two of the poems for children and with a sense of guilt at the desertion of her family made a trip to New York.

[267]

She made the weary rounds in one day, 'a heart-breaking day, going from publisher to publisher.' In two places she saw responsible persons and everywhere her verses were turned down. 'But one man was very kind to me, and to that publishing house I later sent *The Circular Staircase*, my first novel. They published it and some eight other books of mine.'

"In her first year of sustained effort at writing, Mrs. Rinehart made about $1,200. She was surrounded by 'sane people who cried me down,' but who were merry without being contemptuous. Her husband has been her everlasting help. He 'has stood squarely behind me, always. His belief in me, his steadiness and his sanity and his humour have kept me going, when, as has happened now and then, my little world of letters has shaken under my feet.' To the three boys their mother's work has been a matter of course ever since they can remember. 'I did not burst on them gloriously. I am glad to say that they think I am a much better mother than I am a writer, and that the family attitude in general has been attentive but not supine. They regard it exactly as a banker's family regards his bank.'"

Most of the work of the twelve years from 1905 to 1917 was done in Mrs. Rinehart's home. But when she had a long piece of work to do she often felt "the necessity of getting away from everything for a little while." So, beginning about 1915, she rented a room in an office building in Pittsburgh once each year while she was writing a novel. It was sparsely furnished and, significantly, it contained no telephone. In 1917 she became a commuter from her home in Sewickley, a Pittsburgh suburb. Her earnings had risen to $50,000 a year and more.

"My business with its various ramifications had been growing; an enormous correspondence, involving business details, foreign rights, copyrights, moving picture rights, translation rights, second serial rights, and dramatisations, had made from the small beginning of that book of poems a large and complicated business.

"I had added political and editorial writing to my other work, and also records of travel. I was quite likely to begin the day with an article opposing capital punishment, spend the noon hours in the Rocky Mountains, and finish off with a love story!

"I developed the mental agility of a mountain goat! Filing cases entered into my life, card index systems. To glance into my study after working hours was dismaying."

More recently, Mrs. Rinehart has become a resident of Washington, D. C. Her husband is engaged in the Government health service and the family lives in the Wardman Park Hotel, having taken the apartment of the late Senator Boies Penrose of Pennsylvania.

iii

"Yet, if I were to begin again, I would go through it all, the rejections at the beginning, the hard work, the envious and malicious hands reached up to pull down anyone who has risen ever so little above his fellows. Not for the money reward, although that has been large, not for the publicity, although I am frank enough to say I would probably miss being pointed out in a crowd! But because of two things: the friends I have made all over the world, and the increased outlook and a certain breadth of perception and knowledge that must come as the result of years of such labour. I am not so intolerant as in those early days. I love my kind better. I find the world good, to work and to play in.

"I sometimes think, if I were advising a young woman as to a career, that I should say: 'First, pick your husband.'

"It is impossible to try to tell how I have attempted to reconcile my private life with my public work without mentioning my husband. Because, after all, it requires two people, a man and a woman, to organise a home, and those two people must be in accord. It has been a sort of family creed of ours that we do things together. We have tried, because of the varied outside interests that pull hard, to keep the family life even more intact than the average. Differing widely as they do, my husband's profession and my career, we have been compelled to work apart. But we have relaxed, rested and played, together.

"And this rule holds good for the family. Generally speaking, we have been a sort of closed corporation, a board of five, with each one given a vote and the right to cast it. Holidays and home matters, and picnics and dogs, and everything that is of common interest all come up for a discussion in which the best opinion wins. The small boy had a voice as well as the biggest boy. And it worked well.

"It is not because we happened to like the same things. People do not happen to like the same things. It is because we tried to, and it is because we have really all grown up together.

"Thus in the summer we would spend weeks in the saddle in the mountains of the Far West, or fishing in Canada. But let me be entirely frank here. These outdoor summers were planned at first because there were four men and one woman in our party. Now, however, I love the open as the men do."

iv

"Writing is a clean profession. The writer gets out of it exactly what he puts in, no more and no less. It is one-man work. No one can help. The writer works alone, solitary and unaided. And, contrary to the general opinion, what the writer has done in the past does not help him in the

[271]

future. He must continue to make good, day after day.

"More than that he must manufacture a new article every day, and every working hour of his day. He cannot repeat himself. Can you imagine a manufacturer turning out something different all the time? And his income stopping if he has a sick headache, or goes to a funeral?"

v

Next to the vitality, the variety of Mrs. Rinehart's work is most noticeable. Her first novel, *The Circular Staircase*, was a mystery tale, and so was her second, *The Man in Lower Ten*. She has, from time to time, continued to write excellent mystery stories. *The Breaking Point* is, from one standpoint, a first class mystery story; and then there is that enormously successful mystery play, written by Mrs. Rinehart in conjunction with Avery Hopwood, *The Bat*. Nor was this her first success as a playwright for she collaborated with Mr. Hopwood in writing the farce *Seven Days*. Shall I add that Mrs. Rinehart has lived part of her life in haunted houses? I am under the impression that more than one of her residences has been found to be suitably or unsuitably haunted. There was that house at Bellport on Long Island —but I really don't know the story. I do know that the family's experience has been such as to provide material for one or more very good mys-

[272]

tery novels. My own theory is that Mrs. Rinehart's indubitable gift for the creation of mystery
yarns has been responsible for the facts. I imagine that the haunting of the houses has been a pro-
jection into some physical plane of her busy sub-
consciousness. I mean, simply, that instead of
materialising as a story, her preoccupation induced a set of actual and surprising circumstances.
Why couldn't it? Let Sir Oliver Lodge or Sir
Arthur Conan Doyle, the Society for Psychical
Research, anybody who knows about that sort of
thing, explain!

Consider the stories about Letitia Carberry.
Tish is without a literary parallel. Well-to-do,
excitement loving, with a passion for guiding the
lives of two other elderly maidens like herself;
with a nephew who throws up hopeless hands before her unpredictable performances, Tish is
funny beyond all description.

Just as diverting, in a quite different way, is
Bab, the sub-deb and forerunner of the present-
day flapper.

Something like a historical romance is *Long
Live the King!*—a story of a small boy, Crown
Prince of a Graustark kingdom, whose scrapes
and friendships and admiration of Abraham Lincoln are strikingly contrasted with court intrigues
and uncovered treason.

The Amazing Interlude is the story of Sara Lee
Kennedy, who went from a Pennsylvania city to
the Belgian front to make soup for the soldiers

[273]

WHEN WINTER COMES TO MAIN STREET

and to fall in love with Henri. . . . But one could go on with other samples of Mrs. Rinehart's abundant variety. I think, however, that the vitality of her work, and not the variety nor the success in variety, is our point. That vitality has its roots in a sympathetic feeling and a sanative humour not exceeded in the equipment of any popular novelist writing in America today.

Books
by Mary Roberts Rinehart

THE CIRCULAR STAIRCASE
THE MAN IN LOWER TEN
WHEN A MAN MARRIES
THE WINDOW AT THE WHITE CAT
THE AMAZING ADVENTURES OF LETITIA CARBERRY
WHERE THERE'S A WILL
THE CASE OF JENNY BRICE
THE AFTER HOUSE
THE STREET OF SEVEN STARS
K
THROUGH GLACIER PARK
TISH
THE ALTAR OF FREEDOM
LONG LIVE THE KING
TENTING TO-NIGHT
BAB, A SUB-DEB
KINGS, QUEENS AND PAWNS
THE AMAZING INTERLUDE
TWENTY-THREE AND A HALF HOURS' LEAVE

DANGEROUS DAYS
MORE TISH
LOVE STORIES
AFFINITIES AND OTHER STORIES
"ISN'T THAT JUST LIKE A MAN?"
THE TRUCE OF GOD
A POOR WISE MAN
SIGHT UNSEEN AND THE CONFESSION
THE BREAKING POINT

Sources
on Mary Roberts Rinehart

"*My Creed: The Way to Happiness—As I Found It*," by Mary Roberts Rinehart. AMERICAN MAGAZINE, October, 1917.

"*Mary Roberts Rinehart as She Appears*," by Robert H. Davis, AMERICAN MAGAZINE, October, 1917.

"*My Public*," by Mary Roberts Rinehart, THE BOOKMAN, December, 1920.

The Women Who Make Our Novels, by Grant Overton, MOFFAT, YARD & COMPANY.

Who's Who in America.

NOTE: *The Out Trail*, by Mrs. Rinehart, containing her experiences as a woman camping out with men, was published in the autumn of 1923. The articles "My Creed," and "Mary Roberts Rinehart as She Appears," referred to above, are now available, together with other material about this author, in a booklet, *Mary Roberts Rinehart: A*

Sketch of the Woman and Her Work, published by George H. Doran Company. Mrs. Rinehart's family have recently begun to participate in the literary enterprise. Dr. S. M. Rinehart, her husband, has just published a collection of popularly-written papers on health, *Symptoms and Symptom Hunting*, and Alan Rinehart, the second son, has begun to write successful short stories. It is probable that by the time this book is off the press a new collection of stories by Mrs. Rinehart, *Temperamental People*, will have been published.

AUDACIOUS MR. BENNETT

i

TO try to put on paper an impression of Arnold Bennett's importance and possible significance for the reader of his books—fiction and nonfiction alike—is to aspire in audacity with Mr. Bennett himself. But the task is made more directly necessary, if no easier, by the immense success of his novel, *Riceyman Steps*. Together with his new book, *Elsie and the Child and Other Stories* (opening with a novelette which continues the fortunes of the lovable heroine of *Riceyman Steps*), this story of a few humble lives in Clerkenwell has reasonably been described in the words: "London has become Arnold Bennett's Sixth Town." The author of the Five Towns has scored his greatest conquest of the reading public since the publication of *The Old Wives' Tale*.

What is Mr. Bennett's secret, or, at least, what is his peculiarity as a writer that makes him unique among the realists, so-called? I will try to give some clue to the difficult answer.

And first let me say that his distinguishing trait as an artist and writer is the same trait that distinguishes him as a person—a wonderful curiosity

[277]

about life and living, an insatiable interest, an
ability to savor the things that in other mouths are
either tasteless or even bad-tasting. It is, for instance, wholly characteristic that Bennett should
have written a book touching on dozens of topics
and called *Things That Have Interested Me;* it is
even more characteristic that he should later have
found necessary a book with the title, *Things That
Have Interested Me; Second Series.* Those who
read so delicious a novel as *Mr. Prohack* and who
fail to perceive in it a genial self-revelation of the
author miss the final thing that the novel affords.
Who is Mr. Prohack? Who, indeed, but Arnold
Bennett, the young-old, or old-young, man from
the Five Towns, living sumptuously in London,
enjoying with an unspoiled and matchless enjoyment the delights that the metropolis has to give?
Naïve? I suppose not; for Bennett's is that perfect or completed sophistication which has recap-
tured—or never lost—the touch with fresh and
simple perceptive power. His attitude represents
—rather, it embodies—the triumph, over all
artificialities, of taste.

If such a declaration tends to arouse incredulity,
the proof seems to me to lie in such a novel as
Riceyman Steps. It had been said that Bennett,
whose honesty enabled him to refer to some of his
own books as "potboilers," would not be able
again to do anything of the quality of *The Old
Wives' Tale* and *Clayhanger.* With the appearance of *Mr. Prohack*, this criticism fell back upon

[278]

ARNOLD BENNETT

the prepared defense—prepared for it by Mr. Bennett—that, after all, *Mr. Prohack* was an extravagant story, owing to its initial assumption of the sudden and unexpected devolution of wealth on a middle-aged nobody. (Although, as Bennett would say, wealth is constantly devolving, with entire unexpectedness, upon middle-aged nobodies.) What really annoyed some of the critics in *Mr. Prohack* was something which always annoys a certain common type of critical mind—it was an inability to tell when Bennett was being serious and when he was being facetious. How can a critic give his artillery the range in such circumstances?

In the case of *Riceyman Steps*, I suppose there cannot be any such awkwardness; for *Riceyman Steps* is pretty safe to be reckoned as "serious" work. Of the many things that might be said about this story of Elsie, the lovable young "char," and her employers, Henry Earlforward, the miser, and Mrs. Arb, who becomes Mrs. Earlforward, I think the thing which will be said most often is, "This is the hand that wrote *The Old Wives' Tale*." And the real point of that comment will lie in the fact that too-knowing persons have been saying lately, "Of course Bennett will never again give us anything to compare with his early work."

Mr. Bennett's special skill, pointed out long ago by the Folletts, has always been his power to make us know people as they seem to themselves;

[279]

we find it in evidence most strongly in such books as *The Old Wives' Tale* and *Riceyman Steps*. Of the latter it is a fact that any outline of the story is totally inadequate to convey the true content of the book. If I say that Elsie works for Mr. and Mrs. Earlforward and cherishes a dream of Joe's return to her; that Henry Earlforward is a marvel, a virtuoso among misers; that Mrs. Earlforward is an adept in the practise of feminine wisdom in marriage; that an entirely natural fate befalls both Mr. and Mrs. Earlforward; and that Elsie enters into happiness after an ordeal which exposes her in a humbly heroic light—if I say so much, or if I go further and meticulously relate the incidents and episodes of the action—how much have I accomplished toward enlightening the prospective reader? Not much. In fact, as little as nothing at all. Because the magic and the distinction of *Riceyman Steps*, as of Bennett's other important fiction, is in the impassioned moment of life itself, in the seeing of their little world with these people's eyes, which to convey requires the writing of just such a book as Bennett has written.

ii

But there is another and very important aspect of Mr. Bennett's art, and one to which almost no attention has been drawn—his special knowledge of women and of the relations of men and women. That little or nothing should have been said about this is not strange, for other men would not recognize Mr. Bennett's expertizing and women would scarcely announce it. But it is true; in their more accessible moments women can be prevailed upon to confirm the suspicion, although women of one sort are likely to assert that Bennett really knows well only women of other sorts—and even this purely defensive assertion can be undermined. This knowledge Bennett has demonstrated both directly and with artistic indirectness. For a direct demonstration one could not ask a better than is afforded by the last two chapters of *Our Women*, with the parallel illustration of a masculine and a feminine view of a typical sex discordance. The artistic presentation of the same profound wisdom is everywhere in *The Old Wives' Tale* and is over 50 per cent. of *Riceyman Steps*.

Again, *How to Make the Best of Life* and *Married Life*, directly; *Mr. Prohack* artistically and indirectly, exhibit Bennett's very remarkable insight into marriage. Our author's audacity has always been evident. One might say that he began by daring to tell the truth about an author, continued by daring to tell the truth about the Five Towns, and has now reached the incredible stage where he dares to tell the truth about marriage.

That marriage is all, no one but Mr. Bennett seems to realize. No one but Mr. Bennett seems to realize that, as between husband and wife, there are no such things as moral standards, there can

[281]

be no such thing as an ethical code, there can be no interposition of lofty abstractions which men call principles and appeal to as they would appeal to a just God, Himself. No one but Mr. Bennett seems to realize that the relation between a man and his wife necessarily transcends every abstraction, brushes aside every ideal of "right" and "wrong."

It would be impossible for the hero of a Bennett novel of recent years to be a character like Mark Sabre in "If Winter Comes." Arnold Bennett's married hero would realize that the health, comfort, wishes, doubts, dissimulations; the jealousies, the happiness or the fancied happiness, and the exterior appearances of the woman who was his wife abolish, for practical purposes, everything else. It is due to Mr. Bennett more than to anyone else that we now understand that while "husband" may be a correct legal designation, "lover" is the only possible æsthetic appellation of the man who is married. If he is not a lover he is nothing.

A forerunner book, *Anna of the Five Towns*, was published in 1902, *The Old Wives' Tale* in 1908, and *Clayhanger* in 1910. What does contemporary literature—to say nothing of enduring literature, in prospect—owe to the work of Arnold Bennett? It is plain, I think, that as a writer he brought to light and perfected a new and invaluable instrumentality, the subjective method, the knack of enabling us to know people as they

[282]

seem to themselves, the triumph of discovering in the commonplace the eternally wonderful. As a person, we owe in part to his example and encouragement the best work of at least two of the foremost living novelists. As a social historian we are in his debt for many genre pictures of more than one class of society and type of character. I am not sure that mankind in general does not owe him most largely for his contribution to what I can only call economics, since it highly concerns the modes of life and the practice of living; and here, of course, I mean his effort to tell women about men and, much more importantly, to tell men about women. It is a strange thing, a marvellous thing, to consider that a provincial English town should have produced in our day a man who really comprehends woman as the great Frenchmen have comprehended her—who has the endowment in this Gallic direction of Flaubert, de Maupassant, Stendhal. It is even stranger, it is positively miraculous, that, being an Englishman, he should have been endowed with the moral courage to tell what he knew and the genius to tell it, as occasion offered, from *The Old Wives' Tale* clear through to *Riceyman Steps*, in the forms and under the strict canons of traditional art.

iii

Beside *The Old Wives' Tale* and *Riceyman Steps*, *Mr. Prohack* is slightly fantastic, a trifle frivolous, no doubt. And yet I love *Mr. Prohack*. I

[283]

think I have by heart some of the wisdom he utters; for instance—

On women: "Even the finest and most agreeable women, such as those with whom I have been careful to surround myself in my domestic existence, are monsters of cruelty."

On women's clubs: "You scarcely ever speak to a soul in your club. The food's bad in your club. They drink liqueurs before dinner at your club. I've seen 'em. Your club's full every night of the most formidable spinsters each eating at a table alone. Give up your club by all means. Set fire to it and burn it down. But don't count the act as a renunciation. You hate your club."

On his wife: "You may annoy me. You may exasperate me. You are frequently unspeakable. But you have never made me unhappy. And why? Because I am one of the few exponents of romantic passion left in this city. My passion for you transcends my reason. I am a fool, but I am a magnificent fool. And the greatest miracle of modern times is that after twenty-four years of marriage you should be able to give me pleasure by perching your stout body on the arm of my chair as you are doing."

On his daughter: "In 1917 I saw that girl in dirty overalls driving a thundering great van down Whitehall. Yesterday I met her in her foolish high heels and her shocking openwork stockings and her negligible dress and her exposed throat and her fur stole, and she was so

[284]

delicious and so absurd and so futile and so sure
of her power that—that—well . . . that chit has
the right to ruin me—not because of anything
she's done, but because she is."

On kissing: "That fellow has kissed my daughter and he has kissed her for the first time. It is
monstrous that any girl, and especially my daughter, should be kissed for the first time. . . . It
amounts to an outrage."

On parenthood: "To become a parent is to accept terrible risks. I'm Charlie's father. What
then? . . . He owes nothing whatever to me or
to you. If we were starving and he had plenty, he
would probably consider it his duty to look after
us; but that's the limit of what he owes us.
Whereas nothing can put an end to our responsibility towards him. . . . We thought it would
be nice to have children and so Charlie arrived.
He didn't choose his time and he didn't choose his
character, nor his education, nor his chance. If he
had his choice you may depend he'd have chosen
differently. Do you want me, on the top of all
that, to tell him that he must obediently accept
something else from us—our code of conduct? It
would be mere cheek, and with all my shortcom-
ings I'm incapable of impudence, especially to the
young."

On ownership: "Have you ever stood outside
a money-changer's and looked at the fine collection
of genuine banknotes in the window? Supposing
I told you that you could look at them, and enjoy

the sight of them, and nobody could do more? No, my boy, to enjoy a thing properly you've got to own it. And anybody who says the contrary is probably a member of the League of all the Arts."

On economics: "That's where the honest poor have the advantage of us. . . . We're the dishonest poor. . . . We're one vast pretence. . . . A pretence resembles a bladder. It may burst. We probably shall burst. Still, we have one great advantage over the honest poor, who sometimes have no income at all; and also over the rich, who never can tell how big their incomes are going to be. We know exactly where we are. We know to the nearest sixpence."

On history: "Never yet when empire, any empire, has been weighed in the balance against a young and attractive woman has the young woman failed to win! This is a dreadful fact, but men are thus constituted."

On bolshevism: "Abandon the word 'bolshevik.' It's a very overworked word and wants a long repose."

iv

The best brief sketch of Arnold Bennett's life that I know of is given in the chapter on Arnold Bennett in John W. Cunliffe's *English Literature During the Last Half Century.* Professor Cunliffe, with the aid, of course, of Bennett's own story, *The Truth About an Author*, writes as follows:

[286]

AUDACIOUS MR. BENNETT

"He was born near Hanley, the 'Hanbridge' of the Five Towns which his novels were to launch into literary fame, and received a somewhat limited education at the neighbouring 'Middle School' of Newcastle, his highest scholastic achievement being the passing of the London University Matriculation Examination. Some youthful adventures in journalism were perhaps significant of latent power and literary inclination, but a small provincial newspaper offers no great encouragement to youthful ambition, and Enoch Arnold Bennett (as he was then called) made his way at 21 as a solicitor's clerk to London, where he was soon earning a modest livelihood by 'a natural gift for the preparation of bills for taxation.' He had never 'wanted to write' (except for money) and had read almost nothing of Scott, Jane Austen, Dickens, Thackeray, the Brontës, and George Eliot, though he had devoured Ouida, boys' books and serials. His first real interest in a book was 'not as an instrument for obtaining information or emotion, but as a book, printed at such a place in such a year by so-and-so, bound by so-and-so, and carrying colophons, registers, water-marks, and *fautes d'impression.*' It was when he showed a rare copy of *Manon Lescaut* to an artist and the latter remarked that it was one of the ugliest books he had ever seen, that Bennett, now in his early twenties, first became aware of the appreciation of beauty. He won twenty guineas in a competition, conducted by a popular weekly, for a humorous condensation of a sensational serial, being assured that this was 'art,' and the same paper paid him a few shillings for a short article on 'How a bill of costs is drawn up.' Meanwhile he was 'gorging' on English and French literature, his chief idols being the brothers de Goncourt, de Maupassant, and Turgenev, and he got a story into the Yellow Book. He saw that he could write, and he determined to adopt the vocation of letters. After a humiliating period of free lancing in Fleet Street, he became assistant editor and later editor of Woman. When he was 31, his first novel, *A Man From the North*, was published, both in England and America, and with the excess of the profits over the cost of typewriting he bought a new hat. At the end of the following year he wrote in his diary:

" 'This year I have written 335,340 words, grand total: 224 articles and stories, and four instalments of a serial called *The Gates of Wrath* have actually been published, and also my book of plays, *Polite Farces*. My work included six or eight short stories not yet published, also the greater part of a 55,000 word serial *Love and Life* for Tillotsons, and the whole draft, 80,000 words of my Staffordshire novel *Anna Tellwright.*'

"This last was not published in book form till 1902 under the title of *Anna of the Five Towns;* but in the ten years that had elapsed since he came to London, Bennett had risen from a clerk at six dollars a week to be a successful 'editor, novelist, dramatist, critic, connoisseur of all arts' with a comfortable suburban residence. Still he was not satisfied; he was weary of journalism and the tyranny of his Board of Directors. He threw up his editorial post, with its certain income, and retired first to the country and then to a cottage at Fontainebleau to devote himself to literature.

"In the autumn of 1903, when Bennett used to dine frequently in a Paris restaurant, it happened that a fat old woman came in who aroused almost universal merriment by her eccentric behaviour. The novelist reflected: 'This woman was once young, slim, perhaps beautiful; certainly free from these ridiculous mannerisms. Very probably she is unconscious of her singularities. Her case is a tragedy. One ought to be able to make a heart-rending novel out of a woman such as she.' The idea then occurred to him of writing the book which afterwards became *The Old Wives' Tale*, and in order to go one better than Guy de Maupassant's 'Une Vie' he determined to make it the life-history of two women instead of one. Constance, the more ordinary sister, was the original heroine; Sophia, the more independent and attractive one, was created 'out of bravado.' The project occupied Bennett's mind for some years, during which he produced five or six novels of smaller scope, but in the autumn of 1907 he began to write *The Old Wives' Tale* and finished it in

[289]

July, 1908. It was published the same autumn, and though its immediate reception was not encouraging, before the winter was over it was recognised both in England and America as a work of genius. The novelist's reputation was upheld, if not increased, by the publication of *Clayhanger* in 1910, and in June, 1911, the most conservative of American critical authorities, the New York Evening Post, could pronounce judgment in these terms:

" 'Mr. Bennett's Bursley is not merely one single stupid English provincial town. His Baineses and Clayhangers are not simply average middle class provincials foredoomed to humdrum and the drab shadows of experience. His Bursley is every provincial town, his Baineses are all townspeople whatsoever under the sun. He professes nothing of the kind; but with quiet smiling patience, with a multitude of impalpable touches, clothes his scene and its humble figures in an atmosphere of pity and understanding. These little people, he seems to say, are as important to themselves as you are to yourself, or as I am to myself. Their strength and weakness are ours; their lives, like ours, are rounded with a sleep. And because they stand in their fashion for all human character and experience, there is even a sort of beauty in them if you will but look for it.' "

Books
by Arnold Bennett

Novels:
A MAN FROM THE NORTH
THE GRAND BABYLON HOTEL
THE GATES OF WRATH
ANNA OF THE FIVE TOWNS
LEONORA
HUGO
A GREAT MAN
THE BOOK OF CARLOTTA
WHOM GOD HATH JOINED
THE OLD ADAM
BURIED ALIVE
THE OLD WIVES' TALE
CLAYHANGER
DENRY THE AUDACIOUS [In England, THE
    CARD]
HILDA LESSWAYS
THE MATADOR OF THE FIVE TOWNS
HELEN WITH THE HIGH HAND
THE GLIMPSE
THE CITY OF PLEASURE
THESE TWAIN
THE LION'S SHARE
THE PRETTY LADY
THE ROLL CALL
MR. PROHACK
LILIAN

Plays:
CUPID AND COMMONSENSE
WHAT THE PUBLIC WANTS
THE HONEYMOON
MILESTONES [With Edward Knoblock]
THE GREAT ADVENTURE
THE TITLE
JUDITH
SACRED AND PROFANE LOVE
THE LOVE MATCH

Sources
on Arnold Bennett

Who's Who [In England].

English Literature During the Last Half Century, by John W. Cunliffe. THE MACMILLAN COMPANY.

Arnold Bennett. A booklet published by GEORGE H. DORAN COMPANY, 1911. (Out of print.)

The Truth About an Author, by Arnold Bennett. GEORGE H. DORAN COMPANY.

The Author's Craft, by Arnold Bennett. GEORGE H. DORAN COMPANY.

Some Modern Novelists, by Helen Thomas Follett and Wilson Follett. HENRY HOLT & COMPANY.

Arnold Bennett, by J. F. Harvey Darton, in the WRITERS OF THE DAY series.

[292]

AUDACIOUS MR. BENNETT

The critical articles on Mr. Bennett and his individual books are too numerous to mention. The reader is referred to the New York Public Library or the Library of Congress, Washington, D. C., and to the Annual Index of Periodical Publications for the last twenty years.

COBB'S FOURTH DIMENSION

i

AS a three-dimensional writer, Irvin S. Cobb has long been among the American literary heavy-weights. Now that he has acquired a fourth dimension, the time has come for a new measurement of his excellences as an author.

Among those excellences I know a man (responsible for the manufacture of Doran books) who holds that Cobb is the greatest living American author. The reason for this is severely logical, to wit: Irvin Cobb always sends in his copy in a perfect condition. His copy goes to the manufacturer of books with a correctly written title page, a correctly written copyright page, the exact wording of the dedication, an accurate table of contents, and so on, all the way through the manuscript. Moreover, when proofs are sent to Mr. Cobb, he makes very few changes. He reduces to a minimum the difficulties of a printer and his changes are always perceptibly changes for the better.

But I don't suppose that any of this would re-

IRVIN S. COBB

dound to Cobb's credit in the eyes of a literary critic.

And to return to the subject of the fourth dimension: My difficulty is to know in just what direction that fourth dimension lies. Is the fourth dimension of Cobb as a novelist or as an autobiographer? It puzzles me to tell inasmuch as I have before me the manuscripts of Mr. Cobb's first novel, *J. Poindexter, Colored*, and his very first autobiography, a volume called *Stickfuls*.

The title of *Stickfuls* will probably not be charged with meaning to people unfamiliar with newspaper work. Perhaps it is worth while to explain that in the old days, when type was set by hand, the printer had a little metal holder called a "stick." When he had set a dozen lines —more or less—he had a "stickful." Although very little type is now set by hand, the stick as a measure of space is still in good standing. The reporter presents himself at the city desk, tells what he has got, and is told by the city editor, "Write a stickful." Or, "Write two sticks." And so on.

Stickfuls is not so much the story of Cobb's life as the story of people he has met and places he has been, told in a series of extremely interesting chapters—told in a leisurely and delightful fashion of reminiscence by a natural association of one incident with another and one person with someone else. For example, Cobb as a newspaper man, covered a great many trials in court; and

[295]

one of the chapters of *Stickfuls* tells of famous trials he has attended.

ii

Now about this novel of Cobb's: Jeff Poindexter will be remembered by all the readers of Mr. Cobb's short stories as the negro body servant of old Judge Priest. In *J. Poindexter, Colored*, we have Jeff coming to New York. Of course, New York seen through the eyes of a genuine Southern darkey is a New York most of us have never seen. There's nothing like sampling, so I will let you begin the book:

"My name is J. Poindexter. But the full name is Jefferson Exodus Poindexter, Colored. But most always in general I has been known as Jeff for short. The Jefferson part is for a white family which my folks worked for them one time before I was born, and the Exodus is because my mammy craved I should be named after somebody out of the Bible. How I comes to write this is this way:

"It seems like my experiences here in New York is liable to be such that one of my white gentleman friends he says to me I should take pen in hand and write them out just the way they happen and at the time they is happening, or right soon afterwards, whilst the memory of them is clear in my brain; and then he's see if he can't get them printed somewheres, which on the top of the other things which I now is, will make me an author

[296]

with money coming in steady. He says to me he will fix up the spelling wherever needed and attend to the punctuating; but all the rest of it will be my own just like I puts it down. I reads and writes very well but someway I never learned to puncture. So the places where it is necessary to be punctual in order to make good sense and keep everything regulation and make the talk sound natural is his doings and also some of the spelling. But everything else is mine and I asks credit.

"My coming to New York, in the first place, is sort of a sudden thing which starts here about a month before the present time. I has been working for Judge Priest for going on sixteen years and is expecting to go on working for him as long as we can get along together all right, which it seems like from appearances that ought to be always. But after he gives up being circuit judge on account of him getting along so in age he gets sort of fretful by reasons of him not having much to do any more and most of his own friends having died off on him. When the State begins going Republican about once in so often, he says to me, kind of half joking, he's a great mind to pull up stakes and move off and go live somewheres else. But pretty soon after that the whole country goes dry and then he says to me there just naturally ain't no fitten place left for him to go without he leaves the United States."

It seems that Judge Priest finally succumbed to an invitation to visit Bermuda, a place where a gentleman can still raise a thirst and satisfy it. Jeff could not stand the house without the Judge in it; and when an opportunity came to go to New York, Jeff went.

iii

The biographer of Cobb is Robert H. Davis, editor of Munsey's Magazine, whose authoritative account I take pleasure in reprinting here— the more so because it appeared some time ago in a booklet which is now out of print. Mr. Davis's article was first printed in The Sun, New York:

"Let me deal with this individual in a categorical way. Most biographers prefer to mutilate their canvas with a small daub which purports to be a sketch of the most significant event in the life of the accused. Around this it is their custom to paint smaller and less impressive scenes, blending the whole by placing it in a large gilded frame, which, for obvious reasons, costs more than the picture—and it is worth more. Pardon me, therefore, if I creep upon Mr. Cobb from the lower left-hand corner of the canvas and chase him across the open space as rapidly as possible. It is not for me to indicate when the big events in his life will occur or to lay the milestones of the route along which he will travel. I know only that they are in the future, and that, regardless of any of his achievements in the past, Irvin Cobb has not yet come into his own.

[298]

COBB'S FOURTH DIMENSION

"The first glimpse I had of him was in a half-tone portrait in the New York Evening World five years ago. This picture hung pendant-like from a title which read 'Through Funny Glasses, by Irvin S. Cobb.' It was the face of a man scarred with uncertainty; an even money proposition that he had either just emerged from the Commune or was about to enter it. Grief was written on the brow; more than written, it was emblazoned. The eyes were heavy with inexpressible sadness. The corners of the mouth were drooped, heightening the whole effect of incomprehensible depression. Quickly I turned to the next page among the stock quotations, where I got my depression in a blanket form. The concentrated Cobb kind was too much for me.

"A few days later I came suddenly upon the face again. The very incongruity of its alliance with laughter overwhelmed me, and wonderingly I read what he had written, not once, but every day, always with the handicap of that half-tone. If Cobb were an older man, I would go on the witness stand and swear that the photograph was made when he was witnessing the Custer Massacre or the passing of Geronimo through the winter quarters of his enemies. Notwithstanding, he supplied my week's laughter.

"Digression this:

"After Bret Harte died, many stories were written by San Franciscans who knew him when he first put in an appearance on the Pacific Coast.

One contemporary described minutely how Bret would come silently up the stairs of the old Alta office, glide down the dingy hallway through the exchange room, and seat himself at the now historic desk. It took Bret fifteen minutes to sharpen a lead pencil, one hour for sober reflection, and three hours to write a one-stick paragraph, after which he would carefully tear it up, gaze out of the window down the Golden Gate, and go home.

"He repeated this formula the following day, and at the end of the week succeeded in turning out three or four sticks which he considered fit to print. In later years, after fame had sought him out and presented him with a fur-lined overcoat, which I am bound to say Bret knew how to wear, the files of the Alta were ransacked for the pearls he had dropped in his youth. A few gems were identified, a very few. Beside this entire printed collection the New England Primer would have looked like a set of encyclopedias. Bret worked slowly, methodically, brilliantly, and is an imperishable figure in American letters.

"Returning to Cobb: He has already written twenty times more than Bret Harte turned out during his entire career. He has made more people laugh and written better short stories. He has all of Harte's subtle and delicate feeling, and will, if he is spared, write better novels about the people of today than Bret Harte, with all his genius and imagination, wrote around the Pioneers. I know of no single instance where one

[300]

man has shown such fecundity and quality as Irvin Cobb has so far evinced, and it is my opinion that his complete works at fifty will contain more good humour, more good short stories, and at least one bigger novel than the works of any other single contemporaneous figure.

"He was born in Paducah, Kentucky, in June, '76. I have taken occasion to look into the matter and find that his existence was peculiarly varied. He belonged to one of those old Southern families —there being no new Southern families—and passed through the public schools sans incident. At the age of sixteen he went into the office of The Paducah Daily News as a reportorial cub.

"He was first drawn to daily journalism because he yearned to be an illustrator. Indeed, he went so far as to write local humorous stories, illustrating them himself. The pictures must have been pretty bad, although they served to keep people from saying that his literature was the worst thing in the paper.

"Resisting all efforts of the editor, the stockholders and the subscribers of The Paducah Daily News, he remained barricaded behind his desk until his nineteenth year, when he was crowned with a two-dollar raise and a secondary caption under his picture which read 'The Youngest Managing Editor of a Daily Paper in the United States.'

"If Cobb was consulted in the matter of this

[301]

review, he would like to have these preliminaries
expunged from his biography. But the public is
entitled to the details.

"It is also true that he stacked up more libel
suits than a newspaper of limited capital with a
staff of local attorneys could handle before he
moved to Louisville, where, for three years, he
was staff correspondent of The Evening Post. It
was here that Cobb discovered how far a humorist
could go without being invited to step out at 6
a.m. and rehearse 'The Rivals' with real horse-
pistols.

"The first sobering episode in his life occurred
when the Goebel murder echoed out of Louisville.
He reported this historic assassination and covered the subsequent trials in the Georgetown court
house.   Doubtless the seeds of tragedy, which
mark some of his present work, were sown here.
Those who are familiar with his writings know
that occasionally he sets his cap and bells aside
and dips his pen into the very darkness of life.
We find it particularly in three of his short stories entitled 'An Occurrence Up a Side Street,'
'The Belled Buzzard,' and 'Fishhead.'   Nothing
better can be found in Edgar Allan Poe's collected
works. One is impressed not only with the beauty
and simplicity of his prose, but with the tremendous power of his tragic conceptions and his art
in dealing with terror.   There appears to be no
phase of human emotion beyond his pen.   Without an effort he rises from the level of actualities

to the high plane of boundless imagination, invoking laughter or tears at will.

"After his Louisville experience Cobb married and returned to Paducah to be managing editor of The Democrat. Either Paducah or The Democrat got on his nerves and, after a comparison of the Paducah school of journalism with the metropolitan brand, he turned his face (see Evening World half-tone) in the direction of New York, buoyed up by the illusion that he was needed there along with other reforms.

"He arrived at the gates of Manhattan full of hope, and visited every newspaper office in New York without receiving encouragement to call again. Being resourceful he retired to his suite of hall bedrooms on 57th Street West and wrote a personal note to every city editor in New York, setting forth in each instance the magnificent intellectual proportions of the epistolographer. The next morning, by mail, Cobb had offers for a job from five of them. He selected The Evening Sun.

"At about that time the Portsmouth Peace Conference convened, and The Sun sent the Paducah party to help cover the proceedings. Upon arriving at Portsmouth, Cobb cast his experienced eye over the situation, discovered that the story was already well covered by a large coterie of competent, serious-minded young men, and went into action to write a few columns daily on subjects having no bearing whatsoever on the conference. These stories were written in the ebullition of

[303]

youth, inspired by the ecstasy which rises from the possession of a steady job; a perfect deluge from the well springs of spontaneity. There wasn't a single fact in the entire series, and yet The Sun syndicated these stories throughout the United States. All they possessed was I-N-D-I-V-I-D-U-A-L-I-T-Y.

"At the end of three weeks, Cobb returned to New York, to find that he could have a job on any newspaper in it. This brings him to The Evening World, the half-tone engraving, which was the first glimpse I had of him, and the dawn of his subsequent triumphs. For four years he supplied the evening edition and The Sunday World with a comic feature, to say nothing of a comic opera, written to order in five days. The absence of a guillotine in New York State accounts for his escape for this latter offence. Nevertheless, in all else his standard of excellence ascended. He reported the Thaw trial in long-hand, writing nearly 600,000 words of testimony and observation, establishing a new style for reporting trials, and gave further evidence of his power. That performance will stand out in the annals of American journalism as one of the really big reportorial achievements.

"At about this juncture in his career Cobb opened a door to the past, reached in and took out some of the recollections of his youth. These he converted into 'The Escape of Mr. Trimm,' his first short fiction story. It appeared in The

Saturday Evening Post. The court scene was so absolutely true to life, so minutely perfect in its atmosphere, that a Supreme Court judge signed an unsolicited and voluntary note for publication, in which he said that Mr. Cobb had reported with marvelous accuracy and fulness a murder trial at which His Honour had presided.

"Gelett Burgess, in a lecture at Columbia College, said that Cobb was one of the ten great American humourists. Cobb ought to demand a recount. There are not ten humourists in the world, although Cobb is one of them. The extraordinary thing about Cobb is that he can turn a burst of laughter into a funeral oration, a snicker into a shudder and a smile into a crime. He writes in octaves, striking instinctively all the chords of humour, tragedy, pathos and romance with either hand. Observe this man in his thirty-ninth year, possessing gifts the limitations of which even he himself has not yet recognised.

"In appraising a genius, we must consider the man's highest achievement, and in comparing him with others the verdict must be reached only upon consideration of his best work. For scintillant wit and unflagging good humour, read his essays on the Teeth, the Hair and the Stomach. If you desire a perfect blending of all that is essential to a short story, read 'The Escape of Mr. Trimm' or 'Words and Music.' If you are in search of pure, unadulterated, boundless terror, the gruesome quality, the blackness of despair and the fear

[305]

of death in the human conscience, 'Fishhead,'
'The Belled Buzzard' or 'An Occurrence Up a
Side Street' will enthrall you.

"Thus in Irvin Cobb we find Mark Twain, Bret
Harte and Edgar Allan Poe at their best. Reckon
with these potentialities in the future. Speculate,
if you will, upon the sort of a novel that is bound,
some day, to come from his pen. There seem to
be no pinnacles along the horizon of the literary
future that are beyond him. If he uses his pen
for an Alpine stock, the Matterhorn is his.

"There are critics and reviewers who do not
entirely agree with me concerning Cobb. But
they will.

"As I write these lines I recall a conversation I
had with Irvin Cobb on the hurricane deck of a
Fifth Avenue 'bus one bleak November afternoon,
1911. We had met at the funeral of Joseph Pulitzer, in whose employ we had served in the past.

"Cobb was in a reflective mood, chilled to the
marrow, and not particularly communicative.

"At the junction of Fifth Avenue and Forty-
second Street we were held up by congested traffic.
After a little manœuvring on the part of a
mounted policeman, the Fifth Avenue tide flowed
through and onward again.

" 'It reminds me of a river,' said Cobb, 'into
which all humanity is drawn. Some of these people think because they are walking up-stream they
are getting out of it. But they never escape. The
current is at work on them. Some day they will

get tired and go down again, and finally pass out to sea. It is the same with real rivers. They do not flow up-hill.'

"He lapsed into silence.

" 'What's on your mind?' I inquired.

" 'Nothing in particular,' he said, scanning the banks of the great municipal stream, 'except that I intend to write a novel some day about a boy born at the headwaters. Gradually he floats down through the tributaries, across the valleys, swings into the main stream, and docks finally at one of the cities on its banks. This particular youth was a great success—in the beginning. Every door was open to him. He had position, brains, and popularity to boot. He married brilliantly. And then The Past, a trivial, unimportant Detail, lifted its head and barked at him. He was too sensitive to bark back. Thereupon it bit him and he collapsed.'

"Again Cobb ceased talking. For some reason —indefinable—I respected his silence. Two blocks further down he took up the thread of his story again:

" '—and one evening, just about sundown, a river hand, sitting on a stringpiece of a dock, saw a derby hat bobbing in the muddy Mississippi, floating unsteadily but surely into the Gulf of Mexico.'

"As is his habit, Cobb tugged at his lower lip.

" 'What are you going to call this novel?'

" 'I don't know. What do you think?'

[307]

" 'Why not "The River"?'

" 'Very well, I'll call it "The River." '

"He scrambled from his seat. 'I'm docking at Twenty-seventh Street. Good-bye. Keep your hat out of the water.'

"Laboriously he made his way down the winding staircase from the upper deck, dropped flat-footed on the asphalt pavement, turned his collar up, leaned into the gust of wind from the South, and swung into the cross-current of another stream.

"I doubt if he has any intention of calling his story 'The River.' But I am sure the last chapter will contain something about an unhappy wretch who wore a derby hat at the moment he walked hand in hand with his miserable Past into the Father of Waters.

"For those who wish to know something of his personal side, I can do no better than to record his remarks to a stranger, who, in my presence, asked Irvin Cobb, without knowing to whom he was speaking, what kind of a person Cobb was.

" 'Well, to be perfectly frank with you,' replied the Paducah prodigy, 'Cobb is related to my wife by marriage, and if you don't object to a brief sketch, with all the technicalities eliminated, I should say in appearance he is rather bulky, standing six feet high, not especially beautiful, a light roan in colour, with a black mane. His figure is undecided, but might be called bunchy in places. He belongs to several clubs, including

The Yonkers Pressing Club and The Park Hill Democratic Marching Club, and has always, like his father, who was a Confederate soldier, voted the Democratic ticket. He has had one wife and one child and still has them. In religion he is an Innocent Bystander.'

"Could anything be fuller than this?"

iv

It was Mr. Davis, also, who in the New York Herald of April 23, 1922, made public the evidence for the following box score:

	1st	2nd
Best Writer of Humour.....	Cobb	......
Best All-Round Reporter....	Cobb	......
Best Local Colourist........	Cobb	......
Best in Tales of Horror.....	Cobb	......
Best Writer of Negro Stories.	......	Cobb
Best Writer of Light Humorous Fiction	Tarkington	Cobb and Harry Leon Wilson
Best Teller of Anecdotes.....	Cobb	Cobb

"Not long ago a group of ten literary men—editors, critics, readers and writers—were dining together. Discussion arose as to the respective and comparative merits of contemporaneous popular writers. It was decided that each man present should set down upon a slip of paper his first, second and third choices in various specified but widely diversified fields of literary endeavour, and that then the results should be compared. Admirers of Cobb's work will derive a peculiar satisfaction from the outcome. It was found that as a writer of humour he had won first place; that as an all round reporter he had first place; that as a handler of local colour in the qualified sense of a power of apt, swiftly-done, journalistic description, he had first place. He also had first place as a writer of horror yarns. He won second place as a writer of darkey stories. He tied with Harry Leon Wilson for second place as a writer of light humorous fiction, Tarkington being given first place in this category. As a teller of anecdotes he won by acclamation over all contenders. Altogether his name appeared on eight of the ten lists."

Cobb lives at Ossining, New York. He describes himself as lazy, but convinces no one. He likes to go fishing. But he has never written any fish stories.

Books
by Irvin S. Cobb

BACK HOME
COBB'S ANATOMY
THE ESCAPE OF MR. TRIMM
COBB'S BILL OF FARE
ROUGHING IT DE LUXE
EUROPE REVISED

[310]

COBB'S FOURTH DIMENSION

PATHS OF GLORY
OLD JUDGE PRIEST
FIBBLE, D.D.
SPEAKING OF OPERATIONS
LOCAL COLOR
SPEAKING OF PRUSSIANS
THOSE TIMES AND THESE
THE GLORY OF THE COMING
THE THUNDERS OF SILENCE
THE LIFE OF THE PARTY
FROM PLACE TO PLACE
"OH, WELL, YOU KNOW HOW WOMEN ARE!"
THE ABANDONED FARMERS
SUNDRY ACCOUNTS
A PLEA FOR OLD CAP COLLIER
ONE THIRD OFF
EATING IN TWO OR THREE LANGUAGES
J. POINDEXTER, COLORED
STICKFULS

Sources
on Irvin S. Cobb

Irvin S. Cobb: Storyteller. Booklet published by
GEORGE H. DORAN COMPANY.

ALIAS RICHARD DEHAN

i

A T that, I think I am wrong. I think the title of this chapter ought to be "Alias Clotilde Graves."

The problems of literary personality are strange. Some time after the Boer War a woman who had been in newspaper work in London and who had even, at one time, been on the stage under the necessity of earning her living, wrote a novel. The novel happened to be an intensive study of the Boer War, made possible by the fact that the writer was the daughter of a soldier and had spent her early years in barracks. England at that time was interested by the subject of this novel. It sold largely and its author was established by the book.

She was forty-six years old in the year when the book was published. But this was not the striking thing. William De Morgan produced the first of his impressive novels at a much more advanced age. The significant thing was that in publishing her novel, *The Dop Doctor* (American title: *One*

Braver Thing), Clotilde Graves chose the pen
name of Richard Dehan, although she was already
known as a writer (chiefly for the theatre) under
her own name.

I do not know that Miss Graves has ever said
anything publicly about her motive in electing the
name of Richard Dehan. But I feel that whatever the cause the result was the distinct emerg-
ence of a totally different personality. There is
no final disassociation between Clotilde Graves
and Richard Dehan. Richard Dehan, novelist,
steadily employs the material furnished in valuable abundance by Clotilde Graves's life. At the
same time the personality of Richard Dehan is so
unusual, so gifted, so lavish in its invention and
so much at home in surprising backgrounds, that
something approaching a psychic explanation of
authorship seems called for.

ii

Clotilde Inez Mary Graves was born at Barracks, Buttevant, County Cork, Ireland, on June
3, 1864, third daughter of the late Major W. H.
Graves of the Eighteenth Royal Irish Regiment
and Antoinette, daughter of Captain George Anthony Deane of Harwich. Thus, the English
Who's Who.

"She numbers among her ancestors admirals
and deans," said The Bookman in 1912.

As the same magazine at about the same time
spoke of her as descended from Charles II.'s naval

[313]

architect, Admiral Sir Anthony Deane, one wonders if Sir Anthony were not the sum of the admirals and the total of the deans. But no; at any rate in so far as the admirals are concerned, for Miss Graves is also said to be distantly related to Admiral Nelson.

I will give you what The Bookman said in the "Chronicle and Comment" columns of its number for February, 1913:

"Richard Dehan was nine years old when her family emigrated to England from their Irish home. She had seen a good deal of barrack life, and at Southsea, where they went to live, she acquired a large knowledge of both services in the circle of naval and military friends they made there, and this knowledge years afterward she turned to account in *Between Two Thieves*. In 1884, Miss Graves became an art student and worked at the British Museum galleries and the Royal Female School of Art, helping to support herself by journalism of a lesser kind, among other things drawing little pen-and-ink grotesques for the comic papers. By and by she resolved to take to dramatic writing and being too poor, she says, to manage in any other way, she abandoned art and took an engagement in a travelling theatrical company. In 1888 her first chance as a dramatist came. She was again in London, working vigorously at journalism, when some one was needed to write extra lyrics for a pantomime then in preparation. A letter of recommendation from an editor to the manager ended in Miss Clo Graves writing the pantomime of *Puss in Boots*. Later a tragedy by her, *Nitocris*, was produced for an afternoon at Drury Lane, and another of her plays, *The Mother of Three*, proved not only a literary, but also a material, success."

Her first novel to be signed Richard Dehan being so successful, an English publisher planned to bring out an earlier, minor work, already published as by Clotilde Graves, with "Richard Dehan" on the title-page. The author was stirred to a vigorous and public protest. In the ensuing controversy someone made the point that the proposed reissue would not be more indefensible than the act of a publishing house in bringing out posthumous "books" by O. Henry and dragging from its deserved oblivion Rudyard Kipling's *Abaft the Funnel*.

I do not know whether the publishing of books is a business or a profession. I should say that it has, at one time or another and by one or another individual or concern, been pursued as either or both.

There have certainly been, and probably are, book publishers who not only conduct their business as a business but as a business of a low order. There have been and are book publishers who, though quite necessarily business men, observe an ethical code as nice as that of any of the recognised professions. Perhaps publishing books should qualify as an art, since it has the characteristics of bringing out what is best or worst in a publisher; and, indeed, if we are to hold that any successful means of self-expression is art, then publishing books has been an art more than once; for unquestionably there are publishers who find self-expression in their work.

This is an interesting subject, but I must not pursue it in this place. Certainly Miss Graves was justified in objecting to the use of her new pen name on work already published under her own name. In her case; as I think, the objection was peculiarly well-founded, because it seems to me that Richard Dehan was a new person. Since Richard Dehan appeared on the title-page of *The Dop Doctor*, there has never been a Clotilde Graves in books. You have only to study the books. *The Dop Doctor* was followed, two years later, by *Between Two Thieves*. This novel has as a leading character Florence Nightingale under the name of Ada Merling. The story was at first to have been called "The Lady With The Lamp"; but the author delayed it for a year and subjected it to a complete rewriting, the result of a new and enlarged conception of the story.

Then came a steady succession of novels by Richard Dehan. I remember with what surprise I read, in 1918, *That Which Hath Wings*, a war story of large dimensions and an incredible amount of exact and easy detail. I remember, too, noting that there was embedded in it a marvellous story for children—an airplane flight in which a youngster figured—if the publisher chose, with the author's consent, to lift this out of its larger, adult setting. I remember very vividly reading in 1920 a collection of short stories by Richard Dehan, published under the title *The Eve of Pascua*. Pascua is the Spanish word for Easter. I wondered where on earth, unless in Spain itself, the author got the bright colouring for his story.

What I did not realise at the time was that Richard Dehan is like that. Now, smitten to earth by the 500-page novel which he has just completed, I think I understand better. *The Just Steward*, from one standpoint, makes the labours of Gustave Flaubert in *Salaambo* seem trivial. It is known with what passionate tenacity and surprising ardour the French master studied the subject of ancient Carthage, grubbing like the lowliest archæologist to get at his finger-tips all those recondite allusions so necessary if he were to move with lightness, assurance and consummate art through the scenes of his novel. But, frankly, one does not expect this of the third daughter of an Irish soldier, an ex-journalist and the author of a Drury Lane pantomime. Nevertheless the erudition is all here. From this standpoint, *The Just Steward* is truly monumental. I will show you a sample or two:

"Beautiful, even with the trench and wall of Diocletian's comparatively recent siege scarring the orchards and vineyards of Lake Mareotis,

[317]

splendid even though her broken canals and aqueducts had never been repaired, and part of her western quarter still displayed heaps of calcined ruins where had been temples, palaces and academies, Alexandria lay shimmering under the African sun. . . .

"The vintage of Egypt was in full swing, the figs and dates were being harvested. Swarms of wasps and hornets, armed with formidable stings, yellow-striped like the dreaded nomads of the south and eastern frontiers, greedily sucked the sugary juices of the ripe fruit. Flocks of fig-birds twittered amongst the branches, being like the date-pigeons, almost too gorged to fly. Half naked, dark or tawny skinned, tattooed native labourers, hybrids of mingled races, with heads close-shaven save for a topknot, dwellers in mud-hovels, drudges of the water-wheel, cut down the heavy grape-clusters with sickle-shaped cooper knives.

"Ebony, woolly-haired negroes in clean white breech-cloths, piled up the gathered fruit in tall baskets woven of reeds and lined with leaves. Copts with the rich reddish skins, the long eyes and boldly curving profiles of Egyptian warriors and monarchs as presented on the walls of ancient temples of Libya and the Thebaïd, moved about in leather-girdled blue linen tunics and hide sandals, keeping account of the laden panniers, roped upon the backs of diminutive asses and carried to the winepresses as fast as they were filled.

[318]

ALIAS RICHARD DEHAN

"The negroes sang as they set snares for fig-birds, and stuffed themselves to the throat with grapes and custard-apples. The fat beccaficoes beloved of the epicurean fell by hundreds into the limed horsehair traps. Greek, Egyptian and negro girls, laughing under garlands of hibiscus, periwinkle and tuberoses, coaxed the fat morsels out of the black men to carry home for a supper treat, while acrobats, comic singers, sellers of cakes, drinks and sweetmeats, with strolling jugglers and jesters and Jewish fortune-tellers of both sexes, assailed the workers and the merrymakers with importunities and made harvest in their own way."

The story is extraordinary. Opening in the Alexandria of the fourth century, it pictures two men, a Roman official and a Jewish steward, who are friends unto death. The second of the four parts or books into which the novel is divided opens in England in 1914. We have to do with John Hazel, the descendant of Hazaël Aben Hazaël, and with the lovely Katharine Forbis, whose ancestor was a Roman, Hazaël Aben Hazaël's sworn friend.

A story of exciting action certainly; it has elements that would ordinarily be called melodramatic—events which are focussed down into realities against the tremendous background of an incredible war. The exotic settings are Egypt and Palestine. It must not be thought that the story is bizarre; the scenes in England, the Eng-

lish slang of John Hazel, as well as the typical
figure of Trixie, Lady Wastwood, are utterly
modern. I do not find anything to explain how
Miss Graves could write such a book; the answer
is that Richard Dehan wrote it.

iii

Miss Graves, of whose antecedents and education we already know something, is a Roman
Catholic in faith and a Liberal Unionist in politics. She lives at The Towers, Beeding, near
Bramber, Sussex. Her recreations are gardening
and driving.

But Richard Dehan knows the early history of
the Christian Church; he knows military life,
strategy, tactics, types; he knows in a most extraordinary way the details of Jewish history and
religious observances; he knows perfectly and as
a matter of course all about English middle class
life; he knows all sorts of things about the East—
Turkey and Arabia and those countries.

This is a discrepancy which will bear a good
deal of accounting for.

Before I try to account for it I will give you a
long passage from *The Just Steward*, describing
the visit of Katharine Forbis and her friend to the
house of John Hazel, lately of London and now
of Alexandria:

"The negro porter who had opened the door, a

huge Ethiopian of ebony blackness, dressed and turbaned in snow-white linen, salaamed deeply to the ladies, displaying as he did so a mouthful of teeth as dazzling in whiteness and sharply-pointed as those of the mosaic dog.

"Then the negro shut the heavy door and locked and bolted it. They heard the car snort and move away as the heavy bolts scrooped in their ancient grooves of stone. But, as they glanced back, towards the entrance, the imperturbable attendant in the black kaftan waved them forward to where another man, exactly like himself in feature, colouring and costume, waited as imperturbably on the threshold of a larger hall beyond. On its right-hand doorpost was affixed a cylinder of metal *repoussée* with an oval piece of glass on that something like a human eye. And the big invisible bees went on humming as industriously and as sleepily as ever:

" 'Bz'zz'z!...Bzz'z!...Bzz m'm'm! . . .'

"Perhaps it was the bees' thick, sleepy droning that made Miss Forbis feel as though she had previously visited this house in a dream, in which, though the mosaic dog had certainly figured, together with a negro who had opened doors, the rows of shoes along the wall, the little creature tripping at her side, the two dark, ultra-respectable men in black tarbushes and kaftans had had no place or part. Only John Hazel had bulked big. He was there, beyond the grave Semitic face of the second Jewish secretary, on the farther side of the torrent of boiling amber sunshine pouring through a central opening in the roof of the inner hall that succeeded the vestibule of the mosaic Cerberus. An atrium some forty feet in length, paved with squares of black and yellow marble with an oblong pool in the midst of it, upon whose still crystal surface pink and crimson petals of roses had been strewn in patterns, and in the centre of which a triple-jetted fountain played.

"The humming of the unseen bees came louder than ever, from a doorway in the wall upon Katharine's right hand, a wall of black polished marble, decorated with an inlaid ornament in porphyry of yellow and red and pale green. The curtain of dyed and threaded reeds did not hide what lay beyond the doorway. You saw a long, high-pitched whitewashed room, cooled by big wooden electric fans working under the ceiling, and traversed by avenues of creamy-white Chinese matting, running between rows of low native desks, before each of which squatted, on naked or cotton-sock-covered heels, or sat cross-legged upon a square native chintz cushion, a coffee-coloured, almond-eyed young Copt, in a black or blue cotton nightgown, topped with the tarbush of black felt or a dingy-white or olive-brown muslin turban, murmuring softly to himself as he made entries, from right to left, in a huge limp-covered ledger, or deftly fingered the balls of coloured clay strung on the wires of the abacus at his side.

[322]

" 'Oh! . . . Wonderful! I'm so Glad you Brought me!'

"Lady Wastwood's emphatic exclamation of pleasure in her surroundings brought cessation in the humming—caused a swivelling of capped or turbanned heads all down the length of three avenues—evoked a simultaneous flash of black Oriental eyes, and white teeth in dusky faces lifted or turned. Then at the upper end of the long counting-house, where three wide glassless windows looked on a sanded palm-garden, and the leather-topped knee-hole tables, roll-top desks, copying ink presses, mahogany revolving-chairs, telephone installations, willow-paper baskets, pewter inkstands and Post Office Directories suggested Cornhill and Cheapside rather than the Orient—one of the olive-faced Jewish head-clerks in kaftans and side-curls coughed—and as though he had pulled a string controlling all the observant faces, every tooth was hidden and every eye discreetly bent on the big limp ledgers again.

"All the Coptic bees were humming sonorously in unison as Katharine went forward to a lofty doorway, framing brightness, where waited to receive her the master of the hive. . . .

"The light beings behind him may have exaggerated his proportions, but he seemed to Trixie the biggest man she had ever seen, and nearly the ugliest. Close-curling coarse black hair capped his high-domed skull, and his stern, powerful, swarthy face, big-nosed and long-chinned, with a

[323]

humorous quirk at the corners of the heavy-lipped mouth, that redeemed its sensuousness, was lighted by eyes of the intensest black, burning under heavy beetle-brows. His khaki uniform, though of fine material and admirable cut, was that of a common ranker, and a narrow strip of colours over the heart, and the fact of his left arm being bandaged and slung, intimated to Lady Wastwood that Katharine's Jewish friend had already served with some degree of distinction, and had been wounded in the War. And drawing back with her characteristic inconquerable shyness, as he advanced to Miss Forbis, plainly unconscious of any presence save hers, Trixie's observant green eyes saw him bend his towering head, and sweep his right arm out and down with slow Oriental stateliness, bringing back the supple hand to touch breast, lips and brow. Whether or not he had raised the hem of Katharine's skirt to his lips and kissed it, Lady Wastwood could not definitely determine. She was left with the impression that he had done this thing."

iv

I should have liked to have given, rather than purely descriptive passages, a slice of the complicated and tense action with which the story brims over, but there is the difficulty that such a scene might not be intelligible to one not having read the story from the beginning. I must resist the tendency to quote any more, having indulged it already to excess, and I am ready to propound my theory of the existence of Richard Dehan.

If you receive a letter from The Towers, Beeding, it will bear a double signature, like this:

RICHARD DEHAN

CLOTILDE GRAVES

Clotilde Graves has become a secondary personality.

There was once a time when there was no Richard Dehan. There now are times when there is no Clotilde Graves.

To a woman in middle age an opportunity presented itself. It was the chance to write a novel around the subject which, as a girl, she had come to know a great deal about—the subject of war. To write about it and gain attention, the novel required a man's signature.

Then there was born in the mind of the woman who purposed to write the novel the idea of a man—of *the* man—who should be the novelist she wanted to be. He should use as by right and from instinct the material which lay inutile at her woman's disposal.

She created Richard Dehan. Perhaps, in so doing, she created another monster like Frankenstein's. I do not know.

Born of necessity and opportunity and a woman's inventiveness, Richard Dehan took over whatever of Clotilde Graves's he could use. He

[325]

is now the master. It is, intellectually and spiritually, as if he were the full-grown son of Clotilde Graves. It is a partnership not less intimate than that.

Books

by Richard Dehan

Novels:

THE LOVER'S BATTLE
THE DOP DOCTOR
BETWEEN TWO THIEVES
THE HEADQUARTER RECRUIT
THE COST OF WINGS
THE MAN OF IRON
OFF SANDY HOOK
EARTH TO EARTH
UNDER THE HERMES
THAT WHICH HATH WINGS
A SAILOR'S HOME
THE EVE OF PASCUA
THE VILLA OF THE PEACOCK
THE JUST STEWARD

Sources

on Richard Dehan

Who's Who [in England].
Private Information.

FRANK SWINNERTON: ANALYST OF LOVERS

i

I T is as an analyst of lovers, I think, that Frank Swinnerton claims and holds his place among those whom we still sometimes call the younger novelists of England.

I do not say this because his fame was achieved at a bound with *Nocturne*, but because all his novels show a natural preoccupation with the theme of love between the sexes. Usually it is a pair of young lovers or contrasted pairs; but sometimes this is interestingly varied, as in *September*, where we have a study of love that comes to a woman in middle life.

The unique character of *Nocturne* makes it very hard to write about Swinnerton. It is true that Arnold Bennett wrote: "I am prepared to say to the judicious reader unacquainted with Swinnerton's work, 'Read *Nocturne*,' and to stand or fall, and to let him stand or fall by the result." At the same time, though the rule is that we must judge an artist by his finest work and a genius by his greatest masterpiece, it is not entirely just

[327]

to estimate the living writer by a single unique
performance, an extraordinary piece of virtuosity,
which *Nocturne* unquestionably is. For anyone
who wishes to understand and appreciate Swinnerton, I would recommend that he begin with
Coquette, follow it with *September*, follow that
with *Shops and Houses* and then read *Nocturne*.
That is, I would have made this recommendation
a few months ago, but so representative of all
sides of Swinnerton's talent is his new novel, *The
Three Lovers*, that I should now prefer to say to
anyone unacquainted with Swinnerton: "Begin
with *The Three Lovers*." And after that I would
have him read *Coquette* and the other books in
the order I have named. After he had reached
and finished *Nocturne*, I would have him turn to
the several earlier novels—*The Happy Family*,
On the Staircase, and *The Chaste Wife*.

ii

The Three Lovers, a full-length novel which
Swinnerton finished in Devonshire in the spring of
1922, is a story of human beings in conflict, and
it is also a picture of certain phases of modern
life. A young and intelligent girl, alone in the
world, is introduced abruptly to a kind of life
with which she is unfamiliar. Thereafter the
book shows the development of her character and
her struggle for the love of the men to whom she
is most attracted. The book steadily moves

[328]

FRANK SWINNERTON

through its earlier chapters of introduction and growth to a climax that is both dramatic and moving. It opens with a characteristic descriptive passage from which I take a few sentences:

"It was a suddenly cold evening towards the end of September. . . . The street lamps were sharp brightnesses in the black night, wickedly revealing the naked rain-swept paving-stones. It was an evening to make one think with joy of succulent crumpets and rampant fires and warm slippers and noggins of whisky; but it was not an evening for cats or timid people. The cats were racing about the houses, drunken with primeval savagery; the timid people were shuddering and looking in distress over feebly hoisted shoulders, dreadfully prepared for disaster of any kind, afraid of sounds and shadows and their own forgotten sins. . . . The wind shook the window-panes; soot fell down all the chimneys; trees continuously rustled as if they were trying to keep warm by constant friction and movement."

The imagination which sees in the movement of trees an endeavour to keep warm is not less sharp in its discernment of human beings. I will give one other passage, a conversation between Patricia Quin, the heroine, and another girl:

" 'Do you mean he's in love with you?' asked Patricia. 'That seems to be what's the matter.'

" 'Oho, it takes two to be in love,' scornfully cried Amy. 'And I'm not in love with him.'

" 'But he's your friend.'

" 'That's just it. He won't recognise that men and women *can* be friends. He's a very decent fellow; but he's full of this sulky jealousy, and he glowers and sulks whenever any other man comes near me. Well, that's not my idea of friendship.'

" 'Nor mine,' echoed Patricia, trying to reconstruct her puzzled estimate of their relations. 'But couldn't you stop that? Surely, if you put it clearly to him . . .'

"Amy interrupted with a laugh that was almost shrill. Her manner was coldly contemptuous.

" 'You *are* priceless!' she cried. 'You say the most wonderful things.'

" 'Well, *I* should.'

" 'I wonder.' Amy moved about, collecting the plates. 'You see . . . some day I shall marry. And in a weak moment I said probably I'd marry him.'

" 'Oh, Amy! Of *course* he's jealous!' Swiftly, Patricia did the young man justice.

" 'I didn't give him any right to be. I told him I'd changed my mind. I've told him lots of times that probably I sha'n't marry him.'

" 'But you keep him. Amy! You do encourage him.' Patricia was stricken afresh with a generous impulse of emotion on Jack's behalf. 'I mean, by not telling him straight out. Surely you can't keep a man waiting like that? I wonder he doesn't *insist*.'

[330]

" 'Jack insist!' Amy was again scornful. 'Not he!'

"There was a moment's pause. Innocently, Patricia ventured upon a charitable interpretation.

" 'He must love you very much. But, Amy, if you don't love him.'

" 'What's love got to do with marriage?' asked Amy, with a sourly cynical air.

" 'Hasn't it—everything?' Patricia was full of sincerity. She was too absorbed in this story to help Amy to clear the table; but on finding herself alone in the studio while the crockery was carried away to the kitchen she mechanically shook the crumbs behind the gas-fire and folded the napkin. This was the most astonishing moment of her day.

"Presently Amy returned, and sat in the big armchair, while, seated upon the podger and leaning back against the wall, Patricia smoked a cigarette.

" 'You see, the sort of man one falls in love with doesn't make a good husband,' announced Amy, as patiently as if Patricia had been in fact a child. She persisted in her attitude of superior wisdom in the world's ways. 'It's all very well; but a girl ought to be able to live with any man she fancies, and then in the end marry the safe man for a . . . well, for life, if she likes.'

"Patricia's eyes were opened wide.

[331]

" 'I shouldn't like that,' she said. 'I don't think the man would either.'

" 'Bless you, the men all *do* it,' cried Amy, contemptuously. 'Don't make any mistake about that.'

" 'I don't believe it,' said Patricia. 'Do you mean that my father—or *your* father . . .?'

" 'Oh, I don't know. I meant, nowadays. Most of the people you saw last night are living together or living with other people.'

"Patricia was aware of a chill.

" 'But *you've* never,' she urged. 'I've never.'

" 'No.' Amy was obviously irritated by the personal application. 'That's just it. I say we *ought* to be free to do what we like. Men do what they like.'

" 'D'you think Jack has lived with other girls?'

" 'My dear child, how do I know? I should hope he has.'

" 'Hope! Amy, you do make me feel a prig.'

" 'Perhaps you are one. Oh, I don't know. I'm sick of thinking, thinking, thinking about it all. I never get any peace.'

" 'Is there somebody you *want* to live with?'

" 'No. I wish there was. Then I should *know*.'

" 'I wonder if you would know,' said Patricia, in a low voice. 'Amy, do you really know what love is? Because I don't. I've sometimes let men kiss me, and it doesn't seem to matter in the least. I don't particularly want to kiss them, or to be kissed. I've never seen anything in all the flirtation that goes on in dark corners. It's amusing once or twice; but it becomes an awful bore. The men don't interest you. The thought of living with any of them just turns me sick.' "

iii

The analysis, in *The Three Lovers*, of Patricia Quin is done with that simplicity, quiet deftness and inoffensive frankness which is the hallmark of Mr. Swinnerton's fiction. And, coming at last to *Nocturne*, I fall back cheerfully upon the praise accorded that novel by H. G. Wells in his preface to it. Said Mr. Wells:

"Such a writer as Mr. Swinnerton sees life and renders it with a steadiness and detachment and patience quite foreign to my disposition. He has no underlying motive. He sees and tells. His aim is the attainment of that beauty which comes with exquisite presentation. Seen through his art, life is seen as one sees things through a crystal lens, more intensely, more completed, and with less turbidity. There the business begins and ends for him. He does not want you or anyone to do anything.

"Mr. Swinnerton is not alone among recent writers in this clear detached objectivity. But Mr. Swinnerton, like Mr. James Joyce, does not repudiate the depths for the sake of the surface.

[333]

His people are not splashes of appearance, but
living minds. Jenny and Emmy in this book are
realities inside and out; they are imaginative creatures so complete that one can think with ease of
Jenny ten years hence or of Emmy as a baby.
The fickle Alf is one of the most perfect Cockneys
—a type so easy to caricature and so hard to get
true—in fiction. If there exists a better writing
of vulgar lovemaking, so base, so honest, so touchingly mean and so touchingly full of the craving
for happiness than this, I do not know of it. Only
a novelist who has had his troubles can understand
fully what a dance among china cups, what a skat-
ing over thin ice, what a tight-rope performance is
achieved in this astounding chapter. A false note,
one fatal line, would have ruined it all. On the
one hand lay brutality; a hundred imitative louts
could have written a similar chapter brutally,
with the soul left out, we have loads of such
'strong stuff' and it is nothing; on the other side
was the still more dreadful fall into sentimentality, the tear of conscious tenderness, the re-
deeming glimpse of 'better things' in Alf or Emmy
that could at one stroke have converted their
reality into a genteel masquerade. The perfection
of Alf and Emmy is that at no point does a 'nature's gentleman' or a 'nature's lady' show
through and demand our refined sympathy. It is
only by comparison with this supreme conversation that the affair of Keith and Jenny seems to
fall short of perfection. But that also is at last

[334]

perfected, I think, by Jenny's final, 'Keith . . .
Oh, Keith! . . .'

"Above these four figures again looms the ma-
jestic invention of 'Pa.' Every reader can appreciate the truth and humour of Pa, but I doubt if
anyone without technical experience can realise
how the atmosphere is made and completed, and
rounded off by Pa's beer, Pa's meals, and Pa's
accident, how he binds the bundle and makes the
whole thing one, and what an enviable triumph
his achievement is.

"But the book is before the reader and I will
not enlarge upon its merits further. Mr. Swinnerton has written four or five other novels before
this one, but none of them compares with it in
quality. His earlier books were strongly influenced by the work of George Gissing; they have
something of the same fatigued greyness of texture and little of the same artistic completeness
and intense vision of *Nocturne*.

"This is a book that will not die. It is perfect, authentic and alive. Whether a large and
immediate popularity will fall to it, I cannot say,
but certainly the discriminating will find it and
keep it and keep it alive. If Mr. Swinnerton were
never to write another word I think he might
count on this much of his work living, when many
of the more portentous reputations of today may
have served their purpose in the world and become no more than fading names."

[335]

iv

Arnold Bennett has described Swinnerton personally in a way no one else is likely to surpass. I will prefix a few elemental facts which he has neglected and then will let him have his say.

Frank Arthur Swinnerton was born in Wood Green, England, in 1884, the youngest son of Charles Swinnerton and Rose Cottam. He married, a few years ago, Helen Dircks, a poet; her slim little book of verse, *Passenger*, was published with a preface by Mr. Swinnerton. His first three novels Swinnerton destroyed. His first novel to be published was *The Merry Heart*. It is interesting to know that Floyd Dell was the first American to appreciate Swinnerton. I make way for Mr. Bennett, who says:

"One day perhaps eight or nine years ago I received a novel entitled *The Casement*. The book was accompanied by a short, rather curt note from the author, Frank Swinnerton, politely indicating that if I cared to read it he would be glad, and implying that if I didn't care to read it, he should endeavour still to survive. I would quote the letter but I cannot find it—no doubt for the reason that all my correspondence is carefully filed on the most modern filing system. I did not read *The Casement* for a long time. Why should I consecrate three irrecoverable hours or so to the work of a man as to whom I had no credentials? Why should I thus introduce foreign matter into

[336]

the delicate cogwheels of my programme of reading? However, after a delay of weeks, heaven in its deep wisdom inspired me with a caprice to pick up the volume.

"I had read, without fatigue but on the other hand without passionate eagerness, about a hundred pages before the thought occurred suddenly to me: 'I do not remember having yet come across one single ready-made phrase in this story.' Such was my first definable thought concerning Frank Swinnerton. I hate ready-made phrases, which in my view—and in that of Schopenhauer—are the sure mark of a mediocre writer. I began to be interested. I soon said to myself: 'This fellow has a distinguished style.' I then perceived that the character-drawing was both subtle and original, the atmosphere delicious, and the movement of the tale very original, too. The novel stirred me—not by its powerfulness, for it did not set out to be powerful—but by its individuality and distinction. I thereupon wrote to Frank Swinnerton. I forget entirely what I said. But I know that I decided that I must meet him.

"When I came to London, considerably later, I took measures to meet him, at the Authors' Club. He proved to be young; I daresay twenty-four or twenty-five—medium height, medium looks, medium clothes, somewhat reddish hair, and lively eyes. If I had seen him in a motorbus I should never have said, 'A remarkable chap'—no more than if I had seen myself in a motorbus. My im-

[337]

pressions of the interview were rather like my impressions of the book: at first somewhat negative, and only very slowly becoming positive. He was reserved, as became a young author; I was reserved, as became an older author; we were both reserved, as became Englishmen. Our views on the only important thing in the world—that is to say, fiction—agreed, not completely, but in the main; it would never have done for us to agree completely. I was as much pleased by what he didn't say as by what he said; quite as much by the indications of the stock inside the shop as by the display in the window. The interview came to a calm close. My knowledge of him acquired from it amounted to this, that he held decided and righteous views upon literature, that his heart was not on his sleeve, and that he worked in a publisher's office during the day and wrote for himself in the evenings.

"Then I saw no more of Swinnerton for a relatively long period. I read other books of his. I read *The Young Idea*, and *The Happy Family*, and, I think, his critical work on George Gissing. *The Happy Family* marked a new stage in his development. It has some really piquant scenes, and it revealed that minute knowledge of middle-class life in the nearer suburbs of London, and that disturbing insight into the hearts and brains of quite unfashionable girls, which are two of his principal gifts. I read a sketch of his of a commonplace crowd walking around a bandstand

[338]

which brought me to a real decision as to his qualities. The thing was like life, and it was bathed in poetry.

"Our acquaintance proceeded slowly, and I must be allowed to assert that the initiative which pushed it forward was mine. It made a jump when he spent a week-end in the Thames Estuary on my yacht. If any reader has a curiosity to know what my yacht is not like, he should read the striking yacht chapter in *Nocturne*. I am convinced that Swinnerton evolved the yacht in *Nocturne* from my yacht; but he ennobled, magnified, decorated, enriched and bejewelled it till honestly I could not recognise my wretched vessel. The yacht in *Nocturne* is the yacht I want, ought to have, and never shall have. I envy him the yacht in *Nocturne*, and my envy takes a malicious pleasure in pointing out a mistake in the glowing scene. He anchors his yacht in the middle of the Thames—as if the tyrannic authorities of the Port of London would ever allow a yacht, or any other craft, to anchor in midstream!

"After the brief cruise our friendship grew rapidly. I now know Swinnerton—probably as well as any man knows him; I have penetrated into the interior of the shop. He has done several things since I first knew him—rounded the corner of thirty, grown a beard, under the orders of a doctor, and physically matured. Indeed, he looks decidedly stronger than in fact he is—he was never able to pass the medical examination

[339]

for the army. He is still in the business of publishing, being one of the principal personages in the ancient and well-tried firm of Chatto & Windus, the English publishers of Swinburne and Mark Twain. He reads manuscripts, including his own—and including mine. He refuses manuscripts, though he did accept one of mine. He tells authors what they ought to do and ought not to do. He is marvellously and terribly particular and fussy about the format of the books issued by his firm. Questions as to fonts of type, width of margins, disposition of title-pages, tint and texture of bindings really do interest him. And misprints—especially when he has read the proofs himself—give him neuralgia and even worse afflictions. Indeed he is the ideal publisher for an author.

"Nevertheless, publishing is only a side-line of his. He still writes for himself in the evenings and at week-ends—the office never sees him on Saturdays.

"Frank Swinnerton has other gifts. He is a surpassingly good raconteur. By which I do not signify that the man who meets Swinnerton for the first, second or third time will infallibly ache with laughter at his remarks. Swinnerton only blossoms in the right atmosphere; he must know exactly where he is; he must be perfectly sure of his environment, before the flower uncloses. And he merely relates what he has seen, what he has taken part in. The narrations would be naught

[340]

ff he were not the narrator. His effects are helped
by the fact that he is an excellent mimic and by
his utter realistic mercilessness. But like all first-
class realists he is also a romantic, and in his
mercilessness there is a mysterious touch of fundamental benevolence—as befits the attitude of one
who does not worry because human nature is not
something different from what it actually is.
Lastly, in this connection, he has superlatively the
laugh known as the 'infectious laugh.' When he
laughs everybody laughs, everybody has to laugh.
There are men who tell side-splitting tales with
the face of an undertaker—for example, Irvin
Cobb. There are men who can tell side-splitting
tales and openly and candidly rollick in them
from the first word; and of these latter is Frank
Swinnerton. But Frank Swinnerton can be more
cruel than Irvin Cobb. Indeed, sometimes when
he is telling a story, his face becomes exactly like
the face of Mephistopheles in excellent humour
with the world's sinfulness and idiocy.

"Swinnerton's other gift is the critical. It has
been said that an author cannot be at once a first-
class critic and a first-class creative artist. To
which absurdity I reply: What about William
Dean Howells? And what about Henry James,
to name no other names? Anyhow, if Swinnerton excels in fiction he also excels in literary criticism. The fact that the literary editor of the
Manchester Guardian wrote and asked him to
write literary criticism for the Manchester Guar-

dian will perhaps convey nothing to the American citizen. But to the Englishman of literary taste and experience it has enormous import. The Manchester Guardian publishes the most fastidious and judicious literary criticism in Britain.

"I recall that once when Swinnerton was in my house I had there also a young military officer with a mad passion for letters and a terrific ambition to be an author. The officer gave me a manuscript to read. I handed it over to Swinnerton to read, and then called upon Swinnerton to criticise it in the presence of both of us. 'Your friend is very kind,' said the officer to me afterward, 'but it was a frightful ordeal.'

"The book on George Gissing I have already mentioned. But it was Swinnerton's work on R. L. Stevenson that made the trouble in London. It is a destructive work. It is bland and impartial, and not bereft of laudatory passages, but since its appearance Stevenson's reputation has never been the same."

Books
by Frank Swinnerton

THE MERRY HEART
THE YOUNG IDEA
THE CASEMENT
THE HAPPY FAMILY
GEORGE GISSING: A CRITICAL STUDY
R. L. STEVENSON: A CRITICAL STUDY

SWINNERTON: ANALYST OF LOVERS

ON THE STAIRCASE
THE CHASTE WIFE
NOCTURNE
SHOPS AND HOUSES
SEPTEMBER
COQUETTE
THE THREE LOVERS

Sources
on Frank Swinnerton

Who's Who [In England].
Frank Swinnerton: Personal Sketches by Arnold Bennett, H. G. Wells, Grant Overton. Booklet published by GEORGE H. DORAN COMPANY, 1920.
Private Information.

THE HETEROGENEOUS MAGIC OF
MAUGHAM

i

NOW, I don't know where to begin. Probably I shall not know where to leave off, either. That is my usual misfortune, to write a chapter at both ends. It is a fatal thing, like the doubly-consuming candle. Perhaps I might start with the sapience of Hector MacQuarrie, author of *Tahiti Days*. I am tempted to, because so many people think of W. Somerset Maugham as the author of *The Moon and Sixpence*. The day will come, however, when people will think of him as the man who wrote *Of Human Bondage*.

This novel does not need praise. All it needs, like the grand work it is, is attention; and that it increasingly gets.

ii

Theodore Dreiser reviewed *Of Human Bondage* for the New Republic. I reprint part of what he said:

[344]

W. SOMERSET MAUGHAM

HETEROGENEOUS MAGIC OF MAUGHAM

"Sometimes in retrospect of a great book the mind falters, confused by the multitude and yet the harmony of the detail, the strangeness of the frettings, the brooding, musing intelligence that has foreseen, loved, created, elaborated, perfected, until, in the middle ground which we call life, somewhere between nothing and nothing, hangs the perfect thing which we love and cannot understand, but which we are compelled to confess a work of art. It is at once something and nothing, a dream of happy memory, a song, a benediction. In viewing it one finds nothing to criticise or to regret. The thing sings, it has colour. It has rapture. You wonder at the loving, patient care which has evolved it.

"Here is a novel or biography or autobiography or social transcript of the utmost importance. To begin with, it is unmoral, as a novel of this kind must necessarily be. The hero is born with a club foot, and in consequence, and because of a temperament delicately attuned to the miseries of life, suffers all the pains, recessions, and involute self tortures which only those who have striven handicapped by what they have considered a blighting defect can understand. He is a youth, therefore, with an intense craving for sympathy and understanding. He must have it. The thought of his lack, and the part which his disability plays in it soon becomes an obsession. He is tortured, miserable.

"Curiously the story rises to no spired climax.

WHEN WINTER COMES TO MAIN STREET

To some it has apparently appealed as a drab, un-relieved narrative. To me at least it is a gor-geous weave, as interesting and valuable at the beginning as at the end. There is material in its three hundred thousand or more words for many novels and indeed several philosophies, and even a religion or stoic hope. There are a series of women, of course—drab, pathetic, enticing as the case may be,—who lead him through the mazes of sentiment, sex, love, pity, passion; a wonder-ful series of portraits and of incidents. There are a series of men friends of a peculiarly inclu-sive range of intellectuality and taste, who lead him, or whom he leads, through all the in-tricacies of art, philosophy, criticism, humour. And lastly comes life itself, the great land and sea of people, England, Germany, France, bat-tering, corroding, illuminating, a Goyaesque world.

"Naturally I asked myself how such a book would be received in America, in England. In the latter country I was sure, with its traditions and the Athenæum and the Saturday Review, it would be adequately appreciated. Imagine my surprise to find that the English reviews were al-most uniformly contemptuous and critical on moral and social grounds. The hero was a weak-ling, not for a moment to be tolerated by sound, right-thinking men. On the other hand, in Amer-ica the reviewers for the most part have seen its true merits and stated them. Need I say, how-

[346]

ever, that the New York World finds it 'the sentimental servitude of a poor fool,' or that the Philadelphia Press sees fit to dub it 'futile Philip,' or
that the Outlook feels that 'the author might have
made his book true without making it so frequently distasteful'; or that the Dial cries 'a most
depressing impression of the futility of life'?

"Despite these dissonant voices it is still a book
of the utmost import, and has so been received.
Compact of the experiences, the dreams, the
hopes, the fears, the disillusionments, the rup-
tures, and the philosophising of a strangely
starved soul, it is a beacon light by which the
wanderer may be guided. Nothing is left out;
the author writes as though it were a labour of
love. It bears the imprint of an eager, almost
consuming desire to say truly what is in his heart.

"Personally, I found myself aching with pain
when, yearning for sympathy, Philip begs the
wretched Mildred, never his mistress but on his
level, to no more than tolerate him. He finally
humiliates himself to the extent of exclaiming,
'You don't know what it means to be a cripple!'
The pathos of it plumbs the depths. The death
of Fannie Price, of the sixteen-year-old mother
in the slum, of Cronshaw, and the rambling
agonies of old Ducroz and of Philip himself, are
perfect in their appeal.

"There are many other and all equally brilliant
pictures. No one short of a genius could rout the
philosophers from their lairs and label them as

individuals 'tempering life with rules agreeable
to themselves' or could follow Mildred Rogers,
waitress of the London A B C restaurant, through
all the shabby windings of her tawdry soul. No
other than a genius endowed with an immense
capacity for understanding and pity could have
sympathised with Fannie Price, with her futile
and self-destructive art dreams; or old Cronshaw,
the wastrel of poetry and philosophy; or Mons.
Ducroz, the worn-out revolutionary; or Thorne
Athelny, the caged grandee of Spain; or Leonard
Upjohn, airy master of the art of self-advance-
ment; or Dr. South, the vicar of Blackstable, and
his wife—these are masterpieces. They are marvellous portraits; they are as smooth as a Vermeer,
as definite as a Hals; as brooding and moving as
a Rembrandt. The study of Carey himself, while
one sees him more as a medium through which
the others express themselves, still registers photo-
graphically at times. He is by no means a brooding voice but a definite, active, vigorous character.

"If the book can be said to have a fault it will
lie for some in its length, 300,000 words, or for
others in the peculiar reticence with which the
last love affair in the story is handled. Until the
coming of Sallie Athelny all has been described
with the utmost frankness. No situation, however crude or embarrassing, has been shirked. In
the matter of the process by which he arrived at
the intimacy which resulted in her becoming preg-
nant not a word is said. All at once, by a slight

[348]

frown which she subsequently explains, the truth is forced upon you that there has been a series of intimacies which have not been accounted for. After Mildred Rogers and his relationship with Norah Nesbit it strikes one as strange. . . .

"One feels as though one were sitting before a splendid Shiraz or Daghestan of priceless texture and intricate weave, admiring, feeling, responding sensually to its colours and tones. Mr. Maugham . . . has suffered for the joy of the many who are to read after him. By no willing of his own he has been compelled to take life by the hand and go down where there has been little save sorrow and degradation. The cup of gall and wormwood has obviously been lifted to his lips and to the last drop he has been compelled to drink it. Because of this, we are enabled to see the rug, woven of the tortures and delights of a life. We may actually walk and talk with one whose hands and feet have been pierced with nails."

iii

I turn, for a different example of the heterogeneous magic of Maugham, including his ability to create and sustain a mood in his readers, to the words of Mr. MacQuarrie, who writes:

"It was Tahiti. With a profound trust in my discretion, or perhaps an utter ignorance of the homely fact that people have their feelings, a London friend sent us a copy of *The Moon and*

[349]

Sixpence. This friend, actually a beautiful, well set up woman of the intelligent class in England (which is more often than not the upper fringes or spray of the *bourgeoisie*), wrote: 'You will be interested in this book, since quite the most charming portion of it deals with your remote island of Tahiti. I met the author last night at Lady B——'s. I think the landlady at the end, Mrs. Johnson, is a perfect darling.'

"Knowing Somerset Maugham as a dramatist, the author of that kind of play which never bored one, but rather sent one home suffused with pleasantness, I opened the book with happy anticipation. Therefore—and the title of the book, *The Moon and Sixpence*, gave a jolly calming reaction—I was surprised and frankly annoyed when I found myself compelled to follow the fortunes of a large red-headed man with mighty sex appeal, who barged his way through female tears to a final goal which seemed to be a spiritual achievement, and a nasty death in a native *fare*. I was alarmed; here was a man writing something enormously strong, when I had been accustomed to associate him with charming London nights— the theatre, perfect acting, no middle class problems, a dropping of one's women folks at their doors and a return to White's and whiskey and a soda. And furthermore, in this book of his, he had picked up Lavina, the famous landlady of the Tiare Hotel, the uncrowned queen of Tahiti, and with a few strokes of his pen, had dissected her, and exposed her to the world as she was. Here I must quote:

" 'Tall and extremely stout, she would have been an imposing presence if the great good nature of her face had not made it impossible for her to express anything but kindliness. Her arms were like legs of mutton, her breasts like giant cabbages; her face, broad and fleshy, gave you an impression of almost indecent nakedness and vast chin succeeded vast chin.'

"This may seem a small matter in a great world. Tahiti is a small world, and this became a great matter. I read the book twice, decided that Somerset Maugham could no longer be regarded as a pleasant liqueur, but rather as the joint of a meal requiring steady digestion, and suppressed *The Moon and Sixpence* on Tahiti. The temptation to lend it to a kindred spirit was almost unbearable, but the thought of Lavina hearing of the above description of her person frightened me and I resisted. For kindred souls, on Tahiti as elsewhere, have their own kindred souls, and slowly but surely the fact that a writer had described her arms as legs of mutton (perfect!) and her breasts as huge cabbages (even better!) would have oozed its way to Lavina, sending her to bed for six days, with gloom spread over Tahiti and no cocktails.

"All of which is a trifle by the way. Yet in writing of Somerset Maugham one must gaze along all lines of vision. And it seemed to me

[351]

that Tahiti in general, and Papeete in particular
should supply a clear one; for here, certainly, in
the days when Maugham visited the island a man
could be mentally dead, spiritually naked and
physically unashamed.   I therefore sought Lavina
one afternoon as she sat clothed as with a garment
by the small side verandah of the Tiare Hotel.
(Lavina was huge; the verandah was a small
verandah as verandahs go; there was just room
for me and a bottle of rum.)

" 'Lavina,' I remarked; 'many persons who
write come to Tahiti.'

" 'It is true,' she admitted, 'but not as the
heavy rain, rather as the few drops at the end.'

" 'Do you like them?' I enquired.

"One makes that kind of remark on Tahiti.
The climate demands such, since the answer can
be almost anything, a meandering spreading-of-
weight kind of answer.

" 'These are good men,' said Lavina steadily,
wandering off into the old and possibly untrue
story of a lady called Beatrice Grimshaw and her
dilemma on a schooner in mid-Pacific, when the
captain, a gentle ancient, thinking that the dark
women were having it all their own way, offered
to embrace Miss Grimshaw, finding in return a
gun pointing at his middle, filling him with
quaint surprise that anyone could possibly offer
violence in defence of a soul in so delightful a
climate.

"After which and a rum cocktail, I said:

[352]

'Lavina, did you see much of M'sieur Somerset Maugham when he was here?'

" 'It is the man who writes?' she inquired lazily.

" 'It is,' I returned.

" 'It is the *beau garçon-ta-ta, neneenha roa?*' she suggested.

" 'Probably not,' I said; 'I suspect you are thinking, as usual, of Rupert Brooke. M'sieur Maugham may be regarded as *beau*, but he is not an elderly waiter of forty-seven, therefore we may not call him a *garçon*.'

" 'It is,' Lavina admitted; 'that I am thinking of M'sieur Rupert, he is the *beau garçon*.'

" 'But,' I said, 'I want to know what you thought of M'sieur Somerset Maugham?'

"Once started on Rupert Brooke, and Lavina would go on for the afternoon!

" 'I respect M'sieur Morn,' said Lavina.

" 'Oh!' thought I; 'if she respects him, then I'm not going to get much.'

" 'His French is not mixed,' she continued, referring to Maugham's Parisian accent; 'I speak much with him, and he listen, with but a small question here, and one there. It is the pure French from Paris, as M'sieur *le Governeur* speak, who is the pig. But when he speak much, then it is like the coral which breaks.'

"Lavina now wandered off permanently; it was impossible to bring her back. Her image of the brittle coral branches was a mild personality di-

[353]

rected at Maugham's stutter, which seldom escapes the most sophisticated observer. For those who interview him always find well cut suitings, clean collars and the stutter, and very little else that they can lay hold of with any degree of honesty. Which only goes to prove my own opinion that Maugham, as an observer, refuses to have his own vision clogged by prying eyes at himself.

"I expect that if my French had been better, I might have got some information about Maugham in Tahiti from the bland and badly built French officials who lurk in the official club near the Pomare Palace. I was reduced, in my rather casual investigation, to questioning natives and schooner captains. Once I felt confident of gaining a picture. I asked Titi of Taunoa. (Titi is the lady who figures a trifle disgracefully in Gauguin's *Noanoa*, the woman he found boring after a few weeks, her French blood being insufficiently exotic to his spirit.)

"Said Titi: 'M'sieur Morn? Yes, him I know; he speak good French, and take the door down from the *fare* on which is the picture done by Gauguin of the lady whose legs are like thin pillows and her arms like fat ropes, very what you call strained, and funny.'

"After which her remarks centred around a lover of her sister, who had just died at the age of seventy, and Titi considered that the denouement made by Manu, the sister, was uncalled for

[354]

at the death bed, since the true and faithful wife stood there surrounded by nine children, all safely born the right side of the sheet. She did mention that the removal of the door from the *fare* caused the wind to enter. And although I often made inquiries, I never gained much information. Tahiti, as a whole, seemed unaware of Maugham's visit.

"They may have adored him; but I suspect he was a quiet joy, the kind native Tahiti soon forgets, certainly not the kind of joy she embodies in her national songs and *himines*. Such are the merry drunkards, inefficient though earnest white hulahula dancers and the plain (more than everyday) sinners who cut up rough with wild jagged edges and cruel tearings.

"His occasional appearance at the French club would raise his status, removing any light touches with his junketings, perhaps turning them into dignified ceremonies. Which, for the Tahitian, approaches the end. The Tahitian never quite understands the white man who consorts with the French officials, although many do. 'For are not these men of Farane,' says the native, 'like the hen that talks without feathers?'—whatever that may mean, but it suggests at once the talkative Frenchman denuding himself on hot evenings, and wearing but the native *pareu* to hide portions of his bad figure.

"But although, in some ways, Maugham hid himself from the natives and pleasant half-castes,

[355]

he saw them all right, and clearly, since the closing pages of the *The Moon and Sixpence* display a magical picture of that portion of Tahiti he found time to explore."

iv

Mr. Maugham now offers us *On a Chinese Screen*, sketches of Chinese life, and *East of Suez*, his new play.

There are fifty-eight sketches in *On a Chinese Screen*, portraits including European residents in China as well as native types. Here is a sample of the book, the little descriptive study with which it closes, entitled "A Libation to the Gods":

"She was an old woman, and her face was wizened and deeply lined. In her grey hair three long silver knives formed a fantastic headgear. Her dress of faded blue consisted of a long jacket, worn and patched, and a pair of trousers that reached a little below her calves. Her feet were bare, but on one ankle she wore a silver bangle. It was plain that she was very poor. She was not stout but squarely built and in her prime she must have done without effort the heavy work in which her life had been spent. She walked leisurely, with the sedate tread of an elderly woman, and she carried on her arm a basket. She came down to the harbour; it was crowded with painted junks; her eyes rested for a moment curiously on a man who stood on a narrow bamboo raft, fishing with cormorants; and then she set about her business. She put down her basket on the stones of the quay, at the water's edge, and took from it a red candle. This she lit and fixed in a chink of the stones. Then she took several joss-sticks, held each of them for a moment in the flame of the candle and set them up around it. She took three tiny bowls and filled them with a liquid that she had brought with her in a bottle and placed them neatly in a row. Then from her basket she took rolls of paper cash and paper 'shoes' and unravelled them, so that they should burn easily. She made a little bonfire, and when it was well alight she took the three bowls and poured out some of their contents before the smouldering joss-sticks. She bowed herself three times and muttered certain words. She stirred the burning paper so that the flames burned brightly. Then she emptied the bowls on the stones and again bowed three times. No one took the smallest notice of her. She took a few more paper cash from her basket and flung them in the fire. Then, without further ado, she took up her basket, and with the same leisurely, rather heavy tread, walked away. The gods were duly propitiated, and like an old peasant woman in France, who has satisfactorily done her day's housekeeping, she went about her business."

WHEN WINTER COMES TO MAIN STREET

V

W. Somerset Maugham was born in 1874, the son of Robert Ormond Maugham. He married Syrie, daughter of the late Dr. Barnardo. Mr. Maugham has a daughter. His education was got at King's School, Canterbury, at Heidelberg University and at St. Thomas's Hospital, London.

Mr. Maugham's father was a comparatively prominent solicitor, responsible for the foundation of the Incorporated Society of Solicitors in England. Somerset Maugham, after studying medicine at Heidelberg, went to St. Thomas's, in the section of London known as Lambeth. He obtained his medical degree there. St. Thomas's just across the river from Westminster proved his medical ruin, and his literary birth. The hospital is situated on the border of the slum areas of South London where much that is hopeless, terrible, and wildly cheerful can be found. Persons are not wanting who hold that the slums of Battersea and Lambeth contain more misery and poverty than Limehouse, Whitechapel and the dark forest surrounding the Commercial Road combined. To St. Thomas's daily comes a procession of battered derelicts, seeking attention from the young men in white tunics who hope to be doctors on their own account some day. To St. Thomas's came Eliza of Lambeth, came Liza's mother, came Jim and Tom. Here is the genesis of Maugham's first serious work, *Liza of Lambeth*.

[358]

HETEROGENEOUS MAGIC OF MAUGHAM

It will be simpler and less confusing to deal with Somerset Maugham in the first instance as a maker of books rather than as a playwright. One cannot help believing that, while not one of his plays can be regarded as a pot boiler, they yet but seldom display that fervent purpose found in his books. Yet in his plays, one finds a greater attention to conventional technique and "form" than one finds in books like *Of Human Bondage* and *The Moon and Sixpence*.

The first book launched by Somerset Maugham, *Liza of Lambeth*, could hardly have been, considering its slight dimensions, a clearer indication of the line he was to follow. It came out at a time when Gissing was still in favour, and the odour of mean streets was accepted as synonymous with literary honesty and courage. There is certainly no lack of either about this idyll of Elizabeth Kemp of the lissome limbs and auburn hair. The story pursues its way, and one sees the soul of a woman shining clearly through the racy dialect and frolics of the Chingford beano, the rueful futility of faithful Thomas and the engaging callousness of Liza's mother.

Somerset Maugham's next study in female portraiture showed how far he could travel towards perfection. *Mrs. Craddock*, which is often called his best book, is a sex satire punctuated by four curtains, two of comedy and two of tragedy. This mixture of opposites should have been enough to damn it in the eyes of a public intent upon classifying everything by means of labels and of making everything so classified stick to its label like grim death. Yet the unclassified may flourish, and does, when its merit is beyond dispute. *Mrs. Craddock* appeared fully a decade before its time, when Victorian influences were still alive, and the modern idea for well to do women to have something to justify their existence was still in the nature of a novelty. Even in the fuller light of experience, Maugham could hardly have bettered his study of an impulsive and exigent woman, rising at the outset to the height of a bold and womanly choice in defiance of social prejudice and family tradition, and then relapsing under the disillusions of marriage into the weakest failings of her class, rising again, from a self-torturing neurotic into a kind of Niobe at the death of her baby.

The ironic key of the book is at its best, in the passage half way through—

"Mr. Craddock's principles, of course, were quite right; he had given her plenty of run and ignored her cackle, and now she had come home to roost. There is nothing like a knowledge of farming, and an acquaintance with the habits of domestic animals, to teach a man how to manage his wife."

vi

As a playwright Mr. Maugham is quite as well known as he is for his novels. The author of

Lady Frederick, *Mrs. Dot*, and *Caroline*—the creator of Lord Porteous and Lady Kitty in *The Circle*—writes his plays because it amuses him to do so and because they supply him with an excellent income. Here is a good story:

It seems that Maugham had peddled his first play, *Lady Frederick*, to the offices of seventeen well-known London managers, until it came to rest in the Archives of the Court Theatre. The Court Theatre, standing in Sloane Square near the Tube station, is definitely outside the London theatre area, but as the scene of productions by the Stage Society, it is kept in the running. However, it might conceivably be the last port of call for a worn manuscript.

It so happened that Athole Stewart, the manager of the Court Theatre, found himself needing a play very badly during one season. The theatre had to be kept open and there was nothing to keep it open with. From a dingy pile of play manuscripts he chose *Lady Frederick*. He had no hopes of its success—or so it is said—but the success materialised. At the anniversary of *Lady Frederick* in London, Maugham thought of asking to dinner the seventeen managers who rejected the play, but realising that no man enjoyed being reminded of a lost opportunity he decided to forgo the pleasure.

The circumstances in which *Caroline* was written give an interesting reflex on Maugham as an artist. This delicious comedy was put on paper

[361]

while Maugham was acting as British agent in Switzerland during the war. Some of its more amusing lines were written in some haste while a spy (of uncertain intentions toward Maugham) stood outside in the snow.

vii

Someone, probably the gifted Hector Mac-Quarrie, whom I fear I have guiltily been quoting in almost every sentence of this chapter, has said that Maugham writes "transcripts, not of life as a tolerable whole, but of phases which suit his arbitrary treatment." It is an enlightening comment.

But Maugham himself is the keenest appraiser of his own intentions in his work, as when he spoke of the stories in his book, *The Trembling of a Leaf*, as not short stories, but "a study of the effect of the Islands of the Pacific on the white man."

The man never stays still. When you think the time is ripe for him triumphally to tour America—when *The Moon and Sixpence* has attracted the widest attention—he insists on going immediately to China. This may be because, though well set up, black-eyed, broad-framed and excessively handsome in evening clothes, he is rather diffident.

Books
by W. Somerset Maugham

Novels:

LIZA OF LAMBETH

THE MAKING OF A SAINT

ORIENTATIONS

THE HERO

MRS. CRADDOCK

THE MERRY-GO-ROUND

THE LAND OF THE BLESSED VIRGIN

THE BISHOP'S APRON

THE EXPLORER

THE MAGICIAN

OF HUMAN BONDAGE

THE MOON AND SIXPENCE

THE TREMBLING OF A LEAF

ON A CHINESE SCREEN

Plays:

SCHIFFBRÜCHIG

A MAN OF HONOUR

LADY FREDERICK

JACK STRAW

MRS. DOT

THE EXPLORER

PENELOPE

SMITH

THE TENTH MAN

GRACE

LOAVES AND FISHES

[363]

WHEN WINTER COMES TO MAIN STREET

THE LAND OF PROMISE
CAROLINE
LOVE IN A COTTAGE
CÆSAR'S WIFE
HOME AND BEAUTY
THE UNKNOWN
THE CIRCLE
EAST OF SUEZ

Sources
on W. Somerset Maugham

Who's Who [In England].
Somerset Maugham in Tahiti: Hitherto unpub‑
   lished article by Hector MacQuarrie.
THE BOOKMAN (London).
Private information.

NOTE: Mr. Maugham spent some time in America in the autumn of 1923, during rehearsals and production of his play, "The Camel's Back." At that time he was not long returned from his penetration of Siam and the Shan States. His secretary, who had accompanied him, had filled a notebook with about 70,000 words of dictated observations—future source material. In November, 1923, Mr. Maugham returned to England and immediately began work on a new novel—his first since *The Moon and Sixpence*—which he said would deal with English people in Hongkong and which he purposed to call *The Painted Veil*, a title derived from a line of Shelley's poetry. It is expected that

[364]

The Painted Veil will be published early in 1925.

Meantime Mr. Maugham had received a small fortune from his share of the royalties of the play, "Rain." This play was based on his short story of the same title, the last of the tales in the volume called *The Trembling of a Leaf*. The story should be read by all whom the play has interested, as the ending is different. Mrs. Thompson in the play is sentimentalized at the very end—a probably unavoidable concession to the theatre audience. It is to be noted that Maugham did not make the play version and did not, in fact, think highly of the play's chances of success!

ROBERT W. CHAMBERS AND THE WHOLE TRUTH

i

ONCE a man came to Robert W. Chambers and said words to this effect:

"You had a great gift as a literary artist and you spoiled it. For some reason or other, I don't know what, but I suppose there was more money in the other thing, you wrote down to a big audience. Don't you think, yourself, that your earlier work—those stories of Paris and those novels of the American revolution—had something that you have sacrificed in your novels of our modern day?"

Mr. Chambers listened politely and attentively. When the man had finished, Chambers said to him words to this effect:

"You are mistaken. I have heard such talk. I am not to blame if some people entertain a false impression. I have sacrificed nothing, neither for money nor popularity nor anything else.

"Sir, I am a story-teller. I have no other gift. Those who imagine that they have seen in my earlier work some quality of literary distinction or some unrealised possibility as an artist missing from my later work, are wrong.

"They have read into those stories their own satisfaction in them and their first delight. I was new, then. In their pleasure, such as it was, they imagined the arrival of someone whom they styled a great literary artist. They imagined it all; it was not I.

"A story-teller I began, and a story-teller I remain. I do pride myself on being a good story-teller; if the verdict were overwhelmingly against me as a good story-teller that would cast me down. I have no reason to believe that the verdict is against me.

"And that is the ground I myself have stood upon. I am not responsible for the delusion of those who put me on some other, unearthly pinnacle, only to realise, as the years went by, that I was not there at all. But they can find me now where they first found me—where I rather suspect they found me first with unalloyed delight."

This does not pretend to be an actual transcription of the conversation between Mr. Chambers and his visitor. I asked Mr. Chambers recently if he recalled this interview. He said at this date he did not distinctly recollect it and he added:

"Probably I said what is true, that I write the sort of stories which at the moment it amuses me to write; I trust to luck that it may also amuse the public.

[367]

WHEN WINTER COMES TO MAIN STREET

"If a writer makes a hit with a story the public wants him to continue that sort of story. It does not like to follow the moods of a writer from gay to frivolous, from serious to grave, but I have always liked to change, to experiment—just as I used to like to change my medium in painting, aquarelle, oil, charcoal, wash, etc.

"Unless I had a good time writing I'd do something else. I suit myself first of all in choice of subject and treatment, and leave the rest to the gods."

As a human creature Chambers is strikingly versatile. It must always be remembered that he started life as a painter. There is a story that Charles Dana Gibson and Robert W. Chambers sent their first offerings to Life at the same time. Mr. Chambers sent a picture and Mr. Gibson sent a bit of writing. Mr. Gibson's offering was accepted and Robert W. Chambers received a rejection slip.

Not only was he a painter but Chambers has preserved his interest in art, and is a welcome visitor in the offices of curators and directors of museums because he is one of the few who can talk intelligently about paintings.

He knows enough about Chinese and Japanese antiques to enable him to detect forgeries. He knows more about armour than anyone, perhaps, except the man who made the marvellous collection of mediæval armour for the Metropolitan Museum of Art, New York.

[368]

ROBERT W. CHAMBERS

One of his varieties of knowledge, observable by any reader of his novels, is lepidoptery—the science of butterflies. He collects butterflies with exceeding ardour. But then, he is a good deal of an outdoor man. He knows horses and books; he has been known to hunt; he has been seen with a fishing rod in his hand.

His knowledge of out-of-the-way places in different parts of the world—Paris, Petrograd—is not usual.

Will you believe me if I add that he is something of an expert on rare rugs?

Of course, I am, to some extent, taking Rupert Hughes's word for these accomplishments; and yet they are visible in the written work of Robert W. Chambers where, as a rule, they appear without extrusion.

ii

And here is the newest Robert W. Chambers novel, *Eris*. Mr. Chambers's *The Flaming Jewel*, a melodrama of the maddest character, was published last spring. *Eris* is really a story of the movie world, and reaches its most definite conclusion, possibly, in a passage where the hero says to Eris Odell:

"Whether they are financing a picture, directing it, releasing it, exhibiting it, or acting in it, these vermin are likely to do it to death. Your profession is crawling with them. It needs delousing."

[369]

But I am not really anxious, in this chapter, to discuss the justice or injustice of the view of motion pictures thus forcibly presented. I have read *Eris* with an interest sharpened by the fact that its hero is a writer. I seem to see in what is said about and by Barry Annan expressions of Mr. Chambers's own attitude of more than casual importance.

Barry Annan is obsessed with the stupidity of the American mass and more particularly with the grossness (as he sees it) of New York City.

"Annan went on with his breakfast leisurely. As he ate he read over his pencilled manuscript and corrected it between bites of muffin and bacon.

"It was laid out on the lines of those modern short stories which had proven so popular and which had lifted Barry Annan out of the uniform ranks of the unidentified and given him an individual and approving audience for whatever he chose to offer them.

"Already there had been lively competition among periodical publishers for the work of this newcomer.

"His first volume of short stories was now in preparation. Repetition had stencilled his name and his photograph upon the public cerebrum. Success had not yet enraged the less successful in the literary puddle. The frogs chanted politely in praise of their own comrade.

"The maiden, too, who sips the literary soup

that seeps through the pages of periodical publications, was already requesting his autograph. Clipping agencies began to pursue him; film companies wasted his time with glittering offers that never materialised. Annan was on the way to premature fame and fortune. And to the aftermath that follows for all who win too easily and too soon.

"There is a King Stork for all puddles. His law is the law of compensations. Dame Nature executes it—alike on species that swarm and on individuals that ripen too quickly.

"Annan wrote very fast. There was about thirty-five hundred words in the story of Eris. He finished it by halfpast ten.

"Re-reading it, he realised it had all the concentrated brilliancy of an epigram. Whether or not it would hold water did not bother him. The story of Eris was Barry Annan at his easiest and most persuasive. There was the characteristic and ungodly skill in it, the subtle partnership with a mindless public that seduces to mental speculation; the reassuring caress as reward for intellectual penetration; that inborn cleverness that makes the reader see, applaud, or pity him or herself in the sympathetic rôle of a plaything of Chance and Fate.

"And always Barry Annan left the victim of his tact and technique agreeably trapped, suffering gratefully, excited by self-approval to the verge of sentimental tears.

[371]

WHEN WINTER COMES TO MAIN STREET

" 'That'll make 'em ruffle their plumage and gulp down a sob or two,' he reflected, his tongue in his cheek, a little intoxicated, as usual, by his own infernal facility.

"He lit a cigarette, shuffled his manuscript, numbered the pages, and stuffed them into his pocket. The damned thing was done."

And again:—

"Considering her, now, a half-smile touching his lips, it occurred to him that here, in her, he saw his audience in the flesh. This was what his written words did to his readers. His skill held their attention; his persuasive technique, unsuspected, led them where he guided. His cleverness meddled with their intellectual emotions. The more primitive felt it physically, too.

"When he dismissed them at the bottom of the last page they went away about their myriad vocations. But his brand was on their hearts. They were his, these countless listeners whom he had never seen—never would see.

"He checked his agreeable revery. This wouldn't do. He was becoming smug. Reaction brought the inevitable note of alarm. Suppose his audience tired of him. Suppose he lost them. Chastened, he realised what his audience meant to him—these thousands of unknown people whose minds he titivated, whose reason he juggled with and whose heart-strings he yanked, his tongue in his cheek."

And this further on:—

"He went into his room but did not light the lamp. For a long while he sat by the open window looking out into the darkness of Governor's Place.

"It probably was nothing he saw out there that brought to his lips a slight recurrent smile.

"The bad habit of working late at night was growing on this young man. It is a picturesque habit, and one of the most imbecile, because sound work is done only with a normal mind.

"He made himself some coffee. A rush of genius to the head followed stimulation. He had a grand time, revelling with pen and pad and littering the floor with inked sheets unnumbered and still wet. His was a messy genius. His plot-logic held by the grace of God and a hair-line. Even the Leaning Tower of Pisa can be plumbed; and the lead dangled inside Achilles's tendon when one held the string to the medulla of Annan's stories."

Our young man is undergoing a variety of interesting changes:

"Partly experimental, partly sympathetically responsive, always tenderly curious, this young man drifted gratefully through the inevitable episodes to which all young men are heir.

"And something in him always transmuted into ultimate friendship the sentimental chaos, where comedy and tragedy clashed at the crisis.

"The result was professional knowledge. Which, however, he had employed rather ruth-

lessly in his work. For he resolutely cut out all
that had been agreeable to the generations which
had thriven on the various phases of virtue and
its rewards. Beauty he replaced with ugliness;
dreary squalor was the setting for crippled body
and deformed mind. The heavy twilight of
Scandinavian insanity touched his pages where
sombre shapes born out of Jewish Russia moved
like anachronisms through the unpolluted sunshine of the New World.

"His were essays on the enormous meanness
of mankind—meaner conditions, mean minds,
mean aspirations, and a little mean horizon to
encompass all.

"Out of his theme, patiently, deftly, ingen-
iously he extracted every atom of that beauty,
sanity, inspired imagination which *makes* the im-
perfect more perfect, creates *better* than the materials permit, *forces* real life actually to assume
and *be* what the passionate desire for sanity and
beauty demands."

There comes a time when Eris Odell says to
Barry Annan:—

" 'I could neither understand nor play such a
character as the woman in your last book. . . .
Nor could I ever believe in her. . . . Nor in the
ugliness of her world—the world you write about,
nor in the dreary, hopeless, malformed, starving
minds you analyse. . . . My God, Mr. Annan—
are there no wholesome brains in the world you
write about?' "

[374]

ROBERT W. CHAMBERS

I think these citations interesting. I do not feel especially competent to produce from them inferences regarding Mr. Chambers's own attitude toward his work.

Eris will be published early in 1923, following Mr. Chambers's *The Talkers*.

iii

Mr. Chambers was born in Brooklyn, May 26, 1865, the son of William Chambers and Carolyn (Boughton) Chambers. Walter Boughton Chambers, the architect, is his brother. Robert William Chambers was a student in the Julien Academy in Paris from 1886 to 1893. He married, on July 12, 1898, Elsa Vaughn Moler. He first exhibited in the Paris Salon in 1889; he was an illustrator for Life, Truth, Vogue and other magazines. His first book, *In the Quarter*, was published in 1893; and when, in the same year, a collection of stories of Paris called *The King in Yellow* made its appearance, Robert W. Chambers became a name of literary importance.

Curiously enough, among the things persistently remembered about Mr. Chambers to this day is a particular poem in a book of rollicking verse called *With the Band*, which he published in 1895. This cherished—by very many people scattered here and there—poem had to do with Irishmen parading. One stanza will identify it.

[375]

WHEN WINTER COMES TO MAIN STREET

"Ses Corporal Madden to Private McFadden:
  'Bedad yer a bad 'un!
  Now turn out yer toes!
  Yer belt is unhookit,
  Yer cap is on crookit,
  Yer may not be drunk,
  But, be jabers, ye look it!
    Wan-two!
    Wan-two!
Ye monkey-faced divil, I'll jolly ye through!
    Wan-two!
    Time! Mark!
Ye march like the aigle in Cintheral Park!'"

In the course of writing many books, Chambers has been responsible for one or two shows. He wrote for Ada Rehan, *The Witch of Ellangowan*, a drama produced at Daly's Theatre. His *Iole* was the basis of a delightful musical comedy produced in New York in 1913. He is a member of the National Institute of Arts and Letters.

Books
by Robert W. Chambers

IN THE QUARTER
THE KING IN YELLOW
THE RED REPUBLIC
THE KING AND A FEW DUKES
THE MAKER OF MOONS
WITH THE BAND
THE MYSTERY OF CHOICE

[376]

ROBERT W. CHAMBERS

LORRAINE
ASHES OF EMPIRE
THE HAUNTS OF MEN
THE CAMBRIC MASK
OUTSIDERS
THE CONSPIRATORS
CARDIGAN
THE MAID-AT-ARMS
OUTDOOR-LAND
THE MAIDS OF PARADISE
ORCHARD-LAND
FOREST LAND
IOLE
THE FIGHTING CHANCE
MOUNTAIN LAND
THE TRACER OF LOST PERSONS
THE TREE OF HEAVEN
THE FIRING LINE
SOME LADIES IN HASTE
THE DANGER MARK
THE SPECIAL MESSENGER
HIDE AND SEEK IN FORESTLAND
THE GREEN MOUSE
AILSA PAIGE
BLUE-BIRD WEATHER
JAPONETTE
THE STREETS OF ASCALON
ADVENTURES OF A MODEST MAN
THE BUSINESS OF LIFE
THE COMMON LAW
THE GAY REBELLION

[377]

WHEN WINTER COMES TO MAIN STREET

WHO GOES THERE?
THE HIDDEN CHILDREN
ATHALIE
POLICE!!!
THE GIRL PHILIPPA
THE BARBARIANS
THE RESTLESS SEX
THE MOONLIT WAY
IN SECRET
THE CRIMSON TIDE
THE SLAYER OF SOULS
THE LITTLE RED FOOT
THE FLAMING JEWEL
THE TALKERS
ERIS

Sources
on Robert W. Chambers

Robert W. Chambers: Article by Rupert Hughes in the COSMOPOLITAN MAGAZINE for June, 1918.

The Men Who Make Our Novels, by George Gordon. MOFFAT, YARD & COMPANY.

Who's Who in America.

Private Information.

NOTE: It is of interest to note Mr. Chambers's authorship of the scenario of the film, "America," produced by D. W. Griffith. This motion picture belongs in the rather restricted but important class of epic pictures derived from American history. "The Birth of a Nation" and "The Covered

Wagon" are other good examples of the type. Certain earlier novels of Mr. Chambers's, especially *Cardigan*, and such a later work as *The Little Red Foot*, enjoy a remarkable and continuing popularity. It was the excellence of these that led to the commission to write the story of "America."

THE CONFESSIONS OF A WELL-MEANING YOUNG MAN, STEPHEN McKENNA

i

IN a sense, all of Stephen McKenna's writing has been a confession. More than any other novelist now actively at work, this young man bases fiction on biographical and autobiographical material; and when he sits down deliberately to write reminiscences, such as *While I Remember*, the result is merely that, in addition to confessing himself, he confesses others.

He has probably had more opportunity of knowing the social and political life of London from the inside than most novelists of his time. In *While I Remember* he gives his recollections, while his memory is still fresh enough to be vivid, of a generation that closed, for literary if not for political purposes, with the Peace Conference. There is a power of wit and mordant humour and a sufficiency of descriptive power and insight into human character in all his work.

While I Remember is actually a gallery of pictures taken from the life and executed with the

STEPHEN MCKENNA

technique of youth by a man still young—pictures of public school and university life, of social London from the death of King Edward to the Armistice, of domestic and foreign politics of the period, of the public services of Great Britain at home and abroad. Though all these are within the circle of Mr. McKenna's narrative, literary London—the London that is more talked about than seen—is the core of his story.

ii

Mr. McKenna's latest novel, *The Confessions of a Well-Meaning Woman*, is a series of monologues addressed by one Lady Ann Spenworth to "a friend of proved discretion." I quote from the London Times of April 6, 1922: "In the course of them Lady Ann Spenworth reveals to us the difficulties besetting a lady of rank. She is compelled to live in a house in Mount street—for how could she ask 'The Princess' to visit her in Bayswater?—and her income of a few thousands, hardly supplemented by her husband's directorships, is depleted by the disbursements needed to keep the name of her only son out of the newspapers while she is obtaining for him the wife and the salary suited to his requirements and capacities. Mr. Stephen McKenna provides us with the same kind of exasperating entertainment that we get at games from watching a skilful and unscrupulous veteran. Her deftness in taking a step

or two forward in the centre and so putting the
fast wing off side; her air of sporting acquiescence
touched with astonishment when a penalty is
given against her for obstruction; her resolution
in jumping in to hit a young bowler off his length;
the trouble she has with her shoe-lace when her
opponent is nervous; the suddenness with which
every now and again her usually deliberate second
service will follow her first; the slight pucker in
her eyebrows when she picks up a hand full of
spades; the pluck with which she throws herself
on the ball when there is nothing else for it; her
dignified bonhomie in the dressing room! We all
know Lady Ann and her tricks, but nothing can
be proved against her and she continues to play
for the best clubs.

"In this story Lady Ann is playing the social
game, and it is a tribute to the skill of Mr. Mc-
Kenna that at the end we hope that the Princess
will be sufficiently curious about her new 'frame
and setting' to continue her visits. . . . We have
used the word 'story' because Lady Ann reports
her machinations while they are in progress and
we are a little nervous about the issue. Her main
service, however, lies in the pictures she draws of
her own highly placed relatives and of a number
of people who at house parties and elsewhere may
help ladies of title to make both ends meet. Chief
among them is her son Will, who even as seen
through her partial eyes, appears a very dishonest,
paltry boy. Her blind devotion to him humanises

both her shrewdness and her selfishness. It is for
his sake that she separates her niece from the fine
young soldier she is in love with and that she almost succeeds in providing the King's Proctor
with the materials for an intervention that would
secure to him the estates and title of his fox-hunt-
ing uncle. There is always a plain tale to put her
down and always the friend of proved discretion
is left with the impression that the tale is the invention of malice; at least we suppose she must
be, for Lady Ann is allowed by people to whom
she has done one injury to remain in a position
to do them another. The difficult medium employed by Mr. McKenna entitles him, however, to
count on the co-operation of the reader; and it is
to be accorded the more readily that to it we owe
the felicity of having her own account of the
steps she took to prevent an attractive but expensive widow from running away with her husband,
and of the party which she gave, according to plan,
to the Princess and, not according to plan, to other
guests let loose on her by her scapegrace brother-
in-law."

iii

Stephen McKenna, the author of *Sonia*, not to
be confused with Stephen McKenna, the transla-
tor of Poltinus, belongs to the Protestant branch
of that royal Catholic sept which has had its home
in the County Monagham since the dawn of Irish
history. Some members, even, of this branch

[383]

have reverted to the old faith since the date of Stephen McKenna's birth in the year 1888 in London.

He was a scholar of Westminster and an exhibitioner of Christ Church, Oxford. After he had taken his degree, his father, Leopold McKenna, an elder brother of the Right Honourable Reginald McKenna, K. C., the last Liberal Chancellor of the British Exchequer, made it possible for him to travel desultorily and to try his luck in the great literary adventure.

On the outbreak of the war, as his health, which is delicate to the point of frailness, debarred him from entering the army, Stephen McKenna first volunteered for service at his old school, and, after a year, joined the staff of the War Trade Intelligence Department, where he did valuable war work for three and a half years. He represented his department on the Right Honourable A. J. Balfour's mission in 1917, to the United States, where he enjoyed himself thoroughly and made himself very popular; and he did not sever his connection with the government service until February, 1919, four months after the conclusion of the armistice.

Stephen McKenna's first three novels—*The Reluctant Lover, Sheila Intervenes* and *The Sixth Sense*—were written and published before their author was 27 years of age! But *Sonia*, the story that made him widely known, was written entirely during the period of his activities on the staff of

Westminster School and at the War Trade Intelligence Department. The book won the public favour more quickly than perhaps any other novel that has appeared in our time.

The success of *Sonia* was largely due to its description in a facile, popular and yet eminently chaste and polished style, of the social and political situation in England for a half generation before and during the early stages of the war. This description Stephen McKenna was peculiarly well-equipped to produce, not only as the near relative of a prominent cabinet minister, but also as an assiduous frequenter of the leading Liberal centre, the Reform Club, on the committee of which he had sat, despite his youthful years, since 1915. The political interest, indeed, is revealed in the subtitle, *Between Two Worlds*, which was originally intended for the actual title.

McKenna's next book, *Ninety-Six Hours' Leave*, appealed to the reader's gayer moods and *Midas and Son*, with its tragic history of an Anglo-American multimillionaire, to the reader in serious temper.

In spite of certain blemishes due to Mr. McKenna's unfamiliarity with American life, I should say that *Midas and Son* is probably his ablest work so far. I think it surpasses even *Sonia*. Mr. McKenna returned to Sonia in his novel, *Sonia Married*. His work after that was a trilogy called *The Sensationalists*, three brilliant studies of modern London in the form of succes-

[385]

sive novels called *Lady Lilith*, *The Education of Eric Lane* and *The Secret Victory*.

iv

Writing from 11, Stone Buildings, Lincoln's Inn, London, in 1920, Mr. McKenna had this to say about his trilogy:

"*Lady Lilith* is the first volume of a trilogy called *The Sensationalists*, three books giving the history for a few years before the war, during and immediately after the war, of a group of sensation-mongers, emotion-hunters or whatever you like to call them, whose principle and practice it was to startle the world by the extravagance of their behaviour, speech, dress and thought and, in the other sense of the word, sensationalism, to live on the excitement of new experiences. Such people have always existed and always will exist, receiving perhaps undue attention from the world that they set out to astonish. You, I am sure, have them in America, as we have them here, and in the luxurious and idle years before the war they had incomparable scope for their search for novelty and their quest for emotion. Some of the characters in *Lady Lilith* have already been seen hovering in the background of *Sonia*, *Midas and Son* and *Sonia Married*, though the principal characters in *Lady Lilith* have not before been painted at full length or in great detail; and these

[386]

principal characters will be found in all three books of the trilogy.

"*Lady Lilith*, of course, takes its title from the Talmud, according to which Lilith was Adam's first wife; and as mankind did not taste of the Tree of Knowledge or of death until Eve came to trouble the Garden of Eden, Lilith belongs to a time in which there was neither death nor knowledge of good or evil in the world. She is immortal, unaging and non-moral; her name is given by Valentine Arden, the young novelist who appears in *Sonia* and elsewhere, to Lady Barbara Neave, the principal character in *Lady Lilith* and one of the principal characters in the two succeeding books."

v

In person, Stephen McKenna is tall, with a slender figure, Irish blue eyes, fair hair, regular features and a Dante profile. He has an engaging and very courteous address, a sympathetic manner, a ready but always urbane wit and great conversational charm. He possesses the rare accomplishment of "talking like a book." His intimates are legion; and, apart from these, he knows everyone who "counts" in London society. He is known never to lose his temper; and it is doubtful whether he has ever had cause to lose it.

His one recreation is the Opera; and during the London season his delightful chambers in Lincoln's Inn are the almost nightly scene of parties collected then and there from the opera house.

vi

A sample of *The Confessions of a Well-Meaning Woman:*

"Lady Ann (*to a friend of proved discretion*): You have toiled all the way here again? Do you know, I feel I am only beginning to find out who my true friends are? I am much, much better. . . . On Friday I am to be allowed on to the sofa and by the end of next week Dr. Richardson promises to let me go back to Mount Street. Of course I should have liked the operation to take place there—it is one's frame and setting, but, truly honestly, Arthur and I have not been in a position to have any painting or papering done for so long. . . . The surgeon insisted on a nursing home. Apparatus and so on and so forth. . . . Quite between ourselves I fancy that they make a very good thing out of these homes; but I am so thankful to be well again that I would put up with almost any imposition. . . .

"Everything went off too wonderfully. Perhaps you have seen my brother Brackenbury? Or Ruth? Ah, I am sorry; I should have been vastly entertained to hear what they were saying, what they dared say. Ruth did indeed offer to pay the expenses of the operation—the belated prick of conscience!—and it was on the tip of my tongue to say we are not yet dependent on her spasmodic

[388]

charity. Also, that I can keep my lips closed about Brackenbury without expecting a—tip? But they know I can't afford to refuse £500. . . . If they, if everybody would only leave one alone! Spied on, whispered about. . . .

"The papers made such an absurd stir! If you are known by name as occupying any little niche, the world waits gaping below. I suppose I ought to be flattered, but for days there were callers, letters, telephone-messages. Like Royalty *in extremis.* . . . And I never pretended that the operation was in any sense critical. . . .

"Do you know, beyond saying that, I would much rather not talk about it? This very modern frankness. . . . Not you, of course! But when a man like my brother-in-law Spenworth strides in here a few hours before the anæsthetic is administered and says 'What is the matter with you? Much ado about nothing, I call it.' . . . That from Arthur's brother to Arthur's wife, when, for all he knew, he might never see her alive again. . . . I prefer just to say that everything went off most satisfactorily and that I hope now to be better than I have been for years. . . ."

Books
by Stephen McKenna

THE RELUCTANT LOVER
SHEILA INTERVENES
THE SIXTH SENSE

WHEN WINTER COMES TO MAIN STREET

SONIA: BETWEEN TWO WORLDS
NINETY-SIX HOURS' LEAVE
MIDAS AND SON
SONIA MARRIED
LADY LILITH
THE EDUCATION OF ERIC LANE
THE SECRET VICTORY
WHILE I REMEMBER
THE CONFESSIONS OF A WELL-MEANING WOMAN

Sources
on Stephen McKenna

Who's Who [In England].
Private Information.

[390]